Grand Army of the Republic, Dept. of California and Nevada

Register of the Department of California

Grand army of the republic, 1886

Grand Army of the Republic, Dept. of California and Nevada

Register of the Department of California
Grand army of the republic, 1886

ISBN/EAN: 9783337221072

Printed in Europe, USA, Canada, Australia, Japan

Cover: Foto ©Andreas Hilbeck / pixelio.de

More available books at **www.hansebooks.com**

REGISTER

OF THE

DEPARTMENT OF CALIFORNIA,

GRAND ARMY OF THE REPUBLIC

1886.

Compiled and Printed by direction and under supervision of the

GENERAL COMMITTEE OF MANAGEMENT,

TWENTIETH NATIONAL ENCAMPMENT.

SAN FRANCISCO:

JOSEPH L. THARP.

1886.

THIS REGISTER of the Department of California, G. A. R., has been compiled and printed under the direction of the General Committee Twentieth National Encampment, for distribution to visiting Comrades, to aid them in finding their old associates of army days.

In addition to registers of Posts, and alphabetical index of names, it contains the names of all Comrades of this Department by States and organizations, an arrangement by which any one will find under State and number of regiment, the names of all his old Comrades of that regiment now living in this Department, with reference to Post, where will be found the further particulars of service and residence. Attention is invited to this feature of the Register, which it is believed will be found of special value and interest.

All Comrades registering at the General Committee Headquarters, Chamber of Commerce, 431 California street, will be presented with a copy.

TABLE OF CONTENTS.

ROSTER OF POSTS

—IN THE—

DEPARTMENT OF CALIFORNIA, G. A. R.

*See, also, additional names in appendix, pages 190, 191 and 192.

TWENTIETH NATIONAL ENCAMPMENT,
G. A. R.

General Committee of Management.

S. W. BACKUS, CHAIRMAN.

STUART TAYLOR, 1st Vice-Chairman.   T. K. NOBLE, 2d Vice-Chairman.

C. Mason Kinne,	Jerome Deasy,	John Lynch
Chas. E. Wilson,	R. H. Orton,	R. E. Houghton,
W. H. Holmes,	Horace Wilson,	Edward S. Salomon.
J. W. Staples,	Wm. H. Wharff,	S. J. Corbett,
D. M. Cashin,	J. M. Davis,	John T. Cutting.
H. T. Hobbert,	J. M. Litchfield,	G. H. Stevens,
W. O. Gould.	A. T. Eggleston,	W. B. Hooper.
W. H. Dimond,		W. R. Smedberg,

H. BARTLING, Secretary.   W. W. MONTAGUE, Treasurer.

Executive Committee.

S. W. BACKUS, Chairman.   C. MASON KINNE, Secretary.

W. H. Holmes,	R. E. Houghton,	W. O. Gould.
J. M. Davis,	E. S. Salomon,	J. W. Staples,
	W. B. Hooper.	

Finance Committee.

W. H. DIMOND, Chairman.   W. W. MONTAGUE, Treasurer.

W. O. GOULD, Vice-Chairman.   J. M. LITCHFIELD, Secretary.

THOS. S TAYLOR. Ass't Secretary.

Gov. Geo. Stoneman,	M. J. Keating,	H. B. Russ,
Hon. Geo. C. Perkins,	L. F. Holtz,	Geo. C. Hickox,
J. L. Tharp,	A. J. Bryant,	A. W. Scott,
C. Kohler,	Peter Dean,	W. H. L. Barnes,
D. J. Staples,	J. W. Shaeffer,	J. F. Kennedy,
J. B. Stetson,	Geo. K. Porter,	H. L. Dodge,
E. B. Pond,	Sidney M. Smith	F. A. Gibbs,
J. E. Kunkler,	A. W. Foster,	R. M. Hamilton,
Chas. Lux,	L. L. Baker,	J. B. Rider,
R. Tobin,	Ignatz Steinhart,	William Dresbach,
Phil. I. Fisher,	Geo. L. Brander,	C. F. Bassett,
John H. Dickinson,	David Cahn,	J. Eppinger,
Timothy Hopkins,	Geo. A. Fisher,	Joseph Elfelt,
A. P. Williams,	Thos. Denigan,	E. A. Denicke,
B. P. Flint,	C. L. Taylor,	H. W. Wieland,
Louis Sloss,	S. H. Seymour,	Columbus Waterhouse,
A. E. Hecht,	D. A. Macdonald	Horace Davis,
G. W. Prescott,	Colin M. Boyd.	J. G. James.
	J. M. Litchfield,	

Auditing Committee.

C. MASON KINNE, Chairman.

Gov. Geo. Stoneman, J. M. Litchfield, J. W. Staples.
W. H. Dimond,

Committee on Programme.

W. H. HOLMES, Chairman.

Adolph Fried. Alex. Forsyth.

Transportation Committee.

T. H. GOODMAN, Chairman. GEO. W. WALTS, Secretary.

R. E. Houghton, R. H. Warfield, John T. Cutting,
J. M. Davies.

Committee on Hotels and Accommodations.

R. E. HOUGHTON, Chairman. W. A. ROBINSON, Secretary.

John Lynch. H. T. Graves, A. T. Eggleston,

Public Halls and Places of Meetings Committee.

R. H. ORTON, Chairman. C. R. THOMPSON, Secretary.

H. T. Hobbert, M. J. Acton, A. S. Hubbard.
F. M. Lovell.

Mechanics' Pavilion Committee.

JOHN T. CUTTING, Chairman. A. L. ROCKWELL, Secretary.

J. H. Gilmore. E. W. Bushnell, Samuel J. Hendy,
J. R. Cowen, Henry Finnegass, Luther Wagoner,
C. F. Bassett, H. W. Frillman, J. J. Shepherd,
T. H. Allen, David Kerr, Asa R. Wells,
W. J. Ruddick, Henry L. Davis, M. A. McLaughlin,
J. C. Bolles,

Press Committee.

JOHN F. SHEEHAN, Chairman.

John P. Irish, Wm. M. Bunker, H. Hudson,
Hugh M. Burke, W. A. Walker, Thos. E. Flynn,
Thos. Flynn, A. B. Henderson, J. Ross Jackson,
M. Greenblatt, Frank E. Myers, T. T. Williams,
M. D. Boruck, J. M. Ward, Sunderland F. Sutherland,
T. J. Vivian,

Decoration Committee.

J. H. GILMORE, Chairman. PETER T. BARCLAY, Secretary.

Wm. B. Hooper, W. B. May, E. Carlson,
Jerome Deasy, A. W. Starbird, K. Melrose,
Asa R. Wells, Franklin B. Sumner, N. T. Messer,
H. J. Babbitt, Geo. Hopps, W. M. Bramhall.
Wm. H. Wharff,

Printing Committee.

S. W. BACKUS, Chairman.

W. H. Holmes,   H. T. Hobbert.

Invitation Committee.

W. R. SMEDBERG, Chairman.

Alex. G. Hawes,   J. C. Innes,   E. Carlscn.
                       D. M. Cashin,

Badge Committee.

W. H. WHARFF, Chairman.

F. J. Symmes,   Wm. H. McNeil,   O. B. Culver.

Reception Committee.

W. H. L. BARNES, Chairman.   N. T. MESSER, Secretary.

Washington Bartlett,	H. P. Bush,	John Hetherington,
R. H. Warfield,	R. P. Hammond, Jr.,	Geo. W. Bowie,
Gov. Geo. Stoneman,	Judge F. W. Lawler,	A. L. Gartley,
Gen'l John Pope,	Geo. W. Elder,	M. H. Bailhache,
W. R. Smedberg,	Otto Norman,	Dr. W. F. McNutt,
E. Carlson,	J. W. Howell,	Dr L. C. Lane,
Joseph L. Tharp,	N. P. Chipman,	Dr. W. E. Taylor,
John Daggett, Lt. Gov.	W. H. Parks,	Dr. Henry Gibbons, Jr.,
W. V. Farwell,	Clay W. Taylor,	Dr. Benj. R. Swan,
R. P. Thomas,	A. W. Randall,	Hon. Walter H. Levy,
J. L. Boone,	B. O. Carr,	Jas. J. E. Hawkins,
J. H. Boalt,	A. Malpas,	Fleet F. Strother,
Gen'l A. V. Kautz,	O. R. Coghlan,	N. W. Spaulding,
Wm. Centre,	J. H. Barbour,	Robt. Westwater,
Geo. E. Whitney,	Geo. M. Bowman,	Dr. W. P. Gibbons,
Alex. G. Hawes,	L. Finnigan,	Dr. T. H. Pinkerton,
W. B. May,	Prof. Allen,	Dr. G. W. Graves,
H. C. Dibble,	H. S. Foote,	John P. Dunn,
G. H. Kimble,	A. G. Bennett,	Dr. W. R. Cluness,
Edw. Pollitz,	E. B. Jerome,	Dr. H. Latham,
A. P. Williams,	L. W. Allum,	Dr. H. Mays,
J. P. H. Wentworth,	Geo. E. Gard,	Dr. W. S. Thorne,
C. E. Royce,	Ira Moore,	Dr. A. W. Saxe,
Chas. S. Neal,	H. A. Burnett,	Major E. B. Beaumont,
E. A. Denicke,	Chas. E. Pinkham,	E. C. Jordan,
H. Bendel,	C. H. Hubbard,	S. D. Waterman,
P. B. Cornwall,	O. P. Dodge,	F. C. Berry,
Robt. Roy,	L. Tozer,	Hon. John F. Finn,
Geo. A. Fisher,	T. W. Sheehan,	Hon. John Hunt,
Ira G. Hoitt,	Rev. E. R. Dille,	Hon. T. H. Rearden,
Louis F. Holtz,	J. R. Laine,	Hon. T. K. Wilson,
W. H. Dimond,	Frank Miller,	Hon. M. A. Edmonds,
Gen. O. O. Howard,	Gen. C. McKeever,	Gen. W. R. Shafter,

Reception Committee—Continued.

Stuart Taylor,
John W. Shaeffer,
Henry Eickhoff,
P. F. Walsh,
Walter Turnbull,
Chas. E. Travers,
Geo. Spaulding,
Ed. L. G. Steele,
F. L. Castle,
C. F. Roberts,

G. A. Putnam,
Frank Smith,
II. H. Linnell,
J. II. G. Weaver,
J. B. Brown,
J. D. II. Chamberlain,
A. Wiley,
W. G. Bonner,
C. W. Long,
W. H. Pratt,

Hon. J. V. Coffey,
Hon. J. F. Sullivan,
Hon. J. G. Maguire,
Hon. D. J. Murphy,
Hon. D. J. Toohy,
Hon. W. H. Van Fleet,
Alfred Daggett,
Thomas Thompson,
Hon. E. M. Gibson,
Hugh Craig.

Excursion Committee.

CHAS. E. WILSON, Chairman.

A. R. Briggs,
J. J. Lyon,
Dr. Chas. T. Deane,
Wm. L. Merry,
Hon. Geo. C. Perkins,
Jacob S. Taber,

Wm. Center,
A. J. Bryant,
F. M. Lovell,
J. M. Donahue,
T. H. Goodman,
D. B. Jackson,
C. F. Crocker,

W. H. PENFIELD, Secretary.

W. T. Fitzgerald,
E. F. Adams,
Wendell Easton,
J. B. Lauck,
F. S. Douty,
H. R. Judah.

Entertainment Committee.

J. M. DAVIS, Chairman.

Frank J. Symmes,

Moses Wasserman,
G. B. Corwin,

A. J. VINING, Secretary.

W. L. Duncan.

Parade and Review Committee.

E. S. SALOMON, Chairman.

James Kip,
Eugene Lehe,
L. L. Bromwell,

P. H. McGrew,
Frank W. Sumner,
C. B. Hutchins,
J. L. Lyon.

T. H. ALLEN, Secretary.

Z. P. Clark,
W. O. Gould,
W. H. Dimond.

Music Committee.

A. T. EGGLESTON, Chairman.

J. H. Culver,
R. M. Apgar,

M. Gray,
J. H. Mork,

W. H. PENFIELD, Secretary.

L. B. Edwards.
Geo. M. McCarty.

Committee on Horses, Carriages and Equipments.

JOHN TUTTLE, Chairman.

C. C. Shattuck,

Andrew Hollywood,

H. T. HOBBERT, Secretary.

H. L. Chambers.

Police and Streets Committee.

D. M. CASHIN, Chairman.

Frank Buxton,
Louis Kruger,

E. F. Loud,
Sam'l Deal,
Wm. J. Mallady,

M. L. G. O'BRIEN, Secretary.

Dan'l McLeod,
R. J. Falls

Grand Banquet Committee.

J. W. Staples, Chairman.

C. R. Thompson,
F. D. Sweetser,
G. G. Burnett,

W. R. Thomas,
M. J. Keating,
R. H. Pond,

Alfred Greenebaum, Secretary.

R. P. Hammond,
Jerome H. Backus.

Camp-Fire Committee.

Will H. Voorhees, Chairman.

Orrin Taber,
H. O. Dibble,

Geo. E. Filkins,
S. Cahen,

Jos. Simonson, Secretary,

David Scannell.

Registration. Rosters and Bulletins.

Horace Wilson, Chairman.

J. D. Ruggles,
George L. Voorhees,

A. G. Bennett,
J. R. Scupham.

J. A. Calhoun, Secretary.

Eugene Wiegand, Compiler.

Fireworks Committee.

J. G. Giesting, Chairman,
E. W. Bushnell,

Jos. Simonson,
F. R. Morton,

W. W. Magary, Secretary
O. H. Blinn.

Army of the Potomac Committee.

E. S. Salomon, Chairman.

B. G. Barney,
R. H. Warfield,
J. W. Howell,

W. H. Fitton,
C. F. Royce,
F. M. Cooley.

W. R. Parnell, Secretary.

W. R. Smedberg,
J. W. Staples.

Loyal Legion Committee.

W. H. Dimond, Chairman.

T. H. Goodman,
J. B. Coghlan,
C. Mason Kinne,
C. R. Thompson,

R. H. Pond,
Winfield Scott,
Chauncey McKeever,
E. S. Salomon,

W. R. Smedberg, Secretary.

Montgomery Fletcher,
W. B. Hooper,
Edward Carlson.

Woman's Relief Corps Committee.

G. H. Stevens, Chairman.

E. K. Russell,

James G. Steele,

T. C. Masteller, Secretary.

Albert Brown.

Mexican Veteran Association Committee.

Wm. L. Duncan,

R. P. Hammond,
Sam'l Deal,

David Scannell.

Programme for the Twentieth National Encampment, G. A. R., To be Held at San Francisco, Cal., August, 1886.

FIRST DAY—MONDAY, AUGUST 2D.

Details from all Posts in the city to be on duty for escort and reception purposes to arriving Comrades and Organizations, in pursuance of general or special orders.

All of the Posts located in this city, as well as any others in this Department who may feel disposed to do so, are requested to establish headquarters in some public hall or rooms where they may be prepared to receive and greet all visiting Comrades as they arrive, continuing same through the week.

Meeting of Executive Committee of the National Council of Administration at National Headquarters, Occidental Hotel, at 2 o'clock p. m.

EVENING, 8 O'CLOCK.

Review of the Second Brigade of the National Guard of California, General W. H. Dimond commanding, at the Mechanics' Pavilion, at 8 o'clock, P. M., tendered to the Commander-in-Chief of the Grand Army of the Republic, to be followed by a Reception and Grand Ball to the Officers and Delegates of the National Encampment, G. A. R., and *of the National Convention of the Woman's Relief Corps.*
"Society of the Army of the Potomac."
Business meeting for Army Corps Societies, 11 o'clock, A. M.
Business meeting of Society of the Army of the Potomac, at 2 o'clock, P. M.
Reception by Mayor of city; Oration, Poem, Etc., Etc., 8 o'clock, P. M.

SECOND DAY—TUESDAY, AUGUST 3D.

Grand Parade—10 A. M.—Grand Parade of the National Encampment, the Grand Army and all kindred societies, in accordance with special programme to be prepared by the Committee on Grand Parade.

EVENING.

8 P. M.—*Parade and escort to Commander-in-Chief and Staff, National Officers and Members of Encampment,* and General reception at the Mechanics' Pavilion, said reception to be tendered to the National Encampment, the Army of the Potomac, the Loyal Legion, Woman's Relief Corps, and all kindred societies with addresses of welcome by the Governor of the State, Mayor of the City, and Department Commander, in accordance with a special programme prepared by the Committee on Reception.

THIRD DAY—WEDNESDAY, AUGUST 4TH.

National Encampment.—10 A. M.—Meeting of the National Encampment in legislative session, to continue through the day.

Meeting of the National Convention of Woman's Relief Corps, at Irving Hall, commencing at 10 o'clock, A. M.

Excursion via the San Francisco and North Pacific Railroad, to Santa Rosa and Sonoma Valley, Cal., and reception by citizens thereof.

EVENING.

Grand Testimonial Concert at the Mechanics' Pavilion, tendered to the Commander-in-Chief of the G. A. R., the Governors of the several States, and other distinguished guests, together with the members of the Grand Army, and other kindred societies, with chorus of one thousand voices, assisted by one hundred musical instruments to render National airs and lyrics.

"Society of the Army of the Potomac." Grand Banquet to the Society, 8 o'clock.

Reception at the several Post Headquarters of G. A. R. throughout the city.

FOURTH DAY—THURSDAY, AUGUST 5TH.

DURING THE DAY.

Meeting of the National Encampment continued.
Meeting of National Convention of Woman's Relief Corps continued.
Excursion to, and reception by the citizens of Santa Cruz, Cal.

EVENING.

Grand Banquet.—Grand Banquet tendered to the Officers and Members of the National Encampment, to be arranged by the Committee on Grand Banquet.

General Reception and Entertainment at the Mechanics' Pavilion and at the various Post Headquarters.

FIFTH DAY—FRIDAY, AUGUST 6TH.

DURING THE DAY.

Meeting of National Encampment continued.
Meeting of the National Convention of the Woman's Relief Corps continued.
Excursion to Monterey, Cal., and Grand Picnic Excursion over the North Pacific Coast Railway.

EVENING.

General Reception at the Metropolitan Temple, at 8 o'clock, tendered by the National Convention of the Woman's Relief Corps, to the National Encampment of the G. A. R.; Society of the Army of the Potomac; Military Order of the Loyal Legion of the U. S.; and all kindred societies, with address of welcome by Sarah E. Fuller, National President Woman's Relief Corps, followed with addresses by the Governor of the State; Mayor of the City; Commander-in-Chief and Department Commander of the G. A. R., and other able representatives of the Grand Army and Relief Corps, together with a Special Musical Programme, to be prepared for the occasion.

Reception at the several Post Headquarters.

SIXTH DAY—SATURDAY, AUGUST 7TH.

DURING THE DAY.

Grand excursion tendered to the Officers and Members of the National Encampment, around the Bay of San Francisco.

EVENING.

Grand Camp-Fire.—Closing exercises of the week with a Grand Camp-fire of the combined forces at the Mechanics' Pavilion.

MONDAY, AUGUST 9TH.

Excursion to Oakland. Grand Reception by the citizens of that city tendered to the newly-elected officers of the National Encampment, and members thereof.

TUESDAY, AUGUST 10TH.

Excursion to San José. Grand Reception by the citizens of that city, tendered to the newly-elected officers of the National Encampment, and members thereof.

WEDNESDAY AND THURSDAY, AUGUST 11TH AND 12TH.

Excursion to Sacramento, via Napa Valley, reaching Sacramento Wednesday evening, August 11th, where a grand reception will be tendered to the newly-elected officers of the National Encampment, together with members thereof, and continued until the following day.

List of Committees.

General Management,
Executive,
Finance,
Auditing,
Programme,
Transportation,
Hotels and Accommodations,
Public Halls and Places of Meetings,
Mechanics' Pavilion,
Press,

Decorations,
Printing,
Invitations,
Badges,
Reception,
Excursions,
Entertainments,
Parade and Review,
Music,
Horses, Carriages and Equipments,
Police and Streets,

Grand Banquet,
Camp Fire,
Registration, Rosters and Bulletins.
Fire-works,
Army of Potomac,
Loyal Legion,
Woman's Relief Corps,
Mexican Veteran Association,
Advisory Committee.

By Order of the General Committee,

H. BARTLING, Secretary.   S. W. BACKUS, Chairman.

DEPARTMENT OF CALIFORNIA.

OFFICERS.

Commander.........................W. R. SMEDBERG...............San Francisco
Sen. Vice Com.....................GEO. E. GARD................Los Angeles.
Jun. Vice Com.....................S. F. DANIELS...................Oakland.
Medical Director............ ....N. S. HAMLIN.................Marysville.
Chaplain.........................W. L. STEPHENS...............St. Helena.

OFFICIAL STAFF.

Assistant Adjutant General....................................THOMAS S. TAYLOR
        San Francisco.
Assistant Q. M. General......... ....R. H. ORTON
        San Francisco.
Inspector..R. S. JOHNSON
        Stockton.
Judge Advocate...W. H. L. BARNES
        San Francisco.
Chief Mustering Officer.......................................L. B. EDWARDS
        Oakland.
Senior Aide-de-Camp.......................................WILL H. VOORHEES
        San Francisco.

COUNCIL OF ADMINISTRATION.

J. H. BARBOUR,   GEO. L. HARRIS
           C. E. ROYCE,
ALLEN T. BIRD,   FRANK D. SWEETZER.

PAST DEPARTMENT COMMANDERS.

W. H. AIKEN..San Francisco
E. CARLSON ....San Francisco
S. W. BACKUS...San Francisco
S. P. FORD ....San Francisco
C. MASON KINNE............................. ....San Francisco
W. A. ROBINSON...San Francisco
J. W. STAPLES..San Francisco
J. M. DAVIS.................. ....San Francisco
R. H. WARFIELD..Healdsburg

DELEGATES TO THE NATIONAL ENCAMPMENT.   ALTERNATES.
  STUART TAYLOR, (at large.)   GEORGE BABCOCK, (at large.)
  W. H. L. BARNES,   A. G. BENNETT,
  T. F. LAYCOCK,   L. B. EDWARDS,
  N. P. CHIPMAN,   P. H. McGREW,
  E. S. SALOMON,   T. H. ALLEN.

SPECIAL AIDE-DE-CAMPS.

C. A. FULLER, Atlanta Post, 92...Fresno
J. L. SKINNER, Sumner Post, 3............................ ....Sacramento
T. A. McLAUGHLIN, Geo. H. Thomas Post, 2......................San Francisco
Z. N. GOLDSBY, J. F. Reynolds Post, 98.............................Santa Cruz
GEO. W. FICKS, Sumner Post, 3...................................Sacramento
T. J. RILEY, Rod Matheson Post, 16.......................... ....Healdsburg
FRANK T. SINGER, W. R. Cornman Post, 57.....................San Bernardino
ED. SCHWARTZ, J. W. Owens Post, 83............................Phœnix, A. T.
J. L. LYON, Appomattox Post, 60........................... ....Oakland
E. R. MERRIMAN, Jno. A. Dix Post, 42..............................San Jose
D. W. FIELD, Stanton Post, 55....................................Los Angeles
H. T. SMITH, Lyon Post, 8 ....Oakland
J. B. FULLER, Corinth Post, 80....................................Marysville
CHAS. JANSEN, Geo. H. Thomas Veteran Guard.....................San Francisco

LINCOLN POST, No. 1.

SAN FRANCISCO, CAL.

OFFICERS, 1886.

S. J. CORBETT...Commander
WM. H. WHARFF...Senior Vice-Commander
GEO. H. FULLER...Junior Vice-Commander
WILL H. VOORHEES..Adjutant
J. C. BOLLES...Quartermaster
GEO. G. GERE, M. D..Surgeon
M. MURPHY..Chaplain
HUGH J. BRADY...Officer of the Day
W. F. RANDALL..Officer of the Guard
T. C. MASTELLER..Sergeant Major
H. T. HOBBERT...Quartermaster Sergeant
JOHN F. WHARFF..Inside Sentinel
MARTIN GOBERTZ...Outside Sentinel
D. J. KING...Librarian

Meeting, every Thursday, at 8 P. M., in Washington Hall, 35 Eddy Street.

NAME.	CO.	SERVICE.	ADDRESS.
Aber W. E...........	E	39th & 51st Wis. Inf...............	832½ Harrison
Aceret Jacob........	K	103d & 17 th Penn.Inf....	708 Gough
Achorn Albion G....	K	44th Mass. Inf....................	930 Folsom
Adam Robert	F	68th N. Y. Inf.	1049 Howard
Aiken W. H.........	E	40th & 44th Wis. Inf...............	709 Kearny
Anderson Richard R.	H	4th Cal. Inf.....................	235 Fifth
Anderson Walter B..	F	4th Mich. Cav........	724 Pacific
Andrews C. F.......	G	5th Kansas Cav....................	2515 Larkin
Anthony A.........,		131st N. Y. Inf	927½ Post
Apgar R. M........:	E	7th Cal. Inf.....................	Oakland
Arnell W. J.........	F	20th Penn. Cav....................	Folsom, Cal.
Ashley Lucius W....	E	32d U. S. Inf.....................	113 Eddy
Babcock G...... ...	E	105th N. Y. Inf....................	P O Box 1971,S.F.
Backus S. W	L	2d Mass. Cav.....................	2119 Buchanan
Baily George W.....	E	3d Maine Inf.....................	22d & Folsom
Banfield J. H........	H	10th Ill. Inf.....................	322 Mason
Bard James........	L	2d Mass. Cav.....................	Trinity Center,Cal
Barker H. L.........	C	2d Maine Inf.....................	1918 Union
Barlow James.......	E	58th N. Y. Inf.....................	620 Taylor
Barnes H. L.........		22d Ohio Inf	Santa Rosa
Barnstead Thomas D	A	2d Mass. Cav.....................	9 Rausch
Barry Robert........		Board of Trade Batt'y.............	21 Prospect Place
Bartlett Joseph L...	B	132d Ind Inf.............	25 Chesley

3

NAME.	CO.	SERVICE.	ADDRESS.
Bauer Gustavus A...	A	9th & 108th Ohio Inf...............	Lott & McAllister
Baum G. A. R.......	B	2d La. Inf.......................	Fifth & Perry
Baxter Wm. H	C	3d & D 16th N. Y. Art...........	529 Sacramento
Feerstetcher F......	I	192d Penn. Inf	Rutherford, Cal.
Bell George.........	F	2d Cal. Cav.....................	Vallejo, Cal,
Bennett G. W		1st Mass. Art..................	Railroad av.,S.S F.
Betts W. Y.....	G	12th N. Y. Inf.................	513 Kearny
Bixby A. O	K	5th Vt. Inf....................	204 Leavenworth
Black Wm	L	9th & 83d N. Y. Inf...........	20th & Alabama
Blackburn B. F.....	A	30th Ohio Inf..................	9 Liberty
Blaisdell H. Q......	D	6th N. H. Inf	South'n Police Sta.
Blanchard Frank A..	C	1st Maine Heavy Art..........	1507 Market
Blesi S.............	B	10th Mo. Cav..................	15 Page
Boardman J. H......	C	61st N. Y. Inf.	215 Fair Oaks
Bogle Joseph H....	G	4th N. Y. Inf................	1027 Sutter
Bolles J. C.........	G	3d & D 23d Mass. Inf.........	Custom House
Bolton W. H........	H	27th Mich. Inf...............	366 Natoma
Bonifield James T..	F	7th Cal. Inf.................	8 Harriett
Bordwell J. W......		7th Mass. Battery.	1055 Mission
Bowley Freeman S..	H	30th U. S. Inf.	2123 Howard
Bownes George	I	2d Cal. Inf..................	Kentucky nr S'Inno
Brady Hugh J......	K	2d Cal. Cav. & F 9th N. Y. Inf...	624 Brannan
Bragdon C. A.......		U. S. S. Brooklyn.............	South S. F.
Brawn A............	I	18th Ill. Inf................	219 Battery
Brewer Harry.......	A	99th Ind. Inf......	913 Bryant
Brewer J. M........	C	15th & E 9th Ind. Inf........	913 Bryant
Brey Thomas S.....	E	1st Maine Inf................	616 Sacramento
Brigaerts Jos......	K	58th Ill. Inf.	14 Bourbin Place
Brittain William...		U. S. Navy...................	435 Twenty-sec'nd
Brock Edward M....		U. S. S. Hartford............	Benicia, Cal.
Brock G. H.........	B	12th Iowa Inf................	Marine Hospital
Brooks Samuel A...		U. S. Navy...................	37 Eddy
Brower Celsus......	K	6th Cal. Inf.................	Bakersfield, Cal.
Brown George H....	F	129th N. Y. Inf..............	707 Front
Brown George L....	M	1st Mass. Cav................	350 San Jose av.
Brown Thomas A ...	D	2d Cal. Inf..................	20 Shotwell
Brush Elden R	D	196th Ohio Inf...............	608 Market
Bryant Samuel A....	A	8th Cal. Inf.................	528 Hayes
Burnham S. S.......	D	3d Vet. Res. Corps...........	121 Minna
Burns John.........		U. S. S. Horace Beals........	845 Mission
Burson W. J........	F	3d Mich. Cav.................	Clerk Gen.P.O.,S.F
Bushnell E. W......	F	12th Conn. Inf...............	686 Twentieth
Butterfield F. L....	C	50th N. Y. Inf...............	834 Howard
Buttner Henry A...	B	3th Bat. D. C. Rifles........	515 Guerrero
Buxton Frank.......	A	20th Mass. Inf. & 12th Mass. Art...	137 Fourth
Callahan T. J......	H	16th Ill. Inf. and 69th N. Y. Inf....	1104 Mission
Calkins Allen St.....	G	105th Ill. Inf...............	Brentwood, Cal.
Campbell J. D......	D	18th Ind. Inf........	406 Tehama
Campbell J. F.......	D	165th N. Y. Inf..............	3½ Larkin
Canham T. P........	F	2d Cal. Cav..................	10 Salmon
Cappelli Antonio ...	D	12th N. Y. Cav...............	419 Grove
Carleton Jerome....	I	1st Mass. Inf................	248 Ellis
Carlisle William....	E	11th Penn. Res.Corps.........	707 Front
Carman W. P........	B	2d Ohio Cav..................	211 Chattanooga
Carr B. J...........	B	3d Ill. Cav........,.........	448 Sixth
Carstens Henry.....		U. S. S. Lancaster...........	1534 Sanchez

NAME.	CO.	SERVICE.	ADDRESS.
Casebolt J. B........	H	40th Ill. Inf.......................	Australia
Cashman C..........	F	3d R. I. Art.......................	156 Clementina
Casser C............		39th N. Y. Inf.....................	22 Brosnan
Cassidy Wm	I	6th U. S. Inf.....................	Presidio, S. F.
Catoir Julius.......	I	55th N. Y. Inf.....................	1402 Pacific
Ciphers D. S........	E	2d Ohio Heavy Art..............	519 Ellis
Clark Joseph	A	6th N. H. Inf......	428 Twenty-fourth
Cl rk Thomas.......		U. S. S. Commodore Morris........	2 Selina Place
Clarkson P. M......	G	2d Cal. Cav........................	1039 Mission
Claudianus C. M.....		U. S. S. Powhattan................	25 Stockton
Cline Eli............	B	5th Ohio Cav.................	13 Stockton
Clough J. F.........		U. S. Navy.......................	1628 Dolores
Coker John R.......	D	36th N. Y. Inf.....................	LaGrande La'ndry
Collins Daniel S....	E	9th U. S. Inf.....................	210 Twenty-fourth
Cone James H......	I	26th Conn. Inf........	1811 O'Farrell
Concy C. W. H	A	33d Mass. Inf. and 3d Mass. Cav...	1920 Fillmore
Conner Wesley......	F	38th Ind. Inf.....................	652 Market
Connolly P..........	K	3d R. I. Heavy Art...............	643 Merchant
Conway P. J........	G	98th U. S. Colored Inf............	557 Sacramento
Cook Charles M.....	H	15th Kansas Cav...................	120 Seventh
Cook Jay H.........	C	1st U. S. Inf.....................	1 Fifth
Corbett S. J., M. D..	D	2d Mass. Cav.....	311 Taylor
Cottle T. C.........	D	16th U. S. Inf....................	21 Delone
Courtenay M. R.....	K	3d U. S. Cav....'...............	250 Tehama
Cowen J. R..........	A	16th N. Y. Inf....................	118 Geary
Cox C..............	D	147th Penn. Inf........	336 O'Farrell
Craig T. H.........	G	84th Penn. Inf....................	1532 Ellis
Crane John	D	9th U. S. Inf.....	140 Minna
Creed Jeremiah.....	C	4th N. Y. Inf. and 25th N. Y. Inf...	929 Battery
Creedon P. H	B	1st Cal. Cav.....	Greenwood, Cal.
Cronin John	F	1st Conn. Art......................	40½ Louisa
Cross R. S..........	D	8th Cal. Inf......................	141 Page
Crozet Eugene Du...	C	47th N. Y. Inf....................	1324 California
Culver Lafayette....	L	14th Mass. Cav. and F 8th N. J. Cav	McAllister & Lott
Cummings P. W.....	D	10th N. Y. Art. and 6th N. Y. Art...	Mission nr 29th
Curran Patrick......	E	52d N. Y. Inf.....................	144 Second
Currie Arthur L.....	F	83d Ohio Inf......................	514 Post
Curtis J............	B	13th Mass. Inf....................	Visalia, Cal
Cusack Thos	G	102d N. Y. Inf..	2617 Harrison
Czerny C. E.........	C	91st Penn. Inf....................	23 Sixth
Dalton M...........		U. S. S. Chicopee.............	
Davis J. M	F	12th Penn. Reserves.............	17 Fremon
Decker Henry C.....	A	57th Ind. Inf. and H 53d Ind. Inf..	8'0 Market
Decker J. H........	D	1st Mass. Art.....................	718 Market
Dennison E. B.....		1st Ohio Inf......................	221 Powell
Devereaux E. W.....	D	1st Maine Cav....................	120 Fourth .
Devine Patrick......		U. S. Navy.......................	
DeWitt James C.....	C	67th N. Y. Inf...................	2 Helen Place
Dibble H. C.........	G	14th N. Y. Cav.	U.S.Apprais'r Bldg
Doherty M..........	H	12th U. S. Inf....................	40 Louisa
Dohoney J..........	A	162d N. Y. Inf....................	70 Brosnan
Doley W. P	B	5th Ky. Inf.......................	1146 Union
Donahue C. J ..	A	14th N. J. Inf....................	8th & Bryant
Donaldson Stuart...	G	33d Mass. Inf.....................	San Lorenzo, Cal.
Donlon Peter.......	K	35th N. J. Inf....................	Antioch, Cal.
Donnelly A. B......		U. S. S. Argosy...................	234 Sixth

NAME.	CO.	SERVICE.	ADDRESS.
Dorrer William......	C	18th Ky. Inf.......................	1744 Market
Doty Newton M.....	C	25th Wis. Inf......................	Internat'nal Hotel
Douglas C. D........	F	2d Cal. Inf........................	P.O.Sta.C,Potrero
Dudley E. II	I	137th Ill. Inf......................	1238 Bush
Dugan John..	H	19th U. S. Inf.....................	2322 Webster
Duhem Victor......	G	5th Cal. Inf.......................	1324 Polk
Duncan James K....	I	6th Mass. Inf.....................	Jackson, Cal.
Dunn Edward.......	H	21st Wis. Inf.....................	San Mateo, Cal.
Dunn Michael C....	D	1st N. Y. Cav....................	2629 Sutter
Dunphy Luke......	M	2d U. S. Art.....................	2010 Polk
Dwelle James II....	C	1st Mich. Cav....................	1014½ Minna
Dyer M..............	F	2d Cal. Inf........................	
Eagan E. M..........		U. S. S. Colorado.................	11 Pearl
Ebert Eckert........	E	20th N. Y. Inf.....................	323 Fifth
Edsall E P.....		30th Ind. Inf.....................	101 Dupont
Einsfeld Peter.... .	I	28th N. Y. Inf.....................	650 Market
Ellinsworth Samuel.	G	3d U. S Inf. and F 23d Penn. Inf..	108 Fourth
Ellis C. L..	E	2d Cal. Cav.	712½ Clementina
Elsus Christie......	I	3d N. Y. Inf......................	1205 Steiner
Emmerich B........	B	13th Conn. Inf....	140 Eleventh
Evans B F..........	K	4th Mass. Art.....................	Boston, Mass.
Ewen Oliver........	D	69th N. Y. Inf....................	5 Market
Fahcy Martin......	I	9th Mass. Inf.....................	Haight & Gough
Fairbairn Richard...	H	43d Ind. Inf...............	219 Clara
Falls R. J..........	E	2d Cal. Cav. and 1st Penn. Inf....	827 Folsom
Farclot Chas. C.....		U. S. Navy.................... ...	6 Turk
Fenn J. H..........	E	91st Penn. Inf..............	1505 Market
Ferber Charles......	F	46th N. Y. Inf..........	1601 Mason
Ficken Henry.......	B	2d Cal. Inf. ....·....	8½ Erie
Fischer Chas........	A	8th N. Y. Inf.....	244 Sutter
Fisher II. C........	E	7th Mass. Inf,....................	24 Mint av.
Flack David........	E	4th Ohio Inf......................	316 Third
Fletcher John......	A	2d Mass. Cav...	Antioch, Cal.
Flick Carl..........		100th N. Y. Inf....................	Menlo Park, Cal.
Foley John.........	A	23d Ill. Inf.......................	321 Austin
Fontaine Victor de la		2d Mass. Inf..................	1629 West Mission
Ford Fred W.......		U. S. S. Niagara..................	137½ Clara
Ford J. P..........	B	6th Cal. Inf................... ...	1307 Stockton
Foster John C.......	B	139th Ill. Inf. and I 47th Ill. Inf..	Salinas, Cal.
Frank Wm. J.......	B	20th Mass. Inf..............	25th nr Diamond
Frazer Hugh........	H	48th Mass. Inf....................	Paciffc Roll'g Mills
French John S.......	M	1st Maine Cav....................	31 Oak Grove av.
Fuller George II....	A	26th Conn. Inf....................	638 Mission
Fuller Wm. A.......	G	4th U. S. Art.....................	Taylor & Ellis
Gardiner F. I.......		U. S. S. North Carolina...........	
Garland D. H	B	1st Mass. Heavy Art....	455 Octavia
Garrett James II....	F	8th N. Y. Inf.....................	106 Hyde
Garrick Michael....	C	9th R. I. Inf.....................	834 Howard
Gateley T. B........		3d Cal. Inf.......................	1706 Hyde
Gere George G., M. D.	F	1st Neb. Cav	120 Post
Gildersleeve R......	E	4th Cal. Inf......................	134 Main
Gleason John.......		U. S. S. Hartford.................	Lafayette, Cal
Glenn W. II........	A	43d Mass. Inf....................	1228 Market
Gobertz Martin......		U. S. S. Tacoma............·......	9 Geary
Goothe Adolph......	K	8th N. Y, Inf.................	Sonoma, Cal.
Goetze Wm.........	M	2d Cal. Cav......................	460 Jessie

NAME.	CO.	SERVICE.	ADDRESS.
Gorman John	A	4th Cal. Inf	731½ Clementina
Goulding Charles N.		U. S. Vols	Brooklyn Hotel
Green Geo. M	I	51st Ind. Inf	833 Howard
Green John E		20th Mass Inf	222 Fourth
Greer Wm. McF	D	1st Mo. Engineers	871 Folsom
Griffin W. W	G	4th U. S. Inf	1008 Alabama
Griswold E	A	137th Ill. Inf	Wadsworth, Nev.
Guggenheimer S	E	10th Ohio Cav	613 Kearny
Gumbringer John	K	7th N. Y. Inf. and 86th N. Y. Inf	San Jose, Cal.
Hackmeier A	D	5th U. S. Inf	435 Pine
Hadley A. F	K	43d Mass. Inf	2 Boston Place
Hagler O. T	H	144th Ill. Inf	119 Bush
Hall J. C	E	33d Wis. Inf	740 Pine
Hamm Jacob	K	26th Ind. Inf. and 33d Ind. Inf	1148 Sutter
Handley C. J	B	1st Oregon Inf	Louisiana & Shasta
Haney Benj. F	I	3d Iowa Cav	Antioch, Cal.
Hanson Feargus	A	7th Iowa Inf	1708 Stockton
Hard David T	A	13th Vermont Inf	243 Chattanooga
Hardenberg J. R., Jr	I	1st Wash. Ter. Inf. & 2d Cal. Cav	Baldwin Hotel
Harger J	C	15th Iowa Inf	26th & Bartlett
Harlow D. T	H	8th Vt. Inf	39 Lafayette
Harris E. B., M. D.		U. S. Army	1413 Bush
Harris Edwin W.	F	39th Wis. Inf	1 Fifth
Hart Henry	H	1st U. S. Cav	1604 Pacific av.
Hartley Erastus	H	31st Ohio Inf	28 Sixteenth
Harvey John	C	9th U. S. Inf	117 Ellis
Hatherly Wm	H	1st U. S. Engineers	9 Minna
Hatch J. Q	H	5th Mass. Inf	1131 Ellis
Hazard A. R		U. S. S. Vincennes	110 Sixth
Healy Wm	C	37th N. Y. Inf	Mission & 30th
Hegan James	D	3d U. S. Cav	5 Bowie av.
Hegeman F	A	1st N. Y. Cav	321 Dupont
Hein Adam	A	10th Conn. Inf	606 Mission
Henderson J. W	C	3d Cal. Inf	22d & Natoma
Hennessey M	G	4th U. S. Art	34 Minna
Hickey James		U. S. Marine Corps	Haight & Lyon
Hicks R. D	I	12th Maine Inf	609 Shotwell
Hill John J	D	5th Cal. Inf	435 Pine
Hillebrand Albert	E	20th N. Y. Inf	1019 Market
Hinds Wm		U. S. Vols	704 Bryant
Hobbert H. T	I	47th Mass. Inf	218 Third
Hohn John	E	4th Ohio Cav	907 Folsom
Hollis Thomas	I	20th Mass. Inf	434 Twenty-second
Holscher Frank H.	E	34th N. Y. Inf	1510 Sanchez
Holtslander J. J	B	13th Ill. Inf	525 Brannan
Holtz L	E	66th N. Y. Inf	360 Seventeenth
Homer James L	H	6th Cal. Inf	227 San Jose av.
Hood William	A	46th Mass. Inf	1012 Twenty-four'h
Hooper William B.		2d Cal. Cav. and U. S. Vols	Occidental Hotel
Hostetter A. G	A	32d Ohio Inf	808 Harrison
Hough John	C	12th N. Y. Inf	5 Mason
House W. E	B	7th Mich. Cav	930 Market
Howard C. S		U. S. S. Albatross	2521 California
Howe W. C	B	1st Ohio Art	9½ Lapidge
Hubbard H. F	H	1st Conn. Art	113 Oak
Hull Clinton T	G	11th Iowa Inf	124 Eleventh

NAME.	CO.	SERVICE.	ADDRESS.
Hunt J. H............		U. S. Navy	1435 Pine
Hurley John........	G	2d Mass. Cav.....................	230 Langton
Hutchings J. M.....	G	2d Cal. Inf......................	2521 California
Hutchinson David..	I	4th Cal. Inf.....	725 Union
Innes John Calder.	I	2d Cal. Inf......................	1019 Post
Irving John A	B	1st Mass. Inf....................	105 Stockton
Jackson Daniel.....		10th N. Y. Art.................:	Berkeley, Cal.
Jaiser Charles.......	I	3d N. J. Inf.....................	Ball's Ferry, Cal.
Jehu W. H	C	3d Cal. Inf......................	235 Stevenson
Jenno Jacob........	E	20th N. Y. Inf. and I 133d N. Y. Inf	208 Fifth
Johnson S. S	L	1st Mass. Art. and 6th Mass. Art...	810 Folsom
Jones R. H..	F	2d Wis. Inf	Concord, Cal.
Jumper George F..	K	7th Maine Inf...................	51 Hoff av.
Kane Hugh........	A	5th Penn. Cav...................	2d av.&Pt.Lobos rd
Karns J	E	155th N. Y. Inf.................	1132 Columbia
Keil Henry........	D	6th N. Y. Inf. and G 15th N. Y. Art.	763 Howard
K ller David C......	A	71st N. Y. Inf..................	Berkeley, Cal.
Kelley Bernard.....	F	99th Penn. Inf..................	755 Folsom
Kenniff J..........		U. S. S. Pensacola..............	16½ Hoff av.
King David J		U. S. S. Wissahickon	637 Ellis
Kingsbury L. W. ...	I	145th N. Y. Inf. and 176th N. Y. In.	1030 Howard
Kinne C. Mason.....		2d Mass. Cav................... ...	711 Jones
Kip James..........	F	28th N. Y. Inf.................. ...	127 Kearny
Knott Wm. E.......	K	1st Cal. Inf....................	1217 Pacific
Knox Benj. F	D	18th Iowa Inf......	2818 Sacramento
Krank Frank W.....	A	4th Minn. Inf...................	120 Jackson
Kraut Charles		U. S. Navy.....................	Suisun, Cal.
Kreling Martin.....	I	8th N. Y. Inf...................	30 Eddy
Krieger Armen......	D	15th N. Y. Inf..................	341 McAllister
Krill Henry........	I	35th Mass. Inf..................	606 Powell
Krono F. W.........	C	2d Cal. Cav....................	1521 Powell
Lakin J. H.	C	5th Mass. Inf..................	108½ Powell
Landgraf Charles...	I	N. J. Cav......................	16th av., S. S. F.
Lansing J. L........	D	4th N. Y. Heavy Art.......	P. O. Station D
Larkins Patrick.....	M	1st U S. Art...................	Fort Mason
Lauxman Geo	I	2d N. Y. Heavy Art.............	207 M'n'tg'm'ry rv.
Laws E. R...........	B	52d Ill. Inf.	1308 Green
Layton Wm. S.......	A	N. J. Inf......................	Antioch, Cal.
Leachey Thomas ...		U. S S. Shenandoah.............	Union & Battery
Leavitt Charles M..	D	9th N. J. Inf...................	1324 California
LeChevallier Francis		U. S. S. Marigold..............	1101 Mission
Lee W. G...........	D	2d Cal. Inf....................	Utah & Santa Clara
Lehan Dennis.......	K	48th Mass. Inf..................	19 Mason
Leonard Geo. D......	A	1st Mass. Heavy Art.............	ArroyoGrande,Cal
Levit Samuel........	E	57th Ind. Inf...................	1221 Webster
Lewis Egbert.......	A	8th Iowa Inf	820 Folsom
Lindrob John.......	A	89th N. Y. Inf..................	27th & Guerrero
Linquist Adolph....	G	2d N. Y. Art......	Mayfield, Cal.
Loesch Valentine....	K	22d Ky. Inf....................	2 Quincy Place
Long Charles H.....	I	1st Md. Inf., P. H. D	2824 Greenwich
Loring E. B.........	A	2d Cal. Cav.	1203 Market
Lovett Eugene R....	K	22d Conn. Inf	226 Nineteenth
Lucas J. S..........	E	3d and 23d Mass. Inf	711 Minna
Lull N. A..........	A	1st Ill. Art...................	19 South Park
Luttringer Emile...	F	55th N. Y. Inf.................	4 Erie
Lynch William......		U. S. S. Stars and Stripes.........	951 Mission

NAME.	CO.	SERVICE.	ADDRESS.
Lyon J. J............	B	1st Mich. Inf., 24th & 21st Mo. Inf.	1114 Broadway
Lyons Ed...........		U. S. Ordnance Department.......	521 Pacific
Mager Henry........		U. S. S. Pensacola.................	37 Pacific
Maguire Thomas....	D	40th N. J. Inf......................	San Francisco
Manley Frank.......	D	7th Ohio Inf.....................	Benicia, Cal.
Manning Nathan W.	K	11th Ind. Inf.....................	Benicia Barracks
Manouk C...........		25th N. Y. Inf....................	142½ Fourth
Marrs Chas.........	A	30th Mass. Inf....................	570 Howard
Martin A. W	H	10th R. I. Inf....................	33 Kearny
Martin Thomas.....	C	3d Mass. Inf.....................	1418 Pacific
Mass Peter H........		U. S. Navy	2207 Larkin
Massie William.....	A	6th N. Y. Sharpshooters....... ..	Churchill Court
Masteller T. C........	G	140th Ill. Inf. and U. S. S. Missouri	407 Leavenworth
Mayer Harry........		U. S. Navy	39 Pacific
Mayle Geo. D.......	E	11th Ohio Inf....................	38 Fourth
Mayo Nathaniel C...	K	4th Mass. Heavy Art..............	1608 Stevenson
McCarty John.......	F	3d N. Y. Light Art...............	767 Howard
McConnell Robert.	B	150th N. Y. Inf..................	421 Fifth
McDermott T......	H	83d N. Y. Inf.....................	1 Everett
McGrath T..........	C	69th N. Y. Inf...................	102 Sansome
McGrew J. M........	E	15th Ind. Inf....................	818 Twentieth
McGue John I.......	L	16th Kansas Inf.................	Haight & Stanyan
McKillip Daniel.....	D	24th Wis. Inf....................	249 Sixteenth
McLaughlin M. A...	D	2d Cal. Cav......................	R. R. & 12th av.
McLean A. A........	L	2d Mass. Cav....................	646 Market
McNeil W. H.......	A	2d Mass. Cav....................	2211 Van Ness av.
Mead Charles F.....	B	4th Mass. Cav.............	448 Guerrero
Meagher Patrick....	A	25th N. J. Inf...................	416 Duncan
Medbury W. C.......	F	1st Bat. Nevada Inf.....	214½ Sixth
Medley J. P........	G	1st N. Y. Cav...................	108 Third
Meserth L..........		50th Penn. Inf.	28th & Mission
Metzler Theodore C.		U. S. Navy..................	1314 Ellis
Miller C. A.........	G	20th Wis. Inf..	406 Fourth
Miller Frank G.....	H	2d U. S. Art......	411 Polk
Miller Geo. A......		U. S. S. Louisville................	561½ Minna
Miller Jerome.......	D	122d Penn. Inf.....	Clay St. Hill R. R.
Miller J. H..........	A	1st Bat. Wis. Art...............	Guaymas, Mexico
Miller William......	A	80th N. Y. Inf..................	760 Folsom
Mills Luther........	K	80th N. Y. Inf..................	1611 Dupont
Miltenberger Chas..	B	9th U. S. Inf....................	3064 Laguna
Milz Peter..........	E	16th N. Y. Art..................	529 Natoma
Moesner August	E	52d N. Y. Inf. and G 16th Conn. Inf	32 Second
Moran Bernard.....	E	5th U. S. Cav...................	Presidio
Morris C. R.........	A	178th N. Y. Inf..................	1807 Polk
Morris John........	A	99th N. Y. Inf...................	
Morris Thomas.....	C	28th N. J. Inf...................	348 Minna
Morrison Howard...	E	1st Cal. Cav....	Tivoli Theatre
Mosberg A..........	H	40th N. Y. Inf...................	700 Mission
Muehe C............	H	27th Mo. Inf....................	19 Oak Grove av.
Muhlner W. F.......	K	27th Conn. Inf..................	362 Tyler
Mullen John........		U. S. Navy.....................	51 Shipley
Mullins Henry B....	H	170th N. Y. Inf..................	112 Eddy
Murphy A. H........	I	91st Penn. Inf..................	2549 Howard
Murphy H. H.......	H	19th Maine Inf..................	27 Debone
Murphy Michael....		163d N. Y. Inf..................	1624 Pacific av.
Murphy Patrick.....		16th Ind. Battery................	What Cheer House

NAME.	CO.	SERVICE.	ADDRESS.
Murphy Timothy...	F	3d R. I. Heavy Art......	13 Welsh
Murray M..........		U. S. S. Roanoke.........	262 Eighth
M yer F. W........	B	5th N. Y. Inf.....................	2404 Post
Nanscawen L.V....	I	29th Wis. Inf.....................	Visalia, Cal.
Nestell Adam........	A	23d U. S. Inf.....................	4th & Stevenson
Newhard James M..	E	25th Mo. Inf.	7th&Webster, Oak.
Newman Peter A....		U. S. S. Mackinaw.................	141½ Minna
Nicolaysen J........		U. S. S. Roanoke.................	116 Leidesdorff
Noble J. D........	C	27th Iowa Inf....................	P. O. Box 2605
Noble T. K.........		128th U. S. Colored Inf...........	2200 Steiner
Noethig Wm.......		3d Mo. Inf.......................	Duncan's Mills
Nolan Patrick.......	F	66th N. Y. Inf....................	1203½ Pacific av.
Nolto A. F.........	L	1st N. Y. Cav....................	Chestnut & Taylor
Norris Hiram J.....	M	3d Ohio Cav......................	238 Fair Oaks
O'Connor John......	F	5th U. S. Cav....................	27 Church
O'Hearn James F....	I	8th Mass. Inf. and 65th Mass. Inf..	Menlo Park, Cal.
O'Rouke J..........	C	215th Penn. Inf.................	735 Brannan
Orton R. H........	F M	1st Cal. Cav....................	419 California, r 12
Owens J. C.........		U. S. S. Augusta.................	410 Hayes
Park Wm. Jay.......	L	16th Mo. Cav....................	2008 Ellis
Parker F. W........	I	5th Mass. Inf...................	520 Noe
Patterson John M...	B	40th Penn. Inf. and B 192 Ohio Inf	20½ Oak
Patterson Wm.......	D	90th Penn. Inf..................	246 Third
Paulsen Chas. A.....		U. S. Navy	Pt. Bonita L'th'se
Payne A. D. L..	B	64th Ohio Inf...................	2729 Pine
Peake Chas..........	G	153d Ill. Inf...................	3 Fulton
Pendergast J. H.....	C	3d N. Y. Inf. and E 25th N. Y. Inf..	812 Jessie
Penalet William....	E	2d N. Y. Inf. and H 48th N. Y. Inf.	Ft. Halleck, Nev.
Pepper Albert E. ..	I	6th Penn. Cav....................	218 Eddy
Peterman C.........	K	79th Penn. Inf..................	36 New M'ntg'm'ry
Philbrook J. M......	B	4th Cal. Inf...........	San Luis Obispo
Pillsbury C. E.......	D	16th Maine Inf......	Pacific Roll'g Mills
Pinney E. H........	B	2d Mass. Cav...................	616 Harrison
Pittman H. C..		U. S. Navy.....................	38 Market, Oakl'd
Platt Charles H.....	E	8th Cal. Inf....................	412 Hyde
Pool J. W..........	M	10th N. Y. Art..................	63 Tehama
Poulson Andrew J..	D	8th Del. Inf....................	1001 Market
Powers Thomas.....		U. S. S. Albatross	637½ Natoma
Price C. M.........		U. S. Navy	112 Eddy
Provost Nelson......		U. S. S. Anacosta...............	Loring, Cal.
Quart Fred J........	A	2d Mass. Cav	Brentwood, Cal.
Quinlan D..........	C	3d Mass. Art. and U. S. Navy......	718 Howard
Quinn Michael......	A	2d U. S. Art....................	516 Ivy av.
Quitzow August.....	E	11th N. Y. Inf..................	969 Mission
Rainville Joseph....	I	1st Ill. Art.	204 Leavenworth
Ralston J. O........	A	12th N. Y. Cav.................	2343 Washington
Randall W. F......	E	14th Maine Inf......	916 Howard
Ramsey W. H.......	K	11th Ill. Inf...................	124¾ Gilbert
Raymond J. W......	C	7th Ohio Inf...................	
Reintanz Q. J.......	L	8th N. J. Cav..................	629 Broadway
Rentschler J. G....	G	8th Ohio Cav...................	1624 Mission
Rhody A. M........	D	28th Penn. Inf..	64 Locust
Richmond H........	K C	15th Ill. Inf...................	1713 Jessie
Richter R..........	C	1st U. S. Dragoons..............	1816 Union
Richwine Solomon..	G	23d Ohio Inf...................	Gridley, Cal.
Riegelhaupt Philip.	A	4th N. Y. Inf....................	546 Howard

NAME.	CO.	SERVICE.	ADDRESS.
Roberts J. P........	H	28th Penn. Inf....	Sierra & Tennessee
Roberts Philip S....	I	51st Ohio Inf......................	Brentwood, Cal.
Roberts Richard M..	B	146th N. Y. Inf...................	727½ Folsom
Robinson Geo. H....	F	2d Cal. Cav......................	San Mateo
Rockwood A. L.....	E	4th Ill. Cav......................	512 Montgomery
Roskamp H. F......	D	55th N. Y. Inf....................	South S. F.
Rouse Gaylord......	D	10th N. Y. Art...................	Antioch, Cal.
Rowe August........	C	15th N. Y. Inf........	5th & Bryant
Ruffs J.............		U. S. S. Vermont.................	Clay St. R.R. Office
Ryan William.......	C	99th N. Y. Inf. and 1st Md. Inf....	1212 Clay
Salisbury John......	D	84th Ill. Inf.....................	Nevada Block
Sanno W. de........		U. S S. New Ironsides............	20½ Willow av.
Satterlee Geo. A.....	A	1st Iowa Inf......................	4 Mason
Sayre M. S.........	E	161st N. Y. Inf....	Middletown, Cal.
Schlaudecker M.....		111th Penn. Inf..................	527 Clay
Schmidt John C.....	G	2d Cal. Inf......................	427 East
Schnoor C. H.......		9th U. S. Inf.....................	St. Helena, Cal.
Schroeder Anthony.		Ind. Light Art....	Cal. av., nr 29th
Schroff C...........		98th Penn. Inf...................	28th&San Bruno rd
Schubert August....	I	6th N. Y. Inf....................	19th & Howard
Schultz Theodore...	K	2d Cal. Inf......................	426 Green
Schussler O.........	C	20th N. Y. Inf....................	503 Filbert
Seagraves E. F......	L	2d Mass. Cav....................	P. O. Box 1935
Sebring J...........	A	23d Ohio Inf.....................	2708 Sutter
Shellenberger Jos...	E	2d U. S. Art......................	1713 Jessie, rear
Shirk A......... ...		U. S. S. Magnolia......	503 Mason
Shute Wm. C........	A	14th Maine Inf...................	547 Mission
Siegel Morris.......	I	3d R. I. Art.....................	1502 Stockton
Simon J. G.........	H	43d Mass. Inf....................	1608 West Mission
Simonds W. S.......	D	16th Vt. Inf.....................	26th & Dolores
Sitton John Jeffrey.	H	24th Mo. Inf.....................	833 Geary
Slane Edward A.....	A	11th Kansas Cav..................	17 Fourth
Smedley J. K.......		Monitor Nantucket...............	2304 Howard
Smith James H......	G	104th Penn. Inf..................	632 Howard
Smith Joshua.......	C	12th Maine Inf...................	1230 Mission
Smith P. J.........	G	11th N. H. Inf...................	35 Eddy
Smith W. H.... ...	I	2d U. S. Inf.....................	1216 Pacific
Smith Wilson O.....	F	3d Maine Inf....................	Bieber, Lassen Co.
Snyder E. P........		U. S. S. Minnesota...............	51 Tehama
Squires William....		25th N. Y Independent Battery....	436 Seventh
Stark Luke.........	B	7th Cal. Inf.....................	529 First
Starr Frederick....		U. S. Navy......................	715 Lombard
Stauffer Benj. F.....	G	95th Ohio Inf....................	1611 Clay
Stearns Wm. R.....	K	53d N. Y. Inf., F 5th N. Y. (Duryea's Zouaves) and F 146th N. Y. Inf....	826 Sutter
Steffens John.......	C	11th Vet. Reserve Corps...........	Kentucky St.Ex.pl
Sterling Hiram.....		U. S. S. Perry...................	717 Clementina
Stevens George.....	E	4th U. S. Cav......	Police Station
Stevens G. H........	K	5th Iowa Inf. & 48th U.S. Col'd Inf.	857 Harrison
Stevens Lucian.....	B	2d N. J. Inf.....................	2514½ Sutter
Steward Henry D...	A	16th Mich. Inf...................	521 Pacific
Stillwell William...	H	10th Penn. Reserve Corps.........	1330 California
Stone W. W.........		U. S. S. Colorado................	31 Liberty
Stott Wm. D........		U. S. S. New Ironsides............	Golden Gate Park
Stromberg B. F....		U. S. S. Pequot..................	Oakland
Strozinski Theophile	O	31st N. Y. Inf....................	405 Fifth

NAME.	CO.	SERVICE.	ADDRESS.
Stuart John.........	A	5th Cal. Inf.....	938 Pacific
Sullavou Samuel....	K	24th U. S. Colored Iuf............	18 Taylor
Sullivan Michael....	A	16th N. Y. Inf......	19 Freelon
Sullivan Timothy...		U. S. S. Louisville	316 California
Sweetland Alonzo...		5th Maine Art....................	631 Stevenson
Sweetser F. D......	C	71st N. Y Inf. and 2d U.S.Sharpsh's	1523 Polk
Tambling V. A......	C	13th U. S. Inf. and G 53d Ill. Inf..	12 Laskie
Taylor R. W.........	I	55th Ill. Inf. & 3d U. S. Colored Inf.	628 Montgomery
Thatcher E. C......	I	57th Penn. Inf...................	2224 Mission
Thomas C. J........	K	17th Penn. Inf...................	35 Eddy
Thomas Edward B...	C	10th Penn. Inf................ ...	25½ Stockton
Thorn Jacob........	E	15th N. Y. Heavy Art.............	801 Mission
Tonna Pietro........	B	46th N. Y. Inf....................	268 Stevenson
Toohey James.......		U. S. Navy	Pt. Reyes L'thouse
Tower Nelson.......	I	10th N. Y. Inf. and A 11th N. Y. Inf	1446½ Minna
Towndrow W. N	D	9th U. S. Inf....................	638 Valencia
Townley Wm........	E	5th Md. Inf.......	R. R. & 6th av.
Travers W. M.......	G	4th N. Y. Art....................	1621 Powell
Trewin Robert......	C	8th Cal. Inf.....................	631 Mission
Tripp Joseph.......	K	1st Mass. Cav....	337 Bryant
Tuggey Wm.........	A	48th Mass. Inf...................	435 Grove
Turner W. R.......	G	2d Mass. Inf.....................	1607 Mission
Ubhaus Ludwig.....	M	14th N. Y. Cav..................	130 Bernard
Ullmer John........	C	8th Kansas Cav..................	German Hospital
Upton John........	B	1st Cal. Inf...	735 Pine
Van de Water H....	G	2d Cal. Inf......	110 23d
Vetterli Jacob.......	A	7th Ill. Cav......	603 Pine
Vining G. H........		Ordnauce Department	6 Metcalfe Place
Volpillac Etienne...	K	2d Cal. Cav......	Pinole, Cal.
Volz Jacob.........	F	54th N. Y. Inf.....	1402 Montgomery
Voorhees Will H....	C	40th Penn.Inf.and A 196th Penn.Inf	844 Mission
Wacker Gus	G	9th N. H. Inf....................	1118 Alabama
Wall O. L...........	H	7th Kansas Cav..................	San Jose
Wallace Edward L..	A	57th Ill. Inf.....................	838 Mission
Walsh Michael.....		21st and 22d Bat. U. V. R. C......	400 Ninth
Wardlow James.....	B	6th U. S. Inf...................	409 Taylor
Warren C. H.......	E	1st Cal. Cav....................	112 Alta
Watson James.......	A	2d Mass. Cav....................	San Rafael
Watts Richard......	G	14th Mass. Inf........	1432 Broadway
Weber R. H........	I	34th N. Y. Inf...................	2515 Larkin
Wedel John M......	E	2d La. Inf.......................	
Wehr Henry........	G	8th N. Y. Inf....................	40 Jackson
Weisheimer Charles.	C	31st N. Y. Inf...................	450 Sixteenth
Wells Eugene.......	K	156th Ill. Inf....................	308 Beale
Welton Walter B....	K	2d Cal. Cav....................	61 Minna
Wentworth N. S....	E	53d N. Y. Inf....................	20th near Harrison
Wenzlik R..........	G	173d N. Y. Inf...................	113 Montgomery
Werner F. F........	A	7th U. S. Inf....................	11th av.nr.N.S.S.F.
Werner G...........	H	54th N. Y. Inf...................	451 Stevenson
Wharff John F......	M	1st Maine Cav................... .	1324 Devisadero
Wharff W. H......	C	11th Maine Inf....................	Green and Laguna
Whitcomb R. K.....	G	9th Maine Inf....................	34 Glen Park ave.
White Joseph.......		U. S. S. Independence............	411 Sansome
Whitesides Alex	G	2d Mo. Cav......................	116 Chattanooga
Whitney John T	A	146th Ill. Inf	504 Third
Whittemore J. B....	A G	1st Cal. Inf......................	535 Post

NAME.	CO.	SERVICE.	ADDRESS.
Wilkins W. J.......		U. S. S. Nansemond...............	109 Cala., r. 17
Wilkins W. P.......	D	100th N. Y. Inf...................	3008 Filmore
Willscn Thomas A..	B	3d U.S.Col'd Inf.& 10th Pa. R.Corps	518 Green
Wilson B...........	G	9th N. H. Inf......................	226 Montgomery
Wilson J. H.........	B	2d Mass. Inf. and U. S. Navy.	318 Broadway
Wilson John E......	H	83d Penn. Inf..........	906 Folsom
Wilson Richard.....	C	4th U. S. Art...........	2014 Filbert
Wilson W. A........	B	8th Cal. Inf......................	26 Minna
Wing William......	E	4th Cal. Inf.....................	100½ Second
Wohltman Otto.....	A	11th N. Y. Cav....................	4 Tehama
Wornes R. C........	B	7th Cal. Inf.....................	Monterey
Yeomans H.		U. S.S Portsmouth........	219 Second
Young J. H.........	D	14th N. Y. Inf....................	510 Stockton
Zabriskie J. H......	K	2d N. J. Inf. and D 114th N. Y. Inf.	706 Jones
Ziegler F. E.........	B	52d N. Y. Inf....................	Wash'in & Saus'm

DRY GOODS!

—— THE ——

MURPHY BUILDING

Cor. Market and Jones Streets.

J. J. O'BRIEN & CO.

PROPRIETORS.

It is pleasant to recall the success which has attended the efforts of J. J. O'Brien as a business man. He opened a small store on Third street, in 1868, when he was 21 years of age and, in a short time his business outgrew the place. Foreseeing the future of Market street, he leased the Arcade building adjoining the Baldwin Hotel, a location then considered out of Town, his growing trade soor, assumed such enormous proportions as necessitated his removal to more extensive premises.

THE MURPHY BLOCK.

This monster institution occupies a total area of 24,000 square feet, and is the best lighted, best appointed, and one of the largest Retail Dry Goods Stores in the United States. Noticable among its advantages is its perfect ventilation, a pleasing change from the suffocating atmosphere of Dry Goods Stores generally. Its counters laid in a continuous line would measure over a quarter of a mile in length and are capable of accommodating a patronage of several thousands. A visit to the ladies' reception rooms, impresses one with the preparations made for the comfort of its patrons. The architecture and decorations are of Moorish design and surpass in elegance and Artistic effect, the famous waiting room of the Bon Marchi in Paris. Its tables are supplied with Journals, Magazines and Writing materials for the convenience of lady visitors. Adjoining this are the ladies toilet and dressing rooms, in charge of a lady attendant. An idea of the immense volume of business transacted in this model establishment, may be gained by a visit during business hours.

In the several departments can be found the choicest products of the most celebrated European manufacturers as well as the cheapest grades of Domestic goods, it being the business principle of the House to cater to the requirements of all classes. Another feature, is the uniform courtesy and anxiety to please, manifested on all occasions, in exchanging goods or refunding money for purchases made when the goods do not give satisfaction.

In fact, it may be said, that the institution is in every way worthy of San Francisco, and an instance of what enterprise, conducted on true business priciples may accomplish.

GEORGE H. THOMAS POST, No. 2.

SAN FRANCISCO, CAL.

OFFICERS, 1886.

CHARLES E. WILSON..Commander
H. BARTLING..Senior Vice-Commander
W. W. MAGARY..Junior Vice-Commander
GEO. M. McCARTY..Adjutant
CHARLES H. BLINN..Quartermaster
C. A. KIRKPATRICK...Surgeon
REV. J. MATTHEWS..Chaplain
CHARLES JANSEN..Officer of the Day
H. S. DEARBORN..Officer of the Guard
P. T. M. WATE..Sergeant Major
F. R. MORTON..Quartermaster Sergeant

Meeting, every Tuesday, In Ruby Hall, Red Men's Building, 320 Post street.

NAME.	CO.	SERVICE.	ADDRESS.
Abrams Robert......		Marine Art......................	Baldwin Theatre
Adams C. W.........		12th Kansas Inf..........	110 Taylor
Adams E. F.........		41st Ohio Inf.....................	329 Sansome
Adams Zeb. B.......	L	2d and 5th Mass Cav.	12 Pine
Ager Loren J.......	F	10th N. Y. Art...................	Sufiol, Cal.
Ager Mark.........	F	20th N. Y. Cav....................	"
Alberti G. W........	E	26th and A 46th Penn. Inf.........	1007 24th
Allen E. T.........	G	7th R. I. Inf...................	416 Market
Ames R. C..	O	41st Wis. Inf..........	Butte City, Mon.
Ammerman J. B....	B	7th N. Y. State Militia............	329 Sansome
Anthony Albert.....	H	9th Mo. and II 59th Ill. Inf.......	114 Sutter
Arnold Geo. H	O	22d N. Y. State Militia............	Baldwin Hotel
Babcock M. S... ..		U. S. Grand Gulf................	Hanford, Cal.
Bacon A. P.........	D	13th Mass. Inf. and F 4th U.S.Vols	S. F. Gaslight Co.
Bacon Francis H....		U. S. Navy......................	313 Ellis
Bacon Martin.......		1st. Bat. Ill. (Yates') Sharpshooters	Alameda
Bagley P. H., Jr.....	E	1st Mass. Inf......	433 Golden Gate av
Bailey E. F.........	H	1st West Va. Art.................	709 McAllister
Bailey Wilson S.....	D	185th Ohio Inf....................	20 Alvarado
Baird A. M.........	A	113th Ill. Inf....	1211 Mission
Baldwin George E...	L	2d Mass. Cav....	1525 California
Balz A.............		6th U. S. Inf...................	444 Twentieth
Banks Chas. W......	I	131st N. Y. Inf..................	Wells, Fargo & Co
Barnard J. Howard..	'	13th U. S. Colored Heavy Art......	10 Beaver
Barnard L. H........	B	1st Mo. Inf..	402 Front

14

NAME.	CO.	SERVICE.	ADDRESS.
Barnes W. H. L......		7th N. Y. State Militia.............	426 California
Barnett George A....	F	122d N. Y. Inf....................	Santa Rosa
Barnett G. P........	G	10th Kansas Inf..................	Wells, Nev.
Barr J. D............	E	162d N. Y. Inf...................	1214 Mason
Bartholow W. E. B..	A	8th Mo. Inf. and K 30th Ill. Inf....	504 Stockton
Battling H..........	I	2d Ill. Cav. and 8th U. S. Art.......	24 Glen Park ave
Bateman C. A., Rev.	B	5th Mo. Cav....................	107 Ash ave
Beach C. W.........	E	2d Wis. Cav.....................	2101 Devisadero
Behan Chas. T.......	E	129th N. Y. Inf. and 10th Vct. Vols.	101 Montgomery
Dondel Herman.....	O	2d and 34th Mo. Inf..............	S.W.cr Clay & Bat.
Bennett G. J........	O	7th Iowa Inf.....................	U. S. Mint
Bent J. T...........		1st Mass. Inf....................	528 Golden Gate av
Bigelow C. L........		4th Maine Bat'y & G 16th Maine Inf.	Mission & Frem'nt
Billings George A...	H	44th Mass. Inf..................	1155 Howard
Blackmon P. S......	B	63d Ind. Inf....................	511 Hayes
Blake Chas. E., M. D.	F	40th U. S. Colored Inf.......	200 Stockton
Blake C. M..........		13th Mo. Inf...................	427 Geary
Blinn Charles H.....	A	1st Vt. Cav...	1527 Post
Boalt J. H...........	M	11th Ohio Cav..................	438 California
Bolton Thomas......	A	27th Mass. Inf..................	805 Howard
Bonestell C. A......	A	5th N. Y. Inf...................	211 Geary
Bonte J. H. C., Rev..		43d Ohio Inf...................	Berkeley, Cal.
Boone J. L		20th Ohio and 1st Oregon Inf......	320 California
Boyd Abraham......	I	129th Ohio Inf..................	Stockton, Cal.
Bramhall B. M......	D	13th Mass.and K 44th U. S. Inf......	Hill nr. Valencia
Bramhall W. M.....	K	9th N.Y,State Militia&6th N.Y.Ba'y	121 Market
Bridges L...........	G	19th Ill. Inf.. Ill. Light Art. and U.	
		S. Vols......................	37 Nevada Block
Briody Philip.......	A	69th N. Y. State Militia...........	1647 Mission
Britz A. J...........	F	197th Ohio Inf..................	1925 Larkin
Bromwell L. L......		U. S. Navy ....:......	318 California
Brooke Charles.....	K	5th Mich. Cav..................	717 Market
Brooks Elisha.......	D	8th Cal. Inf....................	1725 Sutter
Brown A. M........		15th U. S. Inf..................	Grand Hotel
Brown George......	B	1st Wis. Cav...................	2629½ Mission
Brown L. L........	G	8th N. Y. Cav..................	2253 Mission
Brown Nathaniel B..	K	56th N.Y.Inf.& 7th N.Y.Ind't Bat'ry	2308 Post
Brown Richard	K	1st Wash. Ter. Inf..............	209 Sansome
Brown Wm..........	O	3d and I 4th N. Y. Cav...........	408 Seventh
Browne J. A........	H	177th N. Y. Inf., 11th N. Y. Bat. and	
		5th N. Y. Heavy Art.............	Brooklyn Hotel
Bumsted E. H.......	E	2d N. Y. Cav...................	18 Hawthorne
Burdell Harvey.....	B	2d and 85th Ohio Inf. and 22d Ohio	
		Light Battery..................	Pt. Reyes, Cal.
Burke Hugh M	B	4th Iowa Inf....	Florence House
Byrnes W. A........		U. S. S. Spieres...............	1939 Stevenson
Camp T. B..........	C	8th Penn. Inf. and 52d Penn. Inf...	320 Sansome
Carels John H......	E	82d Penn. Inf..................	634 Sutter
Carlson Edward.....		4th and 8th Cal. Inf.............	585 Market
Carmody A. F... ...	B	11th N. Y. Inf.................	C. P. R. R. Co.
Carpenter F. H......	D	17th Conn. Inf.................	373 10th, Oakland
Carroll C. E.........	G	5th Mass. Inf..................	942 Twenty-second
Casey John.........	C	8th Conn. Inf..................	1129 Folsom
Cawley John........	H	3d Union League Reg't and Navy..	609 Lombard
Cazeau Charles......	M	8th N. Y. Cav..................	206 Nineteenth
Chadwick A. J.......	K	13th Vt. Inf...................	1435 California

NAME.	CO.	SERVICE.	ADDRESS.
Chandler L. M.......	H	52d Mass. Inf., 1st La. Cav. and U. S. S Ohio.........................	1001 Folsom
Chapman O.........	K	13th N. Y. Heavy Art...............	647 Jessie
Cheever M. R.......	G	4th Vt. Inf..........	1401 7th av., E.Oak
Chever E. E........	H	89th Ill. Inf.....	26 Montgomery
Clark A. D..........	E	9th U. S. Inf.....................	Wm. Tell House
Clark Z. P...........	G H	1st Wis. Inf......................	210 Sansome
Clarke Geo. E........	K	1st R. I. Cav.....................	227 Fair Oaks
Clement L. H.......	H	4th Vt. Inf.....................	Bella Vista Hotel
Cobb W, B..........		U. S. S. Kansas.................	Palace Hotel
Coghlan J. B.......		U. S. Navy......................	Navy Pay Office
Coleman H. G......	A	7th Cal. Inf.....................	Salinas City, Cal.
Collier W. B........	C	1st Bat. Penn. Inf..............	cor. Pine & Taylor
Collins Benj., Jr....	G	6th Cal. Inf....................	509 Clay
Collins R. U........		U. S. S. Tejuca and Suwanee.....	2502 Leavenworth
Connolly John......		U. S. Navy.....................	Baldwin Hotel
Cooley E. K.........		U. S. S. Albatross	15th av,. S. S. F.
Coon David........	H	122d Ill. Inf....................	234 Bush
Corwin G. B........	A	10th N. Y. Cav.................	925 Market
Cowen William A....	K	41st and F 110th Ohio Inf........	232 Jessie
Cox M. S...........	D	40th Iowa Inf....	Wright's Station
Crane A. O..........	G	13th N. Y. Inf................	"
Crary B. F., Rev....		3d Minn. Inf...................	1041 Market
Creary W. E........	F	3d Mich. Inf. and Vet. Res.......	Cheyenne, Wyo. T.
Cressy E. P.........		3d U. S. Cav...................	609 Folsom
Crocker John H.....	A	13th Mass. Inf.................	1103 Bush
Crowell M. L.......	E	8th Conn. Inf..................	Wells, Fargo & Co.
Cruden Albert......		U. S. Navy	1024 Montgomery
Culver M. L........	G	8th N. H. Inf.................	213 Shotwell
Cummings F.... ...	G	5th Mass. Inf.................	1722 Sutter
Currey S. T.........	K	46th Ill. Inf..................	1007 Powell
Currie Jas..........	A	9th N. Y. Inf....	652 Market
Curtis J. B.........	D	17th Conn. Inf...............	735 Market
Cushing H.C.......		4th U. S. Art.................	Baltimore, Md.
Cutler A. D.........	B	6th Mass. Inf.................	613 Eddy
Cutting J. T........	B	Chicago Light Art.............	25 California
Dakin E. A..........	H	1st Conn. Art.................	320 Sansome
Dalton Edward......	F	69th and E 31st N. Y. State Militia..	12 Elizabeth
Dane H. O..........	F	41st Mass. Inf................	120 Sutter
Darby G. W........	I	13th N. Y. State Militia........	510 Clay
Davidson R. P......	F	3d Cal. Inf...................	1001 Sutter
Davis George A......	G	60th Mass. and F 17th Vt. Inf......	Tulare, Cal.
Deacon William.....		U. S. Navy	811 Twentieth
Dearborn H. S.......	F	17th Mass. Inf................	10 Stevenson
Dee W............		U. S. Navy.	647 Jessie
Denicke E. A........		10th N. Y. Inf. and Signal Corps...	539 California
De Puy Anson A....	G	2d Cal. Inf....................	401 Sixth
De Remio A. M......	C	15th Wis. Inf. and I 16th N. Y. Cav.	203 Sacramento
Dewing James......	A	18th Conn. Inf................	420 Bush
Dimond W. H......		A. A. G. U. S. Vols.............	202 Market
Donnelly E., M. D...		2d Penn. Res. and 2d Penn. Cav...	832 Howard
Donohue Michael....		U. S. Navy	P. M. S. S. Grenada
Dorman R. G.......	B	1st N. Y. Cav.................	West Berkeley,Cal
Dorr L. L., M. D ...		13th Mass. Inf................	118 Dupont
Douty F. S..........		U. S. S. Constitution	C. P. R. R. Co.
Downer E...........		117th and 48th N. Y. Inf.......	Greaterville, Ar.

NAME.	CO.	SERVICE.	ADDRESS.
Downer P. R........	A	12th Vt. Inf.....	Office R.M.S., P.O.
Drahms A., Rev.....	B	17th Ill. Cav......................	Sonoma, Cal.
Dudley James S.....		2d U. S. Art......	2229 Jackson
Durkee E. H........	C	39th Wis. Inf....	120 Ellis
Eakin C. P.........		1st U. S. Art....................	Fort Canby, W. T.
Earle H. H..........	I	19th Maine Inf....	529 Market
Earnest C. A...	G	2d and A 30th Ohio Inf....	Angel Island
Eastman G. W.......	C	1st Bat. Cal. Mountaineers....	216 Bush
Eckart W. R........		U. S. Navy......................	2295 Sacramento
Eckler Robert......	D	130th Ill Inf....................	1709½ Jessie
Edgerly Samuel A...	E	24th Mass. Inf...................	216 Montgom'ry av
Eggleston A. T.	B	137th N. Y. Inf.................	124 Post
Elleau H...........	C	11th N. Y. Inf. (Ellsworth Zouaves)	
	E	12th N. Y. Inf...................	208 Sutter
Ellinwood C. N.,M.D.		74th Ill. Inf...................	1723 Pine
Elliott W. L........		U. S. Mounted Rifles and U. S. Cav	1920 Franklin
Ellis D. O..........	K	8th Kansas Inf...	31 Julian ave.
Erickson Conrad....		U. S. S. Savannah...............	Saucelito
Farnum C. A........		U. S. Vols.....................	cr.O'Farrell & Polk
Farnum O. J........	B	22d N. Y. State Militia	109 Fifth
Farrell James...... .	A	122d N. Y. Inf...................	Unit'd Carriage Co
Fay M. C...........		U. S. S. Mount Vernon	217 Sansome
Fenn Thos. W...:...	F	23d N. Y. Inf...................	423 California
Field C. L..........	G	23d and A 30th Maine Inf..........	329 O'Farrell
Fields J. L.........	G	25th and 32d Maine Inf......	1819½ Lyon
Fish M. W., M. D...		11th Mo. Inf....................	East Oakland
Fisher George A ...	A	23d Mass. Inf. and Signal Corps...	109 California
Fisher Joseph......		74th Ohio Inf...................	U. S. Mint
Fisher P. I.........	E	7th N. Y. State Militia..............	14 Battery
Fitton W. H........	I & B	5th Penn. Cav....................	317 Stockton
Flack G. D..........	I	1st Wis. Cav..................	2909 Folsom
Fletter F. J........	G	73d Ind. Inf....................	214 California
Forbes F. M........	C	7th Ohio Inf....................	1024 Larkin
Ford F. C...........		U. S. Vols.....................	1008 Bush
Ford S. P..........	E	5th Cal. Inf....................	620 Filbert
Forsyth Alex. C. ...	A	128th Ohio Inf..................	215 Bush
Fortier S. M........		U. S. S. Ohio	Oakland
Foster Geo. H.......	K	44th Mass. Inf..................	313 California
Frank J. J..........	K	41st N. Y. Inf...................	Box 1540, P. O.
French H. C., M. D..		17th Mich. Inf..................	2512 Mission
French John D.....	E	15th Conn. Inf..................	109 California
French T. J........	I	19th Ill. Inf...................	2337 Mission
Fried A...............	A	6th N. Y. S. M. and A 66th N. Y. Inf	1836 Sutter
Fuger F............	A	4th U. S. Art...................	Presidio Barracks
Gage A. H..........	B	3d Iowa Cav....................	1422 Market
Gamble G. H........		1st Ill. Art.,8 Ill.Cav.and 9 U.S.Cav.	Saucelito
Gardner I. G........	E	111th N. Y. & K 20th U. S. Col'd Inf.	401 California
Garratt R. M.......	E	96th Ill. and 14th and 44th U. S. Colored Inf......................	Alameda
Garretson Sam'l W..	A	21st N. J. Inf...................	419 California
Geary W. L.........		28th Penn. Inf..................	2121 Bush
Geiselman W.......	A	6th and 13th Mo. Cav..............	1720 Gold'nGate av
Giddings B. F.......	B	17th Vt. Inf....................	215 Bush
Giosting J. G........	B	108th Ohio Inf..................	1928 Pine
Gillespie A. M......	I	43d Wis. Inf....................	Ellensburg, Or.
Gilmore A. N,.......		U. S. S. State of Georgia..........	1206 Market

NAME.	CO.	SERVICE.	ADDRESS.
Gilmore .. H........	F	6th Cal. Inf....................	304 Montgomery
Gimpel M. C	H	8th N. Y. Inf....	2637 Market
Glass W. C	B	1st Mass. Heavy Art.........	204 Sacramento
Goddard O. M......	F	1st N. Y. Cav......................	33 Market
Goe S. E............	D	8th Ohio Cav..................	21½ Post
Golding Thomas....		U. S. S. Susquehanna..............	607 Turk
Goodman T. H......	A	2d Cal. Cav......................	C. P. R. R. Co.
Gordon C. W........	H	4th Cal. Inf...............	320 Sansome
Gordon J. A.........	I	4th Mich. Inf.......................	1025 Hyde
Gorman O...........	D	37th N. Y. Inf...................	813 Jessie
Gould W. O........	E	5th and 14th Kansas Cav...........	418 California
Graham Adam S.....	D	53d Mass. Inf..................	809 Leavenworth
Gregory S. O........		9th and 29th Ind. Inf.............	Alma, Sa'ta ClaraCo
Gregg V. A.........	E	25th Iowa Inf. and Vet. Res.......	San Luis Obispo
Grimmer C. A......	H	183d Ohio Inf....................	U. S. Mint
Grisiner J. R........	A	192d N. Y. Inf.	Baldwin Theatre
Griswold N. W......	K	30th Mass. and 75th U. S. Col'd Inf.	1223Gold'nGate av
Guptill H. M.......		14th Mass. Light Battery	PortLudlow, W.T.
Hageman George....	K	41st N. Y. Inf......................	723 Bush
Hall D. S............	K	4th Ohio Inf....................	1304 McAllister
Hallett Chas. O.....	F	2d & 5th Mass. Inf. & 103d U.S.Vt.Vls	119 Pine
Hamilton T. J.......	H	22d Ill. Inf........................	64 Minna
Hamlin Chas. H.....	E	9th N. H. Inf.......................	577 Market
Harmon Collins B...	I	24th Wis. Inf..................	Haywards
Harris George F....	I	5th Mass. Inf.....................	U. S. Mint
Harris George L.....		U. S. S. Varuna...............	"
Hart W. H. H......		Hinckley's Scouts and F 44th Iowa Inf.................	1917 Baker
Hartshorn E. F......	I	9th N. Y. State Militia.........	New York City
Harvey L. S........	D	11th Maine and 28th Mass. Inf.....	1013 Market
Hausman J..........	D	4th U. S. Art....................	7 Howard Court
Haveley W. T.......	A	12th Ohio Inf.....................	123 Powell
Hawes Alexander G..	E	9th and 149th Ill. Inf.............	220 Sansome
Hawes W. H....		U. S. Navy	P.M.S.S. San Jose
Hawks A. D.........	C	28th Wis. Inf....................	1822 Hyde
Hawley W. G........	A	28th Wis. Inf....................	Hanford, Cal.
Hayes John J........		U. S. Marine Corps...............	129 Third
Healy W.............	H	4th N. Y. Heavy Art...........	644 Natoma
Heath J. A..........	K	35th Mass. Inf.....................	Walnut Creek ,Cal.
Henderson Geo.....	C	3d Md. Inf......................	1153 Mkt. Oakland
Herrmann Chas. L..	K	9th Ill. Cav.....................	36 New Mont'gy
Hertwick C. F......	A	1st U. S. Light Art......	Alameda
Hinkley S. S........	A	13th Mass. Inf.....................	46 Market
Hobart B. F........	E	28th Maine Inf...................	18 Bartlett
Hoffman Sam'l......	H	67th Penn. Inf..................	Grove & Gough
Holloway A. E......	E	61st Mass. Inf....................	322 Shotwell
Holmes Walter H...	B	8th N. Y. S. M. and B 170th N. Y. Inf	221 Sansome
Hood Geo. J.........	A	10th Ohio Cav....................	Saucelito, Cal.
Hooker H. B........	B	4th Cal. Inf.....................	Alameda Ferry
Hoppe Adolph......	B	5th N. Y. Inf..................	1715 Sacramento
Hosley Geo. A......		U. S. S. Princeton...	21 Derby Place
Houghton R. E......	D	2d Mass. Inf......................	315 California
Hovey S. D..........	G	19th and K 31st Mass. Inf.........	430 California
Howard H. Z........		U. S. S. Savannah...............	Oc'no S. S. Co, Whf
Howard M. B........	G	29th and I 61st Mass. Inf...........	432 Valley
Howard Volney......	F	12th Mass. Inf....................	144 Rose av.

NAME.	CO.	SERVICE.	ADDRESS.
Howe Thomas H....	F	78th and 102d N. Y. Inf............	1025 Mission
Howell J. W.........	K	142d Penn. Inf....	235 Kearny
Huggins John C.....	F	2d Wis. Inf......................	12 Market, r 3
Hughes J. E.........	H	8th Cal. Inf............	Los Angeles
Hundermer Herman	F	7th N. Y. Inf. and F 22d N. Y. Inf..	1210 Treat av.
Hunter Nathaniel.	L	1st Conn. Heavy Art and U. S. A..	614 Merchant
Hutchins C. B.,M.D.		116th N. Y. Inf...................	617 Bush
Irwin D............	G	3d R. I. Inf	1 Seymour av.
Itsell A. J..........	K	10th Mich. Cav....	1832 O'Farrell
Ivory John A.......	H	1st Neb. Cav. and F 13th Mo. Cav..	1003 Market
Jackson J. A........	K	20th Ohio Inf. and Benton Cadets.	321 Seventeenth
Jahn Hermann.....	A	8th N Y. Inf. & 32d N.Y.Light Bat'y	Grand Opera H'se
Jansen Charles......	E	32d Mass. Inf....................	Liberty nr Church
Jenks Albert........		36th Ill. Inf....................	Palace Hotel
Jones Clinton......	K	1st N. H Heavy Art..............	M'ntgom'ry&Sutt'r
Jones Leon E.......	B	12th Penn. Cav.................	1535 Mission
Judd Edward D.....	F	6th & H 1st Mich. Inf. & U. S. Vols.	25 Sansome
Judell Hermann L.	D	1st Wash. Ter. Inf..............	2018 Mission
Kautz A. V..... ...		U. S. Army.....................	Angel Island
Kearny Fred. J......	D	2d Cal. Inf.....................	503 Post
Keeler J. M.........	H	5th Conn. Inf..................	1921 Sacramento
Kelley George W....	H	103d Penn. Inf...	Alameda
Kelly Michael.......		3d Iowa Battery.................	18 First
Kelpe Charles......	D	2d La. Inf.....................	164½ Jessie
Kenny C. A.........		104th N. Y. Inf................	S. F. Stock Exch
Kidder G. E.........	H	27th Maine Inf. and U.S.S. Malvern	2138 Mission
Kirkpatrick C.A.,M.D		3d and 8th Cal. Inf..............	920 Market
Klipstein E. W......		7th U. S. Inf. and U. S. Med. Dept.	142 Seventh
Knowlton Joseph, Jr.	A	8th Cal. Inf....................	613 Market
Kunkler J. E., M. D..		1st Cal. Cav....................	514 Kearny
La Blanc J..........	C	118th Penn. Inf.....	1721 Devisadero
Lamb L. M.........	F	9th U. S. Inf..................	Chico, Cal.
Lamb W. E.........	H	20th Wis. Inf. and F 1st Wis. Cav..	528 California, r 4
Lamp H , Jr.........	K	150th N. Y. Inf................	Sansome & Pine
Lancaster Charles E.		34st N. J. and 1st Mo. Inf..	North San Juan
Lane Nathan W.,Rev	I	49th N. Y. Inf................	Lodi, Cal.
Lane S.......... ...	F	10th Maine Inf................	1322 Eddy
Lane Wm. B.........		3d U. S. Cav..................	Occidental Hotel
Law William.......	H	8th N. Y. State Militia...........	1520 Howard
Leavitt A. H.......	C	9th Maine Inf.................	7 Kearny
Lemen O. T........	C	13th and H 45th Ohio Inf.........	Mazatlan, Mexico
Lester A. W........	B	Chicago Light Art...............	Albion, Mich
Libbing Henry H....	B	92d Ill. Inf. and E Marine Reg't...	631½ Natoma
Litchfield J. M......	A	23d and D 32d Maine Inf..........	415 Montgomery
Littlefield C. G......	I	38th Mass. Inf..................	Neo Ban, Chicago
Livingstone R. R....		U. S. Marines..................	6½ Harriet
Logan H. C.........	I	115th and H 33d Penn. Inf., and C	
		2d N. J. Inf....................	605 Market
Lond E. F..........	L	2d Mass. Cav...................	708 Buchanan
Lovell F. M.........	H	13th N. Y. Cav.................	207 Powell
Lowrie W. H........	F	165th N. Y. Inf................	310 Kearny
Ludwick E. A........	K	112th N. Y. Inf................	U. S. Mint
Lutz W. E..........		U. S. Navy	401 California
Lynch John.........	A	114th Ohio Inf.................	Benicia, Cal
Macdonough Joseph	A	63d N. Y. Inf.....	41 Market
Mackey John........	E	54th, B 115th and A 43d Ind. Inf....	27th and Noe

NAME.	CO.	SERVICE.	ADDRESS.
Magary W. W........	E	7th N. Y. State Militia.............	21 Montgomery
Magill A. E..........	K	14th Mtch. Inf....................	221 Sansome
Malpas Alfred.......	I	2d N. J. and G 40th N. Y. Inf......	Saratoga, Cal.
Manning Sidney.....	O	98th N. Y. Inf....................	787 Folsom
Marden E. D........	D	2d and C 12th Maine Inf..........	851 Market
Markley John F....	K	197th Penn. Inf..................	115 Beale
Marsilliot M. G.....	I	27th Wis. Inf. and U. S. Navy......	Rev. Cut. Hartley
Marvin J. B.........	F	15th Conn. Inf...................	513½ Valencia
Mateer R. W.........	I	9th Penn. Cav....................	1112 Franklin,Oak.
Mathews Harvey....	I	1st U. S. Sharpshooters...........	1514 Hyde
Mathews J. H.......		U. S. S. Iroquois.......	B'rkly,P. O.box142
Matthews J., Rev...		19th Ky. Inf.....................	119 Haight
Mayo R. C..........	A	17th Mass. Inf...................	721 Valencia
McAllister W.F.,M.D	D	9th Kansas Cav. and U. S. Army...	Wash'gt'n&Sans'm
McArthur J. A.......		11th Ohio Battery................	Market St. C. R. R
McCallister H. C ...	F	1st Oregon Inf...................	17 Fourth
McCarty George M..	B	46th Ind. Inf....................	119 Haight
McCauley T. B.......	B	49th Ind. Inf....................	122 Turk
McCollister H. H....	B	6th Mich. Cav...................	Brooklyn Hotel
McElroy W.........	E	3d U. S. Art..........	1129 Folsom
McEwen Warren L...	E	2d Mass. Cav....................	1318 Jones
McGrath Daniel.....	B	1st Cal. Inf.....................	244 Minna
McHugh Felix.......	A	10th Ohio Inf....	1317 Green
McIntosh J. R	D	2d Mass. Cav....	730 Guerrero
McJunkin Hugh K..	K	3d Penn. Art.....................	402 Montgomery
McKenney H. M...	K	92d Ill. Inf.....................	238 Montgomery
McKenney J. T......	G	4th Maine Inf......	1613 Bent'n,Alame.
McLaughlin T. A....	A	13th N. Y. Cav...................	1018 Webster
McNeil Alex., M. D..	A	11th Mich. Inf......	120½ Turk
McNulty Jas. M.,M.D		1st Cal. Inf. and U. S. Vols.......	118 Dupont
McNutt W. F., M. D.		U. S. Navy......................	121 Montgomery
McPherson B. R.....	D	3d Mo. Inf. and U. S. Navy.......	1040 Polk
Mears Frederick....		U. S. Army......	Ft. Sisseton,D'kota
Meehan J. P.........	K	25th N. Y. State Militia...........	613 Market
Megilligan W. B.....		1st Del. Battery.................	35 Eddy
Melrose K..........		U. S. S. Wissahickon.............	2205 Larkin
Merrill Frank H.....	B	1st Bat. U. S. Inf...............	224 Noe
Messer N. T.........	D	20th Mass. Inf..................	1811 Pierce
Meyer Adolph.......		U. S. S. Saranac........	Geary nr Blake
Miller Hamilton W...	C	51st N. Y. Inf...................	Sansome & Pine
Miller Henry R	F	2d Cal. Cav.....................	1426 8th, Oakland
Molière J. W., M. D .	G	76th Ind. Inf....	511 Mason
Monaghan Hugh	G	5th N. Y. Heavy Art.............	1011 Vallejo
Moore Benjamin	E	5th Mass Inf......	62 Perine
Moore F. M..........	H	4th Wis. Cav....................	917 Larkin
Morton F. R........	H	19th Wis. Inf...................	2118 Steiner
Moulton D. S........	A	11th Ind. Inf. and E 4th Ind. Cav..	Custom House
Musgrave Joseph....	F	7th N. Y. S. M...................	C. P. R. R. Co.
Nass Andrew........	H	4th Minn. Inf....................	221 Fourth
Neal Charles S..		U. S. S. Shamrock...............	230 Montgomery
Newell J. T.........	I	44th Mass. Inf. & C 4th Mass. H. Art	916 Van Ness av.
Nicoll Frederic E....		U. S. Navy.....................	24 Bennington
Noggle D. L.........		12th and 4th Wis. Batteries.......	U. S. Mint
Norgrove John......	F	1st Maine and H 1st N. Y. Lt. Art.	12 Geary
Norton Harvey......	B	23d N. Y. Inf. and G 1st N. Y. Cav..	1530 Jackson
Norwood W. E.......	F	26th Maine Inf..................	2028 Scott

NAME.	CO.	SERVICE.	ADDRESS.
Nowlin T. W........	I	10th Iowa Inf.....	230 Montgomery
O'Connor T. M......	A	69th N. Y. State Militia...........	500 Eddy
Orans John........	K	30th Ill. Inf. & A 45th Vet.Res.Corps	204 Ritch
Osborn A. A.........		U. S. S. Vermont................	401 Market
Osborn C. H........	K	7th N. Y. State Militia............	1229 Webster, Oak.
Osborne Wm. H.....	I	105th Ohio Inf....................	Haywards, Cal.
Osbourne S.........	F	46th Ind. Inf.....................	65 Nevada Block
Osgood Hosea......	E	2d Cal. Cav......................	430 Valley
Ostrander W. W.....	H	149th N. Y. Inf...................	132 Sixth
Ott James M........	M	12th Penn. Cav...................	28th St. Car House
Owen J. A...........	D	98th N. Y. Inf....................	2421 Sutter
Page J. H...........	K	14th N. Y. Cav...................	1631 O'Farrell
Parker S. M........	I	2d Cal. Inf......................	48 Louisa
Parkhurst Daniel W.	I	4th Cal. Inf......	120 Liberty
Parnell W. R........		4th N. Y. Cav. and U. S. A........	Berkeley, Cal.
Pease G. M., M. D...		54th Mass. Inf. and U. S. Navy....	125 Turk
Penfield W. H......		U. S. S. Mackinaw...............	B'naV'sta&Oak,Ala
Pennell R. J........		U. S. S. Mayflower...............	810 Capp
Peterson C. H.......	C	7th Cal. Inf.....................	313 Page
Phelps E. D........	K	1st R. I. Cav....................	Brooklyn Hotel
Pillsbury E. S......	M	1st Maine Cav...................	324 Pine
Pinkson H..........	E	1st N. Y. Inf....................	1517 Hyde
Platt E. J...........	A	10th N. Y. Inf....	312 Eddy
Pond Henry.......	C	8th N. J. Inf. & C 1st U.S. Md. Rifles	Presidio
Pond R. H..		12th U. S. Inf...................	307 California
Powers Geo. H.,M.D.		60th Mass. Inf..................	215 Geary
Pracht Max.........		U. S. Navy.....................	813 Union
Prinz Ewald........	F	5th N. Y. Cav....................	36 New M'ntgomry
Quinn John E.......		32d and K 17th Mass. Inf......	1029 Post
Rainsbury John.....	K	21st N. Y. Cav..................	713 Minna
Rankin A. L., Rev..		113th Ill. Inf....................	314 Seventeenth
Ransom S...........		U. S. S. Sagamore...............	327 Third
Rapp John A........	K	52d Penn. Inf...................	Nevada City
Rearden T. H........	E	84th Ohio Inf....................	216 Bush
Reutschler F.......	G	8th Ohio Cav....................	642 Mission
Reynolds H. C......		U. S. Navy.....................	Old City Hall
Richardson E. H....		U. S. Navy	122 Sutter
Richit H. V..........	B	1st Wash. Ter. Inf...............	Presidio
Riley L. K..........	D	121st Ohio Inf...................	Cherokee, Cal.
Ritter M. V. ...	C	23d Ohio Inf....................	1220 Valencia
Roberts John H.....	B	9th N. Y. Inf....................	419 Eddy
Roberts S. H........	I	1st N.Y.Mt. Rifles & M 4th N.Y.Cav.	1073 Bro'dw'y,Oak.
Robinson C. R......	E	2d Maine Inf....................	R. M. S. Post-office
Robinson J. H......	H	1st Ohio Inf....................	929½ Howard
Robinson R. W. E...	K	2d N. H. Inf....................	510 Geary
Robinson W. A......		2d Mass. Cav...................	563½ Minna
Rockwell A. L......		40th Wis. Inf...................	220 Sansome
Rosecrans W. S.....		23d Ohio Inf. and U. S. Vols.......	Washington, D. C.
Ross W. W..........	D	108th N. Y. Inf. and Vet. Reserves.	857 Market
Royal William......	E	44th N. Y. & F 9th U. S. Colored Inf	318 California
Royce C. E	E	44th N. Y., 6th and 29th U. S. Col-	
		ored Inf.......................	507 Montgomery
Ruggles J. D........		2d Wis. Inf.....................	2210 Jackson
Russell E. C........	E	104th Ill. Inf....................	407 O'Farrell
Ryan James.	F	14th N. Y. Heavy Art.............	8 Liberty
Salsbury W. H	C	18th Maine Inf..................	Spear & Mission

NAME.	CO.	SERVICE.	ADDRESS,
Sanborn W. H.......	F	10th N. Y. Heavy Art..............	Suñol, Cal.
Saxton Rufus		U. S. Army......................	Louisville, Ky.
Sayers J. R.........		Halleck's Guards.................	1807 Pierce
Schenck Casper......	G	9th Ind. Inf. and U. S. Navy.......	Norfolk, Va.
Schenck C. W.......	F	29th Ind. Inf.....................	913½ Mission
Schenck W. T. Y....	F	110th U. S. Colored Inf...........	256 Market
Schoenherr A.......	A	41st N. Y. and 11th Conn. Inf......	Stockt'n& O'Farr'll
Scott Walter........		U. S. Navy	2231 Geary
Scott Winfield, Rev..	C	126th N. Y. Inf....	Angel Island
Scoville J. J.........	K	1st Wis. Cav.....................	2223 Pacific av.
Scripture H. D......	G	7th N. Y. Cav....................	430 Montgomery
Scupham J. R.	H	1st Ill. Art. and B Mo. Eng........	306 Pine, r 2
Seamans W. H.... .	K	30th Mass. Inf....................	Los Angeles
Searles W. A........	G	1st Mass. Inf.....................	602 Montgomery
Seibert J. M.........	F	93d Penn. Inf....................	Wells, Fargo & Co·
Shattuck C. C........	B	1st R. I. and G 5th N. H. Inf., and	1208 Jackson
		H 1st N. H. Art.	
Shattuck J. H.......	H	1st N. H. Heavy Art..............	1110 Mason
Shaw H. B..........	I	11th R. I. Inf....................	Cor. Powell & Sut'r
Shawhan F. K.......	D	123d Ohio Inf....................	420 Bush
Shepheard J. J		2d Cal. Inf...............	U. S. Naval Office
Sherwood A. T......	D	21st Wis. Inf....................	330 Sutter
Simonson Joseph ...	C	7th N. Y. State Militia...........	122 Sutter
Skivington J. F.....	B	44th Penn. Militia................	Risdon Iron Works
Slessinger L........	E	10th Ind. Inf....................	2513 Sacramento
Small I. H..........	G	11th Maine Inf...................	134 Twenty-sixth
Smart George C.	B	76th N. Y. Inf....................	35 Eddy
Smedberg W. R....		Nat RiflesDist.of Col.& U.S.Army..	316 California
Smith B. G.........	K	13th Wis. Inf....................	Candelaria, Nev.
Smith David C......	E	105th N. Y. Inf..................	2030 Mission
Smith F............	F	9th U. S. and H 6th Cal. Inf......	316 Montgomery
Smith G. J..........	A	2d N. Y. State Mil'a, or 82 N. Y. Inf	329 Sutter
Smith Leonard F....	E	2d Mass. Cav....................	416 Folsom
Smith L. P..........	I	14th and K 67th Ohio Inf.........	1822 Jessie
Smith S. E..........	I	44th Ind. Inf....................	149 Ninth
Smith W. H.........		U. S. Navy	126½ Silver
Smitten C. H........		U. S. S. Union..................	1321 Filmore
Snively J. B.........	H	38th Ind. Inf....................	Monterey, Cal.
Sonday John	D	10th Ohio Inf. and D 5th U. S. Vet	
		Vols.	Cheyenne, Wyo. T.
Spencer George W...	D	15th Penn. Cav..................	316 California
Spinning G. L., Rev.	C	1st Kansas Cav..................	1018 21st
Sprague Homer B. ..	B	11th La.(Corps D'Afrique) and 13th	Mills Seminary,
		Conn. Inf.....................	Oakland
Stanbridge A. H.....	E	99th N. Y. Inf...................	15 Clinton
Staples D. J.........		Washington Clay Bat.............	711 Taylor
Staples J. W........	A	78th N. Y. Inf...................	219 Sansome'
Starr M. A..........	F	49th Penn. Inf...................	Haywards, Cal.
Sternberg E.........	F	17th Mo. Inf....................	773½ Folsom
Stocking Clark B....	A	5th Cal. Inf. and E 1st Vet. Cal. Inf	Stockton, Cal.
Stone Frank F.......	K	45th Mass. Inf. & 1st Mass. Cav....	410 Pine
Strickland S. E......	G	4th U. S. and 16th Tenn. Cav.......	318 California
Stump Irwin C.......	G	18th Penn. Inf. and Q. M. Dep't...	612 Fell
Sullivan Patrick....		U. S. Navy......................	501 Post
Sumner W..........	E	23d Mich. Inf....................	2 Martha Place
Swan B. R., M. D....	A	23d N. Y. State Militia...........	P. O. Box 1869

NAME.	CO.	SERVICE.	ADDRESS.
Sweetland W.P., M.D		U. S. Vols..........................	405 Hayes
Swineford Calvin N	A	140th Ill. Inf.......................	19 Montgomery
Symmes F. J........		U. S. Navy	122 Sutter
Taintor S. B........	I	2d Mich. Cav. and D 136th U. S. Colored Troops...................	507 Montgomery
Talcott H. D........		110th N. Y. Inf....................	328 Montgomery
Taylor Stuart M.....		55th N. Y. Inf. and U. S. Vols......	Bohemian Club
Taylor Thomas S....	D	7th N. Y. State Militia.............	216 Powell
Taylor W. E., M. D..		U. S. Navy........................	215 Geary
Tharp J. L..........	B	7th and K 126th Ill. Inf	504 Buchanan
Thomas H. E.......	A	94th N. Y. Inf.....	Custom House
Thomas Joel L......	F	2d Cal. Cav.......................	505 Fell
Thomas R. P.......		1st N. Y. Cav.....................	204 Sacramento
Thompson C. R......		12th U. S. Col'd Troops & U. S. Vols	326 Montgomery
Thompson J. D......	G	1st and 8th Iowa Cav....	Lakeville, Cal.
Thompson Olif.....	C	22d Wis. Inf......................	527 Franklin
Tickner H. L........	G	1st Cal. Cav......................	3022 California
Tidball T. T........	K	5th Cal. Inf......................	Joion, Cal.
Tirtlot W. M........	F	105th Ill. Inf.....................	U. S. Mint
Todd Charles D.	A	17th Mich. Inf.....................	815 Shotwell
Todd David B., M. D	D	1st Mich. Engineers..............	Teneriffe&R.R. av.
Toohey Cornelius...	H	14th U. S. Inf.....................	432 Pine
Tower L. N..........	H	8th Cal Inf.......................	17 Fremont
Towle W. W.........	A	16th Vt. Inf.......................	602 Third
Trimble J. G........	A	2d U. S. Cav......................	Berkeley, Cal.
Turpin F. L........	D	148th Penn. Inf. & I 21st Penn. Cav	537 Sacramento
Tuttle John.... ...	F	97th N. Y. Inf.....................	537 Haight
Unwin Edward......	L	5th N. Y. Cav	4 Chatham Place
Upham B. H.........	H	8th Vt. Inf.......	Berkeley, Cal.
Van Inwagen Leona'd	E	111th N. Y. Inf....	404 Front
Van Wyck H. L......		U. S. Navy........................	308 Pine
Vaughn George	F	6th Cal. Inf.......................	2223 Post
Vining A. J.........	K	24th Mass. Inf.....................	2112 Pine
Voorhees James.....	E	5th Cal. Inf.......................	405 Kearny
Waguer C. B........		U. S. Vols........................	Yountville, Cal.
Wagner John, M. D..	B	52d Ohio Inf......................	2025 Mission
Wagner Theodore...	G	34th N. J. Inf. & D 4th U.S. Col'd Art	Berkeley, Cal.
Wallace Uriah.......	M	1st Conn. Heavy Art..............	1620 Polk
Wallazz E. A.......	A	104th Penn. Inf....................	509 Hayes
Wallis George H. W.		42d, 80th, 123d N.Y.Inf. & 3d U.S.Inf	329 Market
Walsh Patrick F.....	E	84th Penn. Inf.....................	1213 Leavenworth
Walts George W.....		18th Ohio Inf......	1 Montgomery
Wands A. H.........	B	18th N. Y., 10th Vet. Res. and 18th U. S. Inf...................	
Warren S. P........		15th Kansas Cav	1511 Clay
Wato P. T. M.......		U. S. S. Little Ada................	239 Shotwell
Waterbury Charles S.	D	6th N. Y. Heavy Art..............	1322 Scott
Waterhouse F. A. ..	E	14th Vt. Inf.......................	2213 Howard
Watts Joseph.......		U. S. Navy........................	1334 Church
Waymire J. A.......	B	1st Oregon and M 1st U. S. Cav....	402 Montgomery
Weber E. C..........	A	122d Ill. Inf......................	5 Market
Welch Charles P.. ..		U. S. Navy........................	1211 Taylor
Wells O. O..........	A	6th Mich. Inf......................	526 Hayes
Wells Ivory........	C	35th Mass. Inf....	1129 Mission
Werner John........	A	1st N. J. Art.....................	616½ Merchant
Westover J. W.......	A	22d Ind. Inf......................	U. S. Mint

NAME.	CO.	SERVICE.	ADDRESS.
Westwater R........	H	85th and B 137th Ohio Inf.........	1019 Pierce
Wheaton George H..	A	131st N. Y. Inf....................	221 Front
Whipple Stephen G.		1st Bat. Cal. Mountaineers & U.S A.	Saratoga, Cal.
White Andrew......	E	165th N. Y. Inf.....	1107 Mason
White Russell.......	E	Mass. Light Battery........... ...	Fire Patrol
Whitefield R. E......	H	40th N. Y Inf......	1006 Jones
Whitten Robert.....	A	U. S. Engineer Corps.............	15½ Sumner
Wiegand Eugene....	B	17th and E 75th Penn. Inf.........	1115 Clay
Wilder F. A.........	K	2d Cal. Cav.....................	Haywards, Cal.
Wilder W. P.........	D	1st Mass. Inf....	210 Fell
Wilhelm Thomas....		8th U. S. Inf....................	Angel Island
Williams George H..	K	12th N. Y. State Militia...........	903 Clay
Williams G. W	C	25th Mass. Inf....................	Worcester, Mass.
Williams W. W......		U. S. Navy.....................	Navy Pay Office
Willis E.............		U. S. S. Winona.................	Market & Bush
Wilson A. P.........	F	2d Maine Inf....	Nucleus Hotel
Wilson Charles E....		2d Maine Cav....................	420 California
Wilson Horace	H	51st Penn. Vol. M.,F 1st Maine Cav.	
	I	12th Maine Inf	1307 Taylor
Wilson J. K.........	I	12th Maine Inf....	1227 Turk
Wilson Parker	B	40th Wis. Inf....................	423 Bush
Wisker F. G.........		U. S. S. Cyane and U.S.S.Jamestown	54 Shipley
Withrow C. W.......	K	30th Wis. Inf................	Ashland, Ohio
Woodard J. H.......	B	10th Ind. Inf.....	58 East 12th,Oakl'd
Worrall Joseph A....	H	131st N. Y. Inf...................	28 Oak Grove av.
Young C. G........	F	5th Mass. Inf...................	25 Davis
Young G. W.........	G	44th Mass. Inf...................	715½ Grove
Youngberg John E..	H	57th Ill. Inf....................	117 Ridley

Southern California

CUCAMONGO FRUIT LANDS

Beautiful Location!
Delightful Scenery!
Unsurpassed Climate!

CHEAP LANDS! PURE WATER! PERFECT TITLE!

Educational Facilities Rarely Equaled.

SITUATED ON THE SOUTHERN PACIFIC RAILWAY!

The L. A. & S. G. V. R. R. soon to Pass Through the Tract.

Pure Mountain Water for Irrigation and Domestic Use, Distributed from
Storage Reservoirs in Iron Pipes under Pressure.

—PRICE FOR A LIMITED PERIOD ONLY—

$70 PER ACRE!

WITH WATER DELIVERED ON THE LAND.

Easy Terms and Low Rates of Interest.

For further particulars apply to or address,

J. C. LYNCH,
Ohio Block, Ontario, Cal.

M. L. WICKS,
Rooms 1 & 4, P. O. Block, Los Angeles, Cal.

M. E. HODGKINS,
Cucamongo, Cal.

E. T. WRIGHT,
Rooms 3 & 4, Downey Block, Los Angeles, Cal.

SUMNER POST, No. 3.

SACRAMENTO CAL.

OFFICERS, 1886.

O. V. KELLOGG..Commander
P. V. WISE..Senior Vice Commander
H. H. SCRIBNER...Junior Vice Commander
W. B. DAVIS..Adjutant
H. BENNETT..Quartermaster
J. R. LAINE...Surgeon
J. W. REEVES..Chaplain
I. S. MOORE..Officer of the Day
L. H. MEGERLEE...Officer of the Guard
E. L. HAWK...Sergeant Major
J. H. CARRINGTON...Quartermaster Sergeant

Meeting, First and Third Thursday.

NAME.	CO.	SERVICE.	ADDRESS.
Adams C. F..........	F	2d Cal. Cav......................	727 J street
Ahrberg Wm. A. F...	L	16th Kansas Cav.........	Colfax
Aiken John J........	A	58th Ill. Inf......................	Sacramento
Albrecht Zillian.....	K	15th Mo. Inf......................	Folsom
Armstrong Henry...	F	7th Mich. Inf....................	Williams
Atwood J. L.........	A	15th U. S. Inf....................	1720 G street
Atwood T. A.........	B	25th Iowa Inf...................	Sacramento
Balch H. G..		U. S. Navy......................	
Banbury J		5th Iowa Inf....................	Pasadena
Banholzer Fred......	B	3d N. Y. Independent Battery......	410 J street
Barbeau John	E	12th Ohio Cav...................	
Barrett Henry...:....	I	53d Penn. Inf....................	1121 8th street
Bateman Wm. T. M..		1st N. J. Cav.................. ...	Alley 7 & 8, I & J
Bell S. D	A	19th Mich. Inf....................	1731 N street
Bemis H A..........	B	10th Kansas Inf....	Sacramento
Bennett H...........		1st Mich. Inf....................	714 7th street
Bentley S. A.........	H	10th Mich. Cav....................	Sacramento Co.
Bodge S. N.........	F	14th Maine Inf....................	Freeport
Bovyer Robt. L......	K	6th Cal. Inf	807 L street
Bradley John........	C	6th Cal. Inf....................	Franklin
Bragg A. L...........	A	6th Maine Inf....................	17th street, E & F
Brainard Gilbert.....	H	29th Ind. Inf....................	Union House, Cal.
Brittingham, F. M...	D	46th Ohio Inf....................	8th and K
Brown C. O..........	O	15th Mo. Cav....................	Bro'n Ho'se, 4 & K
Brown John P.......	A	1st Ill. Light Art.................	Florin

NAME.	CO.	SERVICE.	ADDRESS.
Bullivant Thos. B,...	B	11th Con. Inf....	Woodland
Bundy W. L..........	I	113th Ill. Inf......................	806 H street
Burke John.........		U. S. S. Mercellita.................	2012 K street
Burnett H. A........	F	2d Cal. Cav........................	717 P street
Byrnes Thos	H	12th U. S. Inf.....................	300 K street
Campbell B F......	D	84th Ohio Inf.................	1016 E street
Carlow W. H.........	G	2d Cal. Cav....	Internat'nal Hotel
Carpenter Oliver....	A	37th Ind. Inf......................	
Carrington J. H. ...	G	22d N. J. Inf......................	2106 K street
Carter J. F..........	F	128th Ind. Inf.....................	1617 14th street
Chipman N. P.......		U. S. Vol..................	Red Bluff
Clark E. R,..........	I	5th N. Y. Inf......................	
Coker W. H.........	D	7th Cal. Inf.......................	County Hospital
Collom J. H.........	B	145th Penn. Inf....................	Sacramento
Coons W. W........	D	2d Cal. Cav.......................	State House
Cornish Geo. F.....	C	2d Wis. Cav.......................	Clarksburg
Crymble John.......	G	8th Wis. Inf.......................	State House
Cuddy M.	B	73d N. Y. Inf......................	1118½ 2d street
Curtis W. R.........	B	38th N. Y. Inf.....................	Sacramento
Daily Michael.......	A	10th Mo. Inf......................	"
Dassonville, A. A....	H	1st Wash. Ter. Inf.................	318 P street
Davis Wm. B.	G	18th Ohio Inf.....................	347 D street
Denton N. N........	G	1st N. Y. Engineers...............	1811 H street
Dickenson A. S......	G	20th Maine Inf....................	Sacramento
Dickenson Lewis....	K	9th Mich Inf......................	Franklin
Dille E. R...........	I	150th Ind. Inf.....................	1517 G street
Dodd Jas...........		U. S. S. Monongahela.............	1822 I street
Dodge O. P.........	K	2d Cal. Cav.......................	1614 G street
Dodge Philander....	G	9th Maine Inf.....................	1027 9th street
Dresher Valentine...	B	1st Cal. Inf.......................	20th, I and J
Dryer John H.......	I	6th Cal. Inf............	313 12th street
Dunton George......	A	150th Ohio Inf....................	Union Hotel
Dysart John.........	E	1st Cal. Cav......................	Colfax
Eaton Chas.........	C	8th Vt. Inf.......................	Sacramento
Estes L. W..........	H	16th N. Y. Cav...... :	12th, F and G
Evans J. L..........	F	4th Cal. Inf .... ..:...........	1416 2d street
Farnsworth S.......	D	23d Iowa Inf......................	1321 4th street
Ficks Geo. W...	K	50th Penn. Inf....................	916½ 7th street
Fisher Geo. S.......	C	1st Oregon Inf....................	1006 7th street
Frazee R. S.........	H	4th N. Y. Inf.....................	18th and F
Gates M E..........	A	7th Cal. Inf	1327 O street
Gent Wm. C........	G	4th Mass. Inf......	905 6th street
Gilnack Walter......	K	1st Con. Heavy Art...............	Sacramento
Gladding C.........	K	72d Ill. Inf.......................	Lincoln
Grant Jas. A........	I	2d Cal. Inf.......................	Warnerville, Mass
Green H L..........	G	31st Mo. Inf......................	Sacramento
Greenlaw C. E......	F	6th Mass. Inf.....................	San Francisco
Hamilton Jas.......	D	11th Con. Inf......	Union House, Cal.
Hayford G. O......	C	11th Maine Inf....................	Sacramento
Hayford J. B.......	M	24 Mass. Cav...,.................	826 14th street
Hawk E. L..........	A	114th Ohio Inf....................	Rocklin
Hazel E. J.	C	6th Penn. Cav....................	Western Hotel
Henenger T. J.......	G	7th Cal. Inf......................	Sacramento
Hopkins A. S........		1st Vt. Inf.......................	J, 3d and 4th
Howard M. E.......	F	12th Ill. Inf......................	Galt, Cal.
Hubbard C. H......		23d Ohio Inf.....................	15th and I

NAME.	CO.	SERVICE.	ADDRESS.
Huebschman J. B...	C	4th Cal. Inf......................	521 K street
Jenks G. W., M. D...		26th Ohio Inf....	Galt, Cal.
Jones J. T.	G	11st Ill. Inf....	Sacramento Co.
Kellogg C. V.......	E	1st Cal. Inf......................	821 J street
Kent J. D..........	G	37th Ill. Inf.....................	826 L street
Kerlin Quinter	A	122d Ohio Inf.	10th and F
Kilborn A	B	6th Cal. Inf......................	Los Gatos
Kimball Ami........	B	8th Maine Inf....................	Colfax
Koch John M.......	I	1st Mo. Engineers.................	Sheridan
Laine J. R..........	G	1st Wis. Inf	K, 9th and 10th
Latham Il..		4th U. S. Engineers............. ...	9th and L
Lehman A. S........	K	28th Mass. Inf...................	Butte, Montana
Lencioni P. L.......	F	14th N. Y. Art...................	
Lewis S. A..........	A	8th U. S. Inf...................	Galt
Lindner Fred.......	B	1st N. Y. Mounted Rifles..........	603 K street
Linnell H. H......	D	th Wis. Inf...................	1232 O street
Madden M..........	C	1st Ohio Light Art...............	Sacramento
Markwart H........	B	3d Mo Inf.....................	Lincoln
Maroney S	D	76th Penn. Inf..................	Western Hotel
Martin H. P........	E	12 3d N. Y. Inf.........	Sacramento
Matlock A. R	C	148th Ind. Inf.................	Red Bluff
Maydwell Wm. B....	A	134th Ill. Inf...................	Sacramento
McAnderson J.......	D	2d U S. Art	San Francisco
McCoy N. A.........	D	7th Cal. Inf....................	24th, H and I
McGouldrick J......	G	4th U. S. Art..................	Sacramento
McKelvy H. A.......	K	35th Iowa Inf.................	9th and L
Medley John C.....	C	6th Cal Inf....................	916 14th street
Megerlee L. H.......	F	2d Cal. Cav....................	4th and L
Meserve J. G........	G	99th Wis. Inf	C'lusa Lodg'g H'se
Meyler T. J.	G	1st Vt. Reserve Corps...........	Red Bluff
Miller Frank........	H	2d Wis. Inf....................	831 N street
Mohr L............	C	1st Mo. Inf.	10th and N
Monroe Wm	D	12.th N. Y. Inf.................	Sacramento
Moore I. S.	F	2d Cal. Cav....	217 M street
Morris J. S. T.	M	2d Penn. Heavy Art.............	Central Stables
Murray J. C........	I	64th Ill. Inf..................	Mormon Island
Nokes R............	B	4th Mass. Inf................	1508 J street
O'Brien Pat..	B	14.th N. H. Inf....	13th and F
Olmstead C W......	M	1st Maine Heavy Art............	Sacramento
Osgood G. N..	L	12th Ind. Inf..................	614 10th street
Painter J. S........	C	12th Mich. Inf.................	1868 P street
Parker John S.......	F	1st Cal. Cav	Galt
Parsons A. E........	A	27th Mass. Inf....	631 I street
Poorman D.	G	160th Ohio Inf.................	1222 F street
Putnam G. A........ .		U. S. Vols.................	721 F street
Ragsdale E S........	I	16th Iowa Inf...............	1808 M street
Rawls Brown........	A	4th Cal. Inf......................	Q & R, 22d & 23d
Reeves J. W........	A	19th Iowa Inf.................	1123 13th street
Renwick T	C	127th Ill. Inf...............	Sacramento Co.
Ridgeway S B.. ..		7th Cal. Inf...................	Colfax
Robertson G. C.....	K	11th Mo. Inf..................	Willows
Robertson J. H......	B	1st Iowa Cav..................	Lincoln
Robinson T. G......	M	9th Ill. Cav..................	1010 N street
Robinson Wm.......	M	9th Ill. Cav..................	Ophir
Roe James..	B	1st Cal. Inf...	Rocklin
Scribner H. H.......	B	8th U. S. V. V. Inf...............	Central House

NAME.	CO.	SERVICE.	ADDRESS.
Shaw Ira C.	C	29th Mass. Inf.	314 N street
Shaw Oliver	K	59th Ill. Inf.	Galt
Sheehan Jno. F.,	A	25th Maine Inf.	San Francisco
Sheehan T. W.	E	24th Maine Inf.	21st, U and V
Shirland E. D.	C	1st Cal. Cav.	605 14th street
Silva Anton		U. S. S. Pawnee	Folsom
Singer Wm.	D	1st Cal. Cav.	Sacramento
Skinner J. L.	D	27th Mass. Inf.	Grand Hotel
Slack F. H.	H	2d N. Y. Cav.	Sacramento
Smith C. Freeman	D	28th Maine Inf.	1823 H street
Smith Frank A.	C	14th Vt. Inf.	1230 H street
Spangler J. M.	C	7th Iowa Cav.	
Stephenson C. H.		4th Independent Ohio Cav.	1030 N street
Stewart S. C.	C	2d U. S. Cav.	Elk Grove
Thomas A. J.	A	2d Cal. Cav.	Sacramento
Thorpe D. N.	I	93d Ill. Inf.	901 8th street
Tozer L.		4th Maine Light Art.	5th and K
Tufts A. C.		8th Mass Inf.	Sacramento
Tully James.	D	146th Ill. Inf.	Clarksburg
Underwood E. N.		13th Tenn. Cav.	Jacinto
Valentine D. A.	F	45th Iowa Inf.	Oakland
Valentine J. H.	F	15th Iowa Inf.	"
Vanderhoof D.	A	1st Nevada Inf.	Galt
Warner Geo. A.	B	2d Cal. Cav.	1215 7th street
Waterbury James.	D	96th Ill. Inf.	Clarksburg
Webber F. H. L.	F	5th Cal. Inf.	1217 L street
Webster Noah.	F	4th Mich. Inf.	Sacramento
Wentworth B. F.	F	98th Penn. Inf.	1721 M street
Wentworth Chas.	H	10th Penn. Reserves.	Alturas, Modoc Co.
White J. B.	D	5th N. Y. Cav.	1206 Q street
White T. H.	C	10th Vt. Inf.	Shingle Springs
Wilson Japhet.	F	2d Cal. Cav.	Sacramento
Winkleman Wm.	I	2d Ohio Cav.	506 K street
Wise Geo.	G	15th Vt. Inf.	1129 H street
Wise M. L.	K	38th Ohio Inf.	605 13th street
Wise P. V.	G	31st U. S Inf.	420 L street
Woerner B.	A	43d Ill. Inf.	517 K street
Woods John L.	G	4th Cal. Inf.	Sacramento

Wm. T. Coleman & Co.
Shipping and Commission Merchants,

San Francisco, Cal., 121 Market Street.
Los Angeles, Cal.
Chicago, 91 Michigan Avenue.
New York, 71 Hudson Street.
London, 4 Bishopsgate St., within E. C.
Liverpool, 54 Drury Buildings.
Astoria Oregon, Flavel's Wharf.

CALIFORNIA PRODUCTS
A Specialty.

California Wines & Brandies,
California Canned Fruits,
California Dried Fruits,
California Raisins,
California Oranges.

Columbia and Sacramento-River

SALMON

And all Pacific Coast Products Suited to Eastern Trade.

CONSIGNMENTS SOLICITED.

☞ Our Facilities are Unrivaled.☜

FARRAGUT POST, No. 4.

VALLEJO, CAL.

OFFICERS, 1886.

D. McCOOL	Commander
JOHN REDDAN	Senior Vice-Commander
JAMES J. BERGIN	Junior Vice-Commander
CHARLES DALY	Adjutant
GEORGE L. VOORHEES	Quartermaster
JONAS F. LONG	Surgeon
WM. H. TAYLOR	Chaplain
L. J. CROWELL	Officer of the Day
A. J. POWERS	Officer of the Guard
——— ———	Sergeant Major
——— ———	Quartermaster Sergeant

Meeting Second and Fourth Thursday.

NAME.	CO.	SERVICE.	ADDRESS.
Bergin James J	L	1st Conn. Art	Vallejo
Blessington James	E	2d Penn. luf	"
Bogle R. B		3d Ky. Cav	"
Boyd W. S	A	66th Ill. Inf	U. S. S. Ranger
Brown Thomas	B	1st Ill. Cav	Vallejo
Bruce Henry		U. S. S. Saranac	"
Buchanan J		U. S. S. Ranger	U. S. S. Ranger
Buckles A. J	E	19th Ind. Inf	Suisun
Buxton Geo. A	F	8th Cal. Inf	Vallejo
Chandler Robert	D	2d N. Y. Vet. Vols	"
Churchill Geo. H	I	47th Wis. Inf	"
Cilly J. W	B	4th Cal. Inf	"
Clark W. H	E	31st Ohio Heavy Art	"
Cleveland R. S	B	1st Wis. Cav	"
Coakley Timothy	K	103d Ill. Inf	"
Collins N. W	A	8th Mass. Inf	San Francisco
Costello James	B	4th Cal. Inf	Vallejo
Crowell L. J	E	12th R. I. Inf	"
Craig Hugh	B	108th N. Y. Inf	"
Craig Robert		U. S. S. Old Ironsides	Benicia
Cully W. S	·	U. S. Marine Corps	Vallejo
Cushing F. W	H	13th Ill. Inf	Custom H., S. F.
Daly Charles	E	1st Wash. Ter. Inf	Vallejo
Donnelly George A		U. S. S. Bienville	"
Duncan John K	G	22d Iowa Inf	Dallas, Texas

29

NAME.	CO.	SERVICE.	ADDRESS.
Farwell Fred........	F	5th N. H. Inf......................	Oakland
Ford John H........	E	20th Mass. Inf..............,..	Vallejo
Fraser James P......	D	22d Penn. Inf..............	"
	A	68th Penn. Inf.....................	
	B	198th Penn. Inf....................	
Griffin Francis M....	H	3d Penn. Inf.................. ..	"
Handlin Joseph J....	B	Purnell Legion, Md.................	"
Hanly William......		U. S. S. Wabash.....	"
Henderson O. L.....	H	8th Cal. Inf..............	"
Josephs William. ..		U. S. S. Sabine..................	"
Kearns John........	F	27th N. Y. Inf.....................	Navy Yard, Mare I.
Long Jonas F.,.....	K	7th Penn. Cav.....................	" "
Lyon George A.....	L	22d Con. Heavy Art....	Sutter St.R.R.,S.F.
McCool D. M........		U. S. S. Sabine..:................	Vallejo
McDermott Robert..	E	1st Oregon Inf....................	"
McKean W. D.......		U. S. Navy.......................	San Francisco
Miller Henry........		U. S. Navy.......................	Navy Yard, Mare I.
Mitchell James......	D	83th N. Y. Inf....................	Vallejo
Newcombe Jonathan	A	3d Maine Inf.............	San Francisco
Reddan John........	G	62d N. Y. Inf....................	Vallejo
Reed H. W..........		U. S. S. Ranger......	U. S. S. Ranger
Roney James........	B	2d Penn. Art......................	Vallejo
Rutherford David...	I	19th Ill. Inf.....................	"
Staples Henry.......		U. S. Marine Corps.................	"
Sullivan W. D.......		U. S. Rec'g Ship Independence.....	"
Taylor Wm. H......		U. S. S. Saranac...................	"
VanKirk Walter B...	A	49th Wis. Inf...........	"
Voorhees Geo. L ...	D	22d Wis. Inf.....	"
Voorhees Jasper C...	D	22d Wis. Inf......................	"
Williams R. A.......		U. S. S. Hartford.................	"
Wilson D. P.........		U. S.S. Powhattan......:..........	Navy Yard Mare I.
Wilson Henry.......		U. S. S. Lackawanna...............	Vallejo

CUSTER POST, No. 5.

CARSON NEVADA.

OFFICERS, 1886.

H. F. BARTINE..Commander
O. A. BRULIN..Senior Vice-Commander
McKEE T. ELSEY...Junior Vice-Commander
C. A. WITHERELL...Adjutant
W. T. HANFORD..Quartermaster
J. McCRIMMON...Surgeon
T. P. MOSELEY..Chaplain
G. A. WILCOX...Officer of the Day
JOHN S. CILLEY..Officer of the Guard
D. H. LENTZ...Sergeant Major
—— ——...Quartermaster Sergeant

Meeting First Wednesday, in Odd Fellow's Hall, Musser St.

NAME.	CO.	SERVICE.	ADDRESS.
Avery D. W	H	3d and 51st N. Y. Inf	Carson
Bartine H. F.	A	8th N J. Inf	"
Bell Geo. H.	G	52d Mass. Inf	"
Baskowitz C. J	D	56th N. Y. Inf	San Francisco, Cal.
Brulin Chas. A	D	7th Ill. Cav	Carson
Burk Samuel	D	24th Wis. Inf	"
Calvert Geo. D.		11th Vt. Inf. and 21st U. S. Inf	"
Cilley John S	I B	1st N. H. Cav	"
Connolly T. J	C	Bat Engineers	"
Crisler W. H	I	187th Ohio Inf	"
Doyle Philip A		U. S. Navy	"
Edson Benjamin	D	10th Ill. Inf.	"
Elsey McKee T	I	47th Iowa Inf	"
Ely John B	C	22d N. J. Inf	"
Ford George F	A	13th Mass Inf	"
Fowler Richard		U. S S. Ceres	"
Gale A. Y	E	10th N H Inf	"
Hanford W. T	I	6th Cal. Inf	"
Hark George	K	34th Ohio Inf	"
Harris Chas. N	F	1st Minn. Inf	"
	G	186th Ohio Inf	
Haynie J. W	G	16th Ohio Inf	"
	C	10th Ohio Cav	
Junkins Henry	B	2d Cal. Cav	"

31

NAME.	CO.	SERVICE.	ADDRESS.
La Forge Peter......	A	13th Ill. Inf.....................	Verdi
Lee S. L..............	H	8th Ill. Inf...........................	Carson
Lentz D. H..........	E	91st Penn. Inf......................	"
McCormick J. H....	F	147th Ill. Inf.......................	Los Angeles, Cal.
McCrimmon J.......	A	9th Minn. Inf.......................	Carson
McCullough Frank	H	40th Ohio Inf.......................	"
Meyer C.............	B	21st Penn. Inf.....	"
	B	98th Penn. Inf...........	
Meyers Geo. H......	K	47th Mo. Inf.......................	"
Moore J. B..........	B	3d Cal. Inf............	Elko
Moseley Thomas P..	B	57th Ind. Inf.......................	Carson
O'Hare Mike........	G	5th U. S. Art.......................	"
Robinson Keeler....	A	144th N. Y. Inf.....................	"
Robinson Marshall..	A	1st Minn. Cav......................	"
Sabin Geo. M.......	K	1st Wis. Inf. and R. E. M. D. V.....	"
Sancho Stephen.....	F	8th Ill. Inf........................	"
Taylor Thomas......	E	13th Wis. Inf..	"
Thaxter George C....		11th Maine Inf.....................	"
White H. C..........	L	4th Iowa Cav......	Brooks, Yolo Co.
Wilcox Geo. A..... .	E	31st Mass. Inf......................	Carson
Witherell C. A.......	K	16th Mich. Inf.......	"
	B & G	2d Mich. Cav.......................	
Zabriskie E. B.....	A	1st Bat. Nevada Vols..............	Candelaria, Nev.

EASTON & ELDRIDGE,
REAL ESTATE AGENTS

AND

General Auctioneers.

House and Insurance Brokers.

RENTS COLLECTED.

618 Market St.   15 and 16 Post St.

Opposite Palace Hotel.

Most Complete Office on the Pacific Coast.

We assume charge of property, hold power of attorney for absentees, collect rents, attend to taxes, insurance, street work, improvements and building.

Real Estate in all parts of the City, business and residence property, blocks and fifty-vara lots sub-divided and sold at auction or private sale.

Personal attention given to the sale of Farming Lands, Stocks, Vessels, Personal Property, Furniture and Art.

Careful appraisements and sales made at public or private sale for Courts, Administrators, Executors, Commissioners, Receivers, Mortgagees and Trustees, faithfully complying with legal forms.

Regular Sale Day, Tuesday.

FRANK BARTLETT POST, No. 6,

OFFICERS, 1886.

HORACE BELL..Commander
J. G. DE TURK..Senior Vice-Commander
L. S. BUTLER...Junior Vice-Commander
SAM. KUTZ...Adjutant
J. S. BUSKIRK...Quartermaster
M. HAGAN..Surgeon
THOS. J. SHREVE..Chaplain
W. J. BROWN...Officer of the Day
WM. D. BARNUM...Officer of the Guard
CHAS. M. FAIRBANKS ....Sergeant Major
F. J. RIBBLE...Quartermaster Sergeant

Meeting every Tuesday.

NAME.	CO.	SERVICE.	ADDRESS.
Adams Henry........	C	8th Cal. Inf......................	Los Angeles
Armstrong Robt.....	I	3.l Ohio Inf......................	Wilmington
Bachman H..........	C	d Penn. Cav	Los Angeles
Baker E. L.....		10th U. S. Inf....................	"
Ballou C. J..........	D	1st Col. Cav.....................	"
Barnum W. D........	A	1st Wash. Ter Inf.................	"
Bartley Jas..........	M	1st N. Y. Engineers...............	"
Bayer Jos...........	B	2d U. S. Inf.....................	"
Dayless Wm.........	B	146th Ill. Inf....................	"
Bennett M.....	D	1st Cal. Native Cav..............	"
Bell Horace.........	B	2d La. Cav....	"
Binkley D H........	F	10th N Y. Inf..................	"
Bont Joseph..... ..	F	16th Ill. Inf...................	"
Bracken M..........		74th N. Y. Inf.	"
Brayton Elijah......		U. S. Signal Corps...............	"
Bridge M............	G	126th Ill. Inf...................	"
Brown Geo. R......		U. S. Navy.....................	"
Brown H. R........	D	3d Wis. Inf.....................	"
Brown L. P.........	E	73d Ind. Inf....................	Long Beach, Cal.
Brown W. J........	E	28th N. Y. Inf.................	Los Angeles
Bruno N............	A	2d R. I. Inf...................	"
Burkle F............	F	39th N. J. Inf.................	San Pedro
Burns John.........	A	2d Mass. Cav...................	Los Angeles
Bushey Jos.........	H	3d Mo. Cav....................	"
Buskirk J. S........	H	51st Penn. Inf.................	"

NAME.	CO.	SERVICE.	ADDRESS.
Butler L. S..........		7th Ohio and 67th U. S. Inf.........	Los Angeles
Cardwell L..........	K	23d Wis. Inf........	"
Carse Levi..........	I	7th Mo. Inf........................	Artesia
Czar G. G..........	D	54th Mass. Inf....................	Pomona
Churchill J. B.......	H	16th N. Y. Heavy Art..............	Los Angeles
Clark Asa........ .	I	14th Kansas Cav....................	"
Coffin Geo..........	A	10th Mich. Inf....................	San Gabriel
Cole Jesse,...... ...	B	57th Ill. Inf......................	Los Angeles
Collier John....	C	4th Iowa Cav......................	"
Collins Thomas......	F	120th Ill. Inf.....................	
Curtin M.	C	5th U. S. Cav.....................	Los Angeles
Curtis L. O.........	F	1st Conn. Inf......................	Newhall
Cutler M. P.........	H	4th Mo. Cav.......	Los Angeles
Dana J. P.......... .	F	5th Cal. Inf......................	"
David Benj.........	I	2d U. S. Art......................	"
Davis John..........	I	126th N. Y. Inf...................	"
Deck J. W..........	K	80th Ill. Inf.....................	"
Decker Wm.........		87th and 38th Ohio Inf....	"
De Turk J. G.......	D	86th Ind. Inf.....................	"
Donlan Thos.......	D	14th U. S. Inf....................	"
Drew S. H..........	D	95th Ill. Inf.....................	Newhall
Dunkleberger I. R...	E	1st Penn. Cav....................	Los Angeles
Dunn Thos. S......	D	9th Ind. Inf.....................	Santa Monica
Du Puy T. J........	D	2d Mich. Inf.....................	Los Angeles
Dutton G. F........	A	17th Ind. Inf....................	"
Ebinger L	F	215th Penn. Inf.................	"
Edmonds C. H		12th and 26th Ill. Inf.............	"
Elliott R. P.........		5th Wis. Light Art............ ...	Santa Monica
Elser Fred..........	C	15th Con. Inf....	Los Angeles
Fairbanks C. M.....	D	7th N. Y. N.G....................	"
Farrell Timothy.....	F	16th N. Y. Inf.................	
Feathers O. J.......	C	127th Penn. Inf..............	Los Angeles
Fitzpatrick W.......	F	1st Cal. Inf.....................	"
Fletcher J. R........	H	147th Ill. Inf................	"
Fonck J. L..........	H	2d Cal. Cav......................	"
Fulton h............	I	6th Iowa Inf.....................	"
Furrey A. J.........	B	4th N. Y. Heavy Art.............	"
Fyke J. D.	G	22d Iowa Inf.....................	"
Gard Geo. E........	H	7th Cal. Inf.....................	"
Garrity Pat..	A	6th N. Y. Heavy Art.............	"
Gates H. O	B	2d N. Y. Cav....................	"
Geigerich G........	C	5th Mich. Cav....................	"
Gilbert W. H.......	H	7th Mo. Cav......................	"
Gillman Henry......	H	33d N. J. Inf....................	"
Glover C. J.... ...	I	27th Mass. Inf..............	"
Goodman J. F......	C	1st Bat. Native Cal. Cav...........	"
Green W. S........	F	83d Ill. Inf.....................	"
Griffin W. H........	H	75th Ill. Inf....................	"
Griffin J. W.........	H	8th Cal. Inf.....................	"
Gripp H............	F	29th Mass. Inf...................	"
Guirado J. F........	B	1st Cal. Cav	"
Guth Martin.......	K	47th Penn. Inf...................	"
Guthrie John........	H	122d Ohio Inf....................	"
Hagan M., M. D.....		51st and 161st Ohio Inf..	"
Hagg John..........	B	4th Ky. Cav.....................	"
Hall Thomas S......	E	92d N. Y. Inf....................	"

NAME.	CO.	SERVICE.	ADDRESS.
Hall W. A...........	H	7th Vt. Inf......	Compton
Ham George P......	H	2d Cal. Cav........................	Los Angeles
Hambrook Thos ...	A	91st Ill. Inf........................	"
Hamilton J. A......	M	11th Ind. Cav......................	"
Hammond N. W.....	D	11th Iowa Inf......	"
Hanratti John.......	F	3d U. S. Art.......................	"
Happs Wm...........	E	1st Col. Cav.......................	"
Harrison L. R.......	F	27th Mich. Inf........	"
Haskin W. A	H	Wash. Ter. Iuf.....................	"
Hawley A. D	B	2d Cal. Inf........................	Newhall
Hawver H. W.......	G	121st N. Y. Inf....................	Los Angeles
Herzog Fred........	I	15th N. Y. Heavy Art.............	"
Hill S. J	C	6th Maine Inf.	"
Hiller H............	A	132d Ill. Inf.......................	"
Hood Benj..........	G	12th N. J. Inf.....................	"
Hoover D...........	C	2d Cal. Cav.......................	"
Hosmer F...........	A	1st Cal. Inf.......................	"
Howard Geo. H......	K	9th Mass. Inf.....	"
Howe E. R	F	44th Mass. Inf....................	
Howe Wm..........	F	4th Cal. Inf.......................	
Jacoby H............	H	27th Penn. Inf....................	Los Angeles
Jenkins C M........	E	2d Mass. Cav......................	"
Johnson R. D.......	A	3d Iowa Cav......................	"
Joyes James........	I	69th N. Y. Inf.....................	Arcata
Kellaher M..........	C	63d N. Y. Inf.....................	Los Angeles
Ketler C. A.........	F	6th Penn. Cav.....................	"
Kidder C. W........	I -	33d N. Y. Inf.....	"
Kinley Isaac........		36th Ind. Inf......................	"
Kirkpatrick J. C....	C	10 Penn. Inf.......................	"
Kirsch Geo........ ...	D	27th Ill. Inf......................	San Pedro
Klaus Moses........	B	2d Cal. Inf.......................	Los Angeles
Kotchwitz E........	C	28th Ohio Inf.....................	"
Kribbs H. S.........	H	5th Wis. Inf.......................	Wilmington
Knrrle Fred........	F	8th Mich. Inf.....................	203 Va. Av. Los A.
Kutz Sam...........	D	91st Ill. Inf......................	
Leake Ed......... ..	F	12th Wis. Inf......................	
Ledbetter M. H.....	D	4th Wis. Inf......................	Los Angeles
Lee H. T...........		4th N. Y. Art.....................	"
Leiste Joseph.......	K	Merril Horse, Mo. Cav.............	"
Levy Aaron........ ...	A	26th Penn. Inf. and Signal Corps..	"
Livermore P. P.		31st Wis. Inf. and 4th U. S.Col'd Inf	Downey, Cal.
Manco R.	G	6th Conn. Inf.....................	Los Angeles
Marsailles J. W......	A	26th U. S. Colored Inf.............	"
Marshall L. H		U. S. Army........................	"
Martin James.......		2d N. H. Inf. and 4th U. S. Art.....	Calico
Mason A. J..........	H	35th Mass. Inf....................	Los Angeles
McCollough E.......	D	39th Ohio Inf.....................	"
McCorvie Frank.....	F	19th Maine Inf....................	Fu'ton Wells, Cal.
McFadden Sam.	·	5th and 13th Ohio Cav.	Los Angeles
McKelvey C. W......		151st Penn. Inf. & U.S.S.Wabash...	"
Meahin N........	C	213th Penn. Inf...................	"
Meyer B. F..........		24th and 21st Mo. Inf.............	El Monte
Meyer M............	H	11th N. J. Inf.....................	
Miles H. C..........	G	36th Ill. Inf......................	Los Angeles
Miller A. H....	I	50th Ind. Inf.....................	"
Mooney D. P....... ·	B	23d Ill. Inf.......................	"

NAME.	CO.	SERVICE.	ADDRESS.
Morey F. C..........		U. S. Navy......................	Los Angeles
Mott John	K	47th N. Y. Inf.....................	"
Moyer J. W....	D	76th Penn. Inf....................	"
Neitzke E...........	I	5th N. Y. Heavy Art.............	"
Norviel Levi	B	123d Ill. Inf.....................	"
Odell A. J..........	A	10th Maine Inf..................	"
Olmstead L. F	C	2d N. Y. Mounted Rifles...........	"
Orr B. F............	E	2d Cal Cav.....................	"
Owens R........	C	65th N. Y. Inf....................	"
Paris C. R...........	G	1st Iowa Cav.......................	Wilmington
Paul Wm.............	K	4th Cal. Inf.....................	Los Angeles
Pegg Elias N.......	A	58th Ohio Inf.......................	"
Petty John..........	I	42d Ill. Inf.....................	"
Phelan Thos. H....	F	12th Vt. Inf.....................	"
Pico Benigno.......	A	1st Cal. Native Cav. Bat........ ..	San Fernando
Platt Jesse..........	F	3d N. Y. Light Art..............	Los Angeles
Ramirez A. M........	D	1st Cal. Native Cav. Bat..........	"
Reed W. E..........		125th Penn. Inf. and 18th Ill. Inf..	"
Real J. F............	L	2d Mass. Light Art.............	"
Redona José........	D	1st Cal. Native Cav. Bat..........	"
Reid Ed.............		4th Mass. Art.....................	"
Rhein James........	A	1st District of Columbia Cav......	"
Rhodes John........	A	2d Ill Cav.......................	"
Ribble F. J..	A	14th Wis. Inf.	"
Rivera J. M..........	D	1st Cal. Native Cav. Bat..........	"
Robarts John.......	D	1st Cal. Native Cav. Bat..........	"
Romans T. D........	C	29th Ind. Inf.....................	"
Roth Fred..........	I	9th U. S. Inf....................	"
Rowe Geo. W.......	H	2d Cal. Cav......................	"
Salmon W. B.......	G	2d Maine Inf....................	"
Sanborn W. K.......	K	2d N. H. Inf.....................	"
Sanford H. P.......	F	6th Kansas Cav..................	Artesia
Santee Milton......		13th Ill. Inf. and 11th Mo. Cav....	Los Angeles
Schlesinger Jacob...		U. S. S. Pocohantas..............	"
Schneider John.		5th U. S. Cav...................	"
Schumacher C. F....	E	5th Penn. Cav..	Tucson, A. T.
Schwartzenberg J...	G	1st N. Y. Cav...................	Los Angeles
Scovell Ira..........	H	74th Ind Inf...................	San Gabriel
Seaton Wm.	C	3d Cal. Inf.	Los Angeles
Sebastian G........	G	11th Ohio Cav..................	"
Shaw G. N..........	I	20th Mass. Inf..................	San Pedro
Shaug W. D	D	4th Cal. Inf....................	San Fernando
Shipman E. M	L	2d Mich Cav....................	Los Angeles
Shreve Thos. J......		11th Mo. Inf. and 2d Mo. Lt. Art	"
Shrier Frank........	G	103d Ohio Inf....................	"
Sittle Casper.......		5th U. S. Cav...................	"
Slocum W. P........	K	2d R. I. Inf.....................	"
Smith C. F..........	H	65th Ill. Inf.......	"
Smith W. J. A.......		14th and 85th Mo. Inf............	"
Spencer W. A.......		76th Ohio Inf. and Vet. Res. Corps	"
Steinbrunn Jacob...	D	98th Penn. Inf..................	"
Stengle J............	D	116th N. Y. Inf...................	Newhall
Stoll Hall..........	C	2th Iowa Inf.....................	Los Angeles
Stoneman George...		U. S. Vols......................	San Gabriel
Strong G. N........		....	Los Angeles
Swaney F. H........		8th Mass. Inf. and 2d Mass. Lt. Art	"

NAME.	CO.	SERVICE.	ADDRESS.
Tilden A. H.........	C	12th Con. Inf......................	Los Angeles
Todd Oscar..........	I	18th Wis. Inf.	"
Turnbull Chas......	E	127th Ill. Inf	"
Tyler O. E..........	B	39th Wis. Inf.....................	"
Underwood Wm. B..	B	9th U. S. Inf.....................	"
Van Horne J........	E	121st N. Y. Inf...................	"
Van Steinberg J. A..	F	84th Ill. Inf.....................	
Wackerly Wm.......	H	9th Minn. Inf....................	Los Angeles
Walker J F..........	E	2d Kansas Inf....................	"
Walsh M. J..........		2d and 4th Cal. Inf..............	"
Warren C. F........		5th Wis. Lt. Art.	"
Weed E. A..........		4th Conn. Inf. and 1st Con. Art....	"
Weid I. A...........		3d Mo. and 82d Ill. Inf...........	"
Wetherman C. D....	F	1st Ark. Inf.....................	"
Williams P. S.......		5th Wis. Lt. Art.................	"
Wilmott L. A.	B	2d Cal. Cav......................	Wilmington
Wise K. D...........	A	91st Ind. Inf.....................	Los Angeles
Wittick H. A........		26th Ill. Inf. and 97th Penn. Inf...	"
Wolfe Geo. W.	L	14th Ill. Cav.....................	"
Wolfer Peter........	F	7th N. Y. Art....................	"
Wonderly W. H.....	E	5th Penn. Cav....................	
Woodin Anson......	I	4th Mo. S. M.....................	
Wright James D.....	E	14th U. S. Inf...................	Los Angeles
Yager M.............	E	1st Cal. Inf.....................	"
Young C. M.........	B	8th N. Y. Cav......	

PHIL SHERIDAN POST, No. 7.

SAN JOSE, CAL.

OFFICERS, 1886.

HENRY T. WELCH..Commander
DANIEL McGINLEY........ ....Senior Vice-Commander
J. T. BOYNTON..Junior Vice-Commander
L. W. DENAN...... ....Adjutant
L. FINNIGAN..Quartermaster
DR. A. H. COCHRANE...Surgeon
REV. JAS. M. NEWELL..Chaplain
J. J. PEARD..Officer of the Day
FRED. BRANDT........... ....Officer of the Guard
ROBERT CAROTHERS...Sergeant Major
O. W. HANSON..Quartermaster Sergeant

Meeting every Thursday.

NAME.	CO.	SERVICE.	ADDRESS.
Anderson H. H......	H	34th Ohio Inf......................	San Jose
Bagley E. M.........		U. S. S. Mohaska..	"
Balling Anthony....	G	3d Cal. Inf......................	"
Bassett G. P....	G	1st Wis. Heavy Art..............	"
Bower N............	I	4th Mo. Inf..........	"
Bowman Alex.......	B	156th Ill. Inf......................	Gilroy
Boynton J. T........	I	3d Maine Inf......................	San Jose
	G	14th Maine Inf....................	
	I	32d Maine Inf....................	
Brandt Fred........	F	35th Mass. Inf....................	"
Brady Terence......	G	2d U. S. Cav....................	"
Brimson T. W........	K	106th N. Y. Inf..................	Gilroy
Brown Luis........	K	22d Mich. Inf......	San Jose
Burgess M. D........	C	7th Cal. Inf....................	"
Burnham John I....		7th Independent Ohio Cav........	"
Butler F. S.........	A	8th Iowa Inf....................	"
Cameron Phil.......	A	1st Vt. Heavy Art	Milpitas
Campbell F. W.....	G	12th Ill. Inf.	San Jose
Carothers Robert....	B	163d Ohio Inf..	"
	A	187th Ohio Inf....................	"
Chapin John A.....	D	104th N. Y. Inf..................	Oakland
Cheney C. R.......	H	15th Ill. Inf....................	Santa Clara
Clendenin L. W.. ..	D	1st Cal. Inf....................	Alma
Close Sam'l L	B	18th Ohio Inf....................	San Jose
Cochrane A. H		15th N. Y. Eng's and U. S. Army..	"

NAME.	CO.	SERVICE.	ADDRESS.
Cole Wallace D.	L	6th N. Y. Heavy Art...............	San Jose
Conant Timothy....	F	4th Minn. Inf...	"
Costello M..........	F	3d U. S. Cav. and U. S. S. Brooklyn.	"
Craw J. P.	B	10th Minn. Inf....................	"
Denan L. W........	B	2d Mass. Cav....................	"
	F	3d U. S. Cav.....................	
Elliot James........	H	12th N. Y. Cav..................	"
Ellis W. F..........	M	1st Minn. Heavy Art.............	Watsonville
Eustice George......	F	7th Wis. Inf.....................	Gilroy
Everhart B. F.......	B	42d Mo. Inf.....................	San Jose
Finigan L...........	D	50th Ohio Inf.....:	"
Foote H S...	I	11th Ind. Inf....................	"
	A	39th Ind. Inf....................	
Gourley James......	D	1st Cal. Inf.....................	"
Grant Geo. W.	I	10th Kan. Inf...................	"
Greo field Milo.....	C	17th Mich. Inf..................	"
Haberdier Oliver....	I	15th Ohio Inf...................	"
Hailstone John B. ..	A	20th Mich. Inf..................	"
Hanson Geo. W......	E	13th N.H.Inf. & U.S.S.Quaker City.	"
Hartman Chas. H. ..	G	12th Mo. Inf..........	"
Harvey A. W........		U. S. S. Fahker..................	"
Haskell Dan N......	G	137th Ohio Inf. G 2d Mo. Inf......	Redding
Hayes J. C..........	F	8th Ill. Inf.....................	San Jose
	H	11th Ill. Inf....................	
Hayford Edw. F....	F	12th Vt. Inf.....................	"
Heagney A. J........	H	15th Iowa Inf...................	"
Hesser H. R.........	A	7th Iowa Inf....................	Soquel
Hibbard M. J........	H	7th Maine Inf..................	Watsonville
Hite M	H	108th Ill. Inf..................	Santa Clara
Holcom Chas. F.....	G	27th Conn. Inf........	San Jose
Hull B. D	H	23d Conn. Inf..................	"
Ingham John.......	H	8th Iowa Inf..................	"
Inman Henry.	B	46th Ill. Inf..................	"
Jahle August........	F	2d U. S. Light Art...............	"
	F	2d Mo. Light Art................	
Judd Charles H.....	E	1st Bat. Nevada Cav.............	"
Kelly James	K	18th Mich. Inf.................	"
Lashbrooks Eli M..	D	2d Wis. Cav.......	"
Lauck George.......	F	12th Ill. Inf..................	Santa Clara
Lesor Lewis.		3d Maine Battery................	San Jose
Mason L. D.........	K	1st Mich. Engineers..............	West Oakland
McClintock E. A....	B	51st Ind. Inf..................	San Jose
McGinley Daniel....		U. S. Navy....................	"
McMahon A.........		52d and 64th Ohio Inf. & U. S. Vols	"
McMurray Sam'l....	C	11th Penn. Reserves	Alameda
McNiff John M......	C	2d Mass. Cav...................	Soquel
Mitchell W. B.......	H	6th U. S. Cav...	Sau Jose
Moody Horace......	I	23d N. Y. Inf. and A12th Wis. Inf..	"
Morphy T. R........	F	3d U. S. Cav....................	"
	I	19th Penn. Cav............	
Morse Obadiah......		U. S. S. Octorora...............	Santa Clara
Nattinger L. L......	E	104th Ill. Inf..................	San Jose
Naylor Benj. F......	D	183d Penn. Inf.................	Gilroy
Newell James M	H	1st Va. Inf.....:..............	Santa Clara
	A	115th Ohio Inf......	
Norton Thos. A......	B	20th Maine Inf..................	San Jose

NAME.	CO.	SERVICE.	ADDRESS.
Oswald Adam........	I	154th Penn. Inf....................	San Jose
Onsley Geo. W......	B	1st Bat. Cal. Mountaineers........	"
Ownly T. P.........	B	28th Ill. Inf......................	"
Parmater John B....	M	5th N. Y. Heavy Art..............	"
Peard John J.	M	2d N. Y. Heavy Art..............	"
Perry Royal S.......	E	100th Ill. Inf.....................	Gilroy
Pettitt James.......	E	6th Tenn. Inf.....................	san Jose
Phelps Geo. M......	A	9th Mich. Inf....................	"
Phifer Jacob J......	F	32d Ill. Inf......................	"
Pomeroy Edgar......	D C	1st Cal. Inf......................	"
Rainey J. W.........	D	22d Mich. Inf....................	"
Rawlings Benj. W...	D	8th N. Y. Heavy Art.............	"
Rayburn G. W.......	L	4th Ill. Cav.....................	"
Rodibaugh D. M ..	K	52d Indiana Inf.................	"
Salisbury N. C......		U. S. S. North Carolina..........	"
Schoenheit Otto.....		20th Ind. Bat....................	"
Schwartz S. F.......	L	16th Penn. Inf...................	"
Scur Richard A.	F	8th Ill. Inf.....................	Santa Clara
Smith Bradley......	G A	9th Maine Inf....................	San Jose
Soper D. J..........	F C	151st N. Y. Inf....	"
Stevens John B.....	C	2d N. H. Inf....................	"
Stewart J. W.......	H	7th U. S. Inf...................	"
Taylor James	K	32d Mass. Inf...................	"
Tennyson D. D......	L	13th Mich. Inf..................	"
Vanhorn B. F.......	H	11th Penn. Inf..................	"
Vestal D. C........	D	1st Cal. Inf....................	"
Weaver E. M........	D	8th Conn. Inf...................	"
Welch Henry T.....	E	1st Maine Cav...................	"
Wendt Albert........	D	144th Ill. Inf..................	"
Wert Frank A.......	G	154th Ind. Inf..................	"
Whitten Wallace....	A	67th Ohio Inf...................	"
Withrow A. A.......	M	2d Mass. Cav....................	Santa Clara
Worcester H. B.....	B	18th Wis. Inf...................	San Jose
Worden Chas. H	B	2d Ohio Cav....................	"
Worthen Geo. W....	H	15th Vt. Inf....................	"
Wright J. B.........	H	16th Mass. Inf..................	"

LYON POST, No. 8.

OAKLAND, CAL.

OFFICERS, 1886.

R. C. J. ADNEY	Commander
LEVI S. BIXBY	Senior Vice-Commander
D. C. SADDLEMIRE	Junior Vice-Commander
R. B. S. YORK	Adjutant
ALFRED W. REINOEHL	Quartermaster
E. H. WOOLSEY	Surgeon
JAMES HILL	Chaplain
C. K. KING	Officer of the Day
HENRY BAYLY	Officer of the Guard
ALBERT S. WINCHESTER	Sergeant Major
HARVEY M. WILSON	Quartermaster Sergeant
ELLIOTT F. SCOTT	Inside Sentinel
LEVI R. BIXBY	Outside Sentinel
RICHARD SCHNEIDER	Organist

Meeting every Tuesday evening, in Grand Army Hall, 419 Thirteenth Street.

NAME.	CO.	SERVICE.	ADDRESS.
Abbott A. F	A	18th N. H. Inf.	1156 Broadway
Adams J. R.	G	2d Col. Inf.	1059 Clay
Adney R. C. J.	B	36th Ohio Inf.	North Temescal
Allen W. W.	F	66th Ill. Inf.	665 Fifth
Allum Leroy W.	C	22d Iowa Inf.	East Oakland
Anderson Thomas	G	168th N. Y. Inf.	479 Orchard
Ash Ferdinand	B	198th Penn. Inf.	575 Fifth
Atkinson George	G	1st Minn. Inf. and 8th Minn. Inf.	1355 Thirteenth av
Babcock Sanford P.	C	152d N. Y. Inf.	1504 Eighth
Bayly Henry	G	2d Cal. Inf.	Emeryville, Cal.
Bell J. K.	A	7th Ohio Cav.	Oakland
Bixby Levi R.	H	7th Cal. Inf.	1463 Brush
Bixby Levi S.	K	35th Mass. Inf.	1470 Brush
Bradford Alonzo	G	1st Mass. Art.	Haywards, Cal.
Bradford A. S.	A	1st N. H. Inf.	1729 Myrtle
Brower H. J.	A	5th Cal. Inf.	832 Market
Brundage J. H.		U. S. S. Nyack	North Temescal
Bryant E. J.	C	5th Maine Inf.	Fifth & Broadway
Buck C. P. H.	F	7th N. Y. Inf. and K 14th N. Y. Cav	539 Thirty-sixth
Buck E. W., M. D.		51st N. Y. Inf.	350 East Fifteenth
Burns Hillary B.	M	11th U. S. Colored Heavy Art.	220 Fifth

NAME.	CO.	SERVICE.	ADDRESS.
Cahill James........	D	9th Conn. Inf....................	1613 Myrtle
Carteron Ed.........	A	13th Mo. Inf.....................	620 Fifth
Carver L. M.........	F	5th Wis. Inf.....................	Oakland
Chapman A. P......	H	113th Ill. Inf............	"
Clapp Geo. P........		U. S. S. Massachusetts..........	Thirty-fifth street
Clark A. O..........	A	65th Ill. Inf....................	819 Castro
Clark R. N..........	G	U. S. Colored Troops............	917 Twenty-fourth
Clarrage E. D.......	F	8th Mass. Inf...................	Oakland
Coburn Jud C.......	F	3d C. 1. Inf....................	Emeryville, Cal.
Coe John T.........	D	8th Mass. Inf...................	5 4 Fifteenth
Cohn Joseph........	F	1st U. S. Art................	Eureka Hotel
Coleman Levi B.....	C	4th Mich Inf....................	618 East 22d
Cook C. C..........		U. S. S. Dragon................	519 Eighth
Cooley F. M........	H	5th Pa. and 11 & 16 U. S. Inf......	1214 Thirtieth
Corrigan John S.....	E	195th Penn. Inf................	Sherman&Adeline
Courvoisier F. L ...	D	93d Ind. Inf....................	941 Linden
Craven A. F........	C	8th Iowa Inf...................	481 Prospect av.
Culver J. O.........		U. S. Army....................	605 M'tgomery S.F.
Cushing A. D........	F	146th Ill. Inf.................	East Oakland
Daniels S. F..... ..	F	105th Ill. Inf..................	Wilson House
Dannaker Wm. A....	H	55th Penn. Inf.................	1781 William
Deasy Thos. A.	E	90th N. Y. Inf.................	Grant's Cot'ge 12th
Dicy Levi.........	E	16th Mich. Inf.................	Arlington House
Dixon Wm. H......	G	51st Mass. Inf.................	1456 Fifteenth
Drais Lemuel K.....	H	39th Ohio Inf..................	Arizona
Edwards John G....	D	72d Ind. Inf..................	520 Tenth
Edwards L. B......	D	72d Ind. Inf	916 California, S.F.
Emlay Oliver.......		1st Mich. Inf.................	1160 Broadway
Ensign Chas. H.....	B	128th N. Y. Inf...............	57 Valley
Erb Eugene W.....	B	1st Conn. Heavy Art...........	B and Hollis
Fairchild Judd H..	A	5 Vt Inf.and C 2d Vet. Res. Corps..	565 Seventeenth
Fitzmaurice John...	F	1st U. S. Art.................	713 Fifteenth
Fitzpatrick Peter...		5th U. S. Art.................	1359 Eighteenth
Gaywood James.....	G	7th Cal. Inf..................	North Temescal
Gibson John.......		U. S. S. St. Mary.............	213 Seventh
Griffin Chas. R......	G	116th Ohio Inf................	Oakland
Harkin D..........	I	6th Mass. Inf.................	1422 Sixth Av.
Harmon R. E........	1	3d U. S. Art..................	368 Fourth
Harper Chas. A.....	F	13th Vt. Inf..................	West Oakland
Harrison Joseph		U. S. S. North Carolina.........	808 Clay
Hossard Richard...	E	23d Ill. Inf...................	Oakland
Hempstead Wm. C. F	1	104th Ill ..Inf...............	729 Tenth
Herrick S. W........	B	10th Wis. Inf.................	810 Myrtle
Hill James.........		1st Ohio Inf..................	818 Clay
Hollywood Andrew .	D	40th N. Y. Inf................	1668 Twelfth
Hollywood Joseph.	H	10th N. Y. Inf................	606 Jessie, S. F.
Hussey W. H. H.....	A	2d Mass. Cav.......	Sacramento, Cal.
Hyde Marcus D....		U. S. Navy...................	119 Tenth
Ingerson Chas. A ..	I	14th N. Y. Heavy Art..........	828 Myrtle
Inwall John H......	I	2d Ohio Cav..................	461 Seventh
Jerome E. B.........	K	14th Ill. Inf.......	1331 Chestnut
		71st Ill. Inf.................	
Johns J. R..........	1	10th Wis. Inf.................	Oakland
Kenna James........		U. S. S. Sangur...............	651 Myrtle
Kerchival J. H......	K	10th Ill. Inf....	C.P.R.R., W.Oakl'd
Kimball Chas. B....		1st Wis. Battery................	1931 Market

NAME.	CO.	SERVICE.	ADDRESS.
King Chas. K.	D	18th N. Y. Cav.	Summer street
Korn Christopher.	I	74th Penn. Inf.	Emeryville, Cal.
Kraft Geo. H.	H	1st U. S. Art.	859 Washington
La Bœuf F.	D	1st Cal. Cav.	762 Jefferson
Lamb Samuel J.	C	114th Ohio Inf.	North Temescal
	K	185th Ohio Inf.	
Lambert John C.	G	62d Ill. Inf.	"
Legler H. T., M. D.		8th N. Y. Inf.	12th & Broadway
Leist Charles.	D	3d U. S. Art.	1668 Thirteenth av
Lemmon John G.	E	4th Mich. Cav.	Oakland
Linderman H. H.	G	8th N. Y. Inf.	Grove and 29th
Lindsey James W.	H	4th Ohio Cav.	1561 Seventh
Lovett W. D.	G	2d Maine Cav.	Yountville, Cal
Mahoney Cornelius.	I	15th Maine Inf.	Oakland
Marsh C. C.		20th Ill. Inf.	360 East 17th
Marshall Samuel W.	C	55th Penn. Inf.	North Temescal
McAlpin A. C.	L	11th N. Y. Cav.	U. S. Mint, S. F.
McConkey E., M. D.	D	3d Ill. Cav.	Oakland
McFeeley Fred. P.	E	74th N. Y. Inf.	1931 Market
McGivern J. W.	D	60th Mass. Inf.	Emeryville, Cal.
McGivney Thos. J.	B	47th Mass. Inf.	1812 Taylor
McGovern Thomas.	H	71st N. Y. Inf.	North Temescal
	D	2d U. S. Inf.	
McGrew P. H.	F	17th Ohio Inf.	1056 Thirteenth av
McLaughlin C. W.	A	17th Ind. Inf.	496 Ninth
Miller C. S.		30th Mass. Heavy Art.	ewland House
Mills W. W.	A	1st Wash. Ter. Inf.	1280 Eighth Av.
Minnett Geo. C.	A	6th Cal. Inf.	1211 Franklin
Mongelez Chas.	B	7th Cal. Inf.	6th and Broadway
Morgan Winfield S	E	17th U. S. Inf.	1312 Thirteenth av
Morse D. A.	F	118th N. Y. Inf.	San Francisco
Moulton Floyd.	B	50th N. Y. Engineers.	631 Fourteenth
Mueller John C.	F	24th Ill. Inf.	366 Fifth
O'Donnell James.		U. S. S. Pensacola.	West Oakland
Olsen R.	G	2d Minn. Inf.	908 Willow
	A	6th Minn. Inf.	
Orelup J. K.	H	3d N. H. Inf.	Oakland
Parker James.	C	44th Ill. Inf.	461 Seventh
	I	9th U. S. Vet. Vols.	
Parmentor Chas. H	G	5th Mass. Inf.	1370 Brush
Patterson A. K.	B	59th N. Y. Inf.	San Francisco
	C	4th N. Y. Art.	
Peer Abram.	B&F	93d N. Y. Inf.	Yountville
Pike E. P.	G	5th N. H. Inf.	14th and Tel. Av.
Pounstone A. L.	C	101st Ohio Inf.	610 Eighteenth
Proksch Lorenz.	B	2d Wis. Cav.	1217 Center
Reany William.	H	3d U. S. Heavy Art.	1219 Peralta
Redington C. H.	C	15th Ill. Inf.	1665 Twelfth
Reeve W. N.	B	41st Ohio Inf.	Ohio
Reinoehl Alfred W.	I	107th Penn. Inf.	818 Brush
Rincke John.	C	24th Mass. Inf.	924 Twenty-fourth
Robinson J. A.	K	8th Ill. Inf.	Livermore, Cal.
Rogers W. H.	G	14th Iowa Inf.	Oakland
Roundy J. L.	G	14th Mass. Inf.	503 East 14th
	B	1st Mass. Art.	
Royce Frank L.	A	138th N. Y. Inf. and 9th N. Y. H. Art.	Tulare City, Cal.

NAME.	CO.	SERVICE.	ADDRESS.
Rudolph August....		U. S. S. Unadilla and Mohongo....	1471 Fifth
Saddlemire D. C.....		11th N. Y. Battery.................	North Temescal
Schauer Henry......	C	35th Mass. Inf....................	611 East 12th
Schneider Richard...	I&D	9th Ohio Inf......................	480 Orchard
Scott Elliott F......	C	1st Nevada Inf...................	North Temescal
Shea Daniel........		U. S. Navy	821 Sixteenth
Simon Joseph.......	G	2d Mo. Inf.......................	1525 Broadway
Smith Chas. H	H	7th R. I. Inf.....................	506 East 18th
Smith Chas. W......	A	6th Minn. Inf....................	Alameda, Cal.
Smith Henry T......	H	20th Ill. Inf.....................	1461 Broadway
Smith H S..........	E	3d Mass. Heavy Art	918 Fifth
Smith James........	I	40th N. Y. Inf...................	Emeryville
Spencer E. W.......	M	1st Wis. Heavy Art..............	1114 Webster
Stewart G. W.......	G	23d Ill. Inf......................	517 Ninth
Stiles H. K		47th N. Y. Inf...................	Center, A and B
Stufflebean Geo. W..	F	25th Mo. Inf.....................	9th and Harrison
Tusher Fred........	H	15th Ill. Inf.....................	953 Willow
Van Arnam H. M ...	A	58th Ill.. Inf....................	1166 Seventh
Vance James M......	E	1st Bat. Nevada Cav.............	802 Henry
Vaughan Silas B.....		18th Ohio Battery...............	Oakland
Wells Henry C......	C	1st Conn. Cav...................	1204 Adeline
West F. M..........	I	5th Iowa Cav....................	Ross House
West Rollin A.......	L	1st Minn. Heavy Art.....	"
Wilcox Chas. H......	F	35th N. Y. Inf...................	380 Tenth
Williams Nicholas..		U. S. S. Constitution............	Oakland
Wilson Harvey M...		30th Maine Inf..................	1210 Franklin
Winchester Albert S.	D	36th Ohio Inf.......	Girard House
	B	39th Ohio Inf....................	955½ Washington
Winkler Jacob......	G	21st N. J. Inf....................	612 Fourth
Woolsey E. H., M. D.	H	33d N. Y. Inf....................	Woolsey Hospital
Wright Geo. H......	B	11th Mich. Inf..................	222 Helen
Wythe Jos. H., M. D..		U. S. Vols......................	965 West
York R. B. S........	I	148th Ind. Inf...................	Hall of Records

THE
Fredericksburg Brewing Co.

SAN JOSE, CALIFORNIA.

General Depot, 539 California Street.

BREWERS AND BOTTLERS OF

LAGER BEER!

—❧ For Export and Draught. ☙—

FAMILIES SUPPLIED.

GRANT POST, No. 9.

MODESTO, CAL.

OFFICERS, 1886.

W. H. THORNBURG..Commander
RICHARD YOUNG...............................Senior Vice-Commander
D. C. COLEMAN................................Junior Vice-Commander
I. S. LOVENTHAL...Adjutant
W. R. PIPER...Quartermaster
JAY HARRISON...Surgeon
W. H. ARMENT...Chaplain
——— ———...Officer of the Day
JOHN BRAIDS..Officer of the Guard
——— ———..Sergeant Major
——— ———...............................Quartermaster Sergeant

Meeting, Second and Fourth Tuesday.

NAME.	CO.	SERVICE.	ADDRESS.
Abbott C. H.........	H	93d Ill. Inf......................	Turlock
Acker Hudson H....	F	21st Iowa Inf....................	Oakdale
Arment W. H........	M	20th Penn. Cav..................	Modesto
Arnold W. H........	K	6th Iowa Inf....................	
Bartch Frederick....		142d U. S. Colored Inf............	Grayson
Beesley Thos........	B	13th Ill. Inf....................	Turlock
Blanchard A. C	B	1st Maine Inf...................	Modesto
Braids John.,.......		U. S. S. Anacosta..............	"
Case J. J......	M	8th Mo. Cav...................	Turlock
Christman Henry....	A	74th Ill. Inf..............	Modesto
Coleman David C....	B	10th Ill. Inf...................	"
Cunningham L.......	E	53d Ill. Inf...................	"
Fuller M. A..........	I	31th Ill. Inf..............	Turlock
Givens W. J.........		U. S. S. Cumberland..	Modesto
Gordon Aaron.......	A	83d Ill. Inf....................	"
Harrison Jay........	F	58th Ill. Inf...................	"
Howard W. A........	B	59th Iowa Inf...................	"
Johnson Chas. W....	B	4th Cal. Inf...................	"
Keeley Conrad......	G	Mead's Cav....................	Oakdale
Laudon D. B........	A	48th Iowa Inf..................	Modesto
Loventhal I. S......	G	18th Ind. Inf.................	"
Lundy Wm..........	D	171st Penn. Inf.................	Hills Ferry
Mann Wesley S......	A	53d Ind. Inf...................	Modesto
McCreedy H. C......	K	2d Cal. Inf....................	"
McCumber Thos. C..	A	53d Wis. Inf...................	"

45

NAME.	CO.	SERVICE.	ADDRESS.
Mitchell G..........	D	10th Iowa Inf.....................	Modesto
Myers Jacob........	H	55th Ohio Inf.....................	"
Palmer W. D........	B	10th Mich. Inf....................	"
Phillips R. O........	C	60th Ill. Inf.....................	"
Piper W. R..........	G	9th Mich. Cav....................	"
Prentiss J. W........	C	26th Conn. Inf..................	"
Richards H. W......	D	13th Conn. Inf..................	Turlock
Roberts Michael.....	L	13th Tenn. Cav.................	Modesto
Sawyer Frederick A.	E	17th Maine Inf.................	Oakdale
Smith W. J..........	K	1st Mo. Engineers.............	Modesto
Thornburg W. H....	A	27th Iowa Inf.................	"
Trammell J. J.......	M	1st Ark. Cav.. /..............	"
Vosburg Isaac.......	F	N. Y. Heavy Art...............	Hills Ferry
Wilson B. B.........	I	96th Ill. Inf..................	Modesto
Wilson Chas. S......	K	42d Ill. Inf..................	"
Wood A. A..........	H	19th Iowa Inf.................	"
Young Richard......		U. S. S. Mackinaw...........	"

PHIL. KEARNEY POST, No. 10.

VIRGINIA CITY, NEVADA.

OFFICERS, 1886.

J. A. ROBERTSON	Commander
A. H. WARD	Senior Vice-Commander
P. G. KING	Junior Vice-Commander
C. H. GALUSHA	Adjutant
B. ARMBRUST	Quartermaster
P. T. KIRBY	Surgeon
W. H. ORMROD	Chaplain
F. A. ST. JOHN	Officer of the Day
W. J. HILL	Officer of the Guard
H. SCHIRLEY	Sergeant Major
V. RITCHIE	Quartermaster Sergeant

Meeting, First Monday.

NAME.	CO.	SERVICE.	ADDRESS.
Ambrust B	D	4th Mo. Cav	Virginia City
Bailey A. B	L	9th N. Y. S. M	Oregon
Bondshu Charles A	A	10th U. S. Inf	Virginia City
Burbank J. P	I	8th N. H. Inf	"
Clark Thos	F	12th U. S. Inf	Candelaria
Dodero Domingo	L	2d Cal. Cav	Gold Hill
Donnelly T. S		U. S. Navy	Virginia City
Dresser F. S	H	47th Wis. Inf	"
Ebner Conrad		4th Ohio Battery	"
Eckerman J. B	E	139th Penn. Inf	"
Folsom P. E	H	20th Maine Inf. & Griffin's Battery	"
Galusha C. H	G	6th Mich. Heavy Art	Gold Hill
Harris E. B		U. S. Vols	San Francisco
Hill W. J	O	7th Cal. Inf	Virginia City
Kennedy Thos	C	11th Vt. Inf	"
King P. G	E	2d Penn. Reserve Corps	Gold Hill
Kirby P. T	K	19th Ohio Inf	Virginia City
Libby T. C	K	1st Maine Battery	"
Lord F. C	L	13th N. Y. Cav	"
McCullough J. S	G	66th Ohio Inf	"
Ormrod W. H	K	129th Penn. Inf	"
Parker Wm. H	B	3d Cal. Inf	"
Ritchie V	A	10th N. Y. Inf	"
Robertson J. A	G	24th Mass. Inf	"
Robinson L. W	F	11th Ind. Inf	"
Schirley Henry	D	9th Wis. Inf	"
Shaw H. G	B	125th Ohio Inf	"
St. John F. A		U. S. S. Brooklyn	"
Sullivan Edward	B	4th U. S. Art	Carson, Nev.
Turman B. I	K	8th Cal. Inf	Dayton
Ward A. H	H	2d Maine Inf	Virginia City
Williams Philemon	D	12th N. Y. Cav	

JOE HOOKER POST, No. 11.

ALAMEDA, CAL.

OFFICERS, 1886.

JOHN ELLSWORTH..Commander
E. B. DUNNING..Senior Vice-Commander
H. W. COTTON..Junior Vice-Commander
O. L. METZGER..Adjutant
JAMES COOK..Quartermaster
W. O. TAYLOR..Surgeon
E. F. M. HURLBUT..Chaplain
WILLIAM SEYMOUR..Officer of the Day
JOHN MYER..Officer of the Guard
R. HAMLIN..Sergeant Major
——— ———...Quartermaster Sergeant

Meeting, First Friday, Masonic Hall, Cor. Park and Santa Clara Ave.

NAME.	CO.	SERVICE.	ADDRESS.
Anderson George...		U. S. Navy..........................	Alameda
Bakker R....		U. S. S. Wm. L. Marcy............	"
Boehse Charles......	A	1st N. Y. Art............	"
Brown M. L.........	I	117th Ind. Inf....................	"
Cole L. L.	B	11th Mich. Inf....................	"
Cook James.	H	2d Penn. Inf.	"
	B	191st Penn. Inf....................	
Cotton H. W.........	A	3d Ind. Mounted Vols............	"
Deane C. T.		12th N. Y. Art....................	San Francisco
DeNice J. H.........	B	8th Ohio Cav.....................	Alameda
Dunning E. B..	D	1st Bat. Nevada Cav.............	"
Ellsworth John.....	G	25th Conn. Inf...................	"
Hamlin Orin E.....	D	45th Ill. Inf. and A 1st Cal. Inf.. ..	"
Hamlin Adrian R....	L	1st Cal. Cav,....................	"
Hart John...........		U. S. Navy	"
Hurlbut E. F. M...		24th N. Y. Battery................	Santa Rosa, Cal.
Hutton E. L........	C	15th Ohio Inf....................	Alameda
Kruger H...........	E	5th U. S. Cav....................	"
Kuster H. C........	B	149th Ill. Inf.	Oakland
Linderman J. C......	C	1st Ohio Light Art................	Alameda
McGown Harvey...	K	71st Ohio Inf....................	"
McMahon J. S.......		U. S. Navy......................	"
Metzger C. L........	I	138th and 155th Ind. Inf..........	"
Miller G. B.........	D	11th Penn. Inf...................	"
Myer John..........	K	122d N. Y. Inf...................	"

48

NAME.	CO.	SERVICE.	ADDRESS.
Poindexter F. H.....	B	20th Ohio Inf......................	Portland, Or.
Porter B. B..........	G	10th N. Y. Cav....................	San Francisco
Prindle H. F........	B	5th Conn. Inf.....................	Alameda
Reynolds J. M.......		10th N. Y. Cav	"
Richardson J........	K	8th Cal. Inf......................	"
See R. J.............	B	19th Ohio Inf......................	"
	A	105th Ohio Inf....................	
Seymour William...	B	2d Mo. Inf......................	"
Taylor D. B.	D	31st Mass. Inf....................	"
Taylor W. O.........		U. S. Vols.......................	"
Theysohn A.........	G	58th N. Y. Inf....................	San Leandro
Todd H. H..........	K	2d N. J. Inf. and I 8th N. J. Inf....	Alameda
Ward A. H..........	H	90th N. Y. Inf.......	"
Welch Denis........	G	4th N. J. Inf...........	"

ROD MATHESON POST, No. 16.

HEALDSBURG, CAL.

OFFICERS, 1886.

JOHN FAVOUR..Commander
LESTER STEVENS.....................................Senior Vice-Commander
J. W. SYLVESTER.....................................Junior Vice-Commander
E. B. METZGER...Adjutant
THOS. J. RILEY..Quartermaster
W. H. BARNES..Surgeon
MILES MORRIS...Chaplain
GEO. SLOCUM...Officer of the Day
D. G. BOWSHER..Officer of the Guard
....Sergeant Major
FRANK PASCHAL..............................Quartermaster Sergeant

Meeting, Second Friday.

NAME.	CO.	SERVICE.	ADDRESS.
Babcock J. H........		U. S. S. Ossippe...................	Healdsburg
Baker J. C..........	D	40th Iowa Inf.....................	"
Barnes W. H........	E	72d Mo. Inf......................	"
Blackmore N. L.....		U. S. S. Valley City............	Cloverdale
Bowsher D. G.......	C	73d Ohio Inf.....................	Healdsburg
Conger C. C........		8th Cal. Inf......................	"
Cook Chas..........	C	4th Cal. Inf......................	Cloverdale
Deaton G. M........	I	23d Ind. Inf......................	Healdsburg
Favour John........	G	2d Cal. Cav......................	"
Franklin J. W.......	F	1st Cal. Bat. Mountaineers......	
Frazier Wm.........	G	1st Mo. Inf.......................	Cloverdale
Gibson Thos. J.....	E	6th Ind. Cav....................	Healdsburg
Heath H. A.........	I	7th N. H. Inf....................	"
Ink Walter S.......	C	85th Ohio Inf....................	Cloverdale
Jahn Ferdinand.....	F	7th Cal. Inf......................	Healdsburg
Joy W. H..........	I	11th Minn. Inf...................	"
Keith A. D.........	G	2d Col. Cav......................	"
Metzger A. V.......	I	155th Ind. Inf...................	"
Metzger E. B.......	C	1st Cal. Cav.....................	"
Morris Miles.......	G	7th Kansas Cav...................	"
Moulton W. M......		9th N. Y. Heavy Art..............	"
Nichols C. A.......	G	67th Ohio Inf....................	Cloverdale
Paschal Frank.....	B	7th Cal. Inf.....................	Healdsburg
Ragsdale J. W......	C	13th Iowa Inf....................	Santa Rosa
Remmel Chas......	F	42d Wis. Inf.....................	Clairville
Riley Thomas J.....	G	2d Iowa Inf......................	Healdsburg
Roesch Frank......	C	4th Wis. Cav....................	"
Ross J. B..........	H	84th Ill. Inf.....................	"
Rowe N............	K	31st N. J. Inf. and K 41st Mo. Inf..	Cloverdale
Scott Julius........		U. S. S. Wabash..................	Healdsburg
Skellenger D. A.....	D	18th Wis. Inf....................	"
Slocum Geo........	K	30th Penn. Inf. and 143d Penn. Inf	"
Smith Wm N.......	D	13th Ohio Inf....................	"
Stevens Lester.....	G	5th Wis. Inf. and 16th Wis. Inf....	"
Sylvester J. W.....	B	44th Mass. Inf...................	"
Van Clief J. H......	A & I	13th N. Y. Inf. and 38th N. Y. Inf..	"
Warfield R. H......		50th N. Y Engineers..............	"
Warner A. L.......	C	105th Ill. Inf....................	"
Wiedemeyer S. J....	D	11th Mo. Inf.....................	"

Members of the G. A. R., Attention!

Special Arrangements for your Entertainment have been made by

WE MIRROR NATURE

INSTANTANEOUS PORTRAITS.
VIEWS OF PACIFIC COAST SCENERY.

FINE ART WORK.
PORTRAITS FROM LIFE OR COPY.

Taber
PHOTOGRAPHER

8 MONTGOMERY ST.

OPPOSITE
Palace Hotel and Masonic Temple.   **SAN FRANCISCO, CAL**

You are heartily Invited to Inspect my

VIEW DEPARTMENT,

Wherein you can see all the beautiful Scenery of California as in a Mirror.

THE PORTRAIT GALLERY

Contains the Likenesses of Prominent Men of California and of all Nations, Photographed by me.

A Portrait of yourself, or Views of this City and State are

the best Souvenirs you can have, for yourself and

your friends, of your visit to San Francisco.

Gold Medal " World's Fair," New Orleans, 1885. Highest Award, Southern
Exposition, Louisville, 1884, and the same again in 1885.
Many more at other places, and earlier dates.

SEDGWICK POST, No. 17.

SANTA ANA, CAL.

OFFICERS, 1886.

C. E. BERRY...Commander
G. M. DOYLE...Senior Vice-Commander
E. C. JONES...Junior Vice-Commander
W. H. DRIPS..Adjutant
R. CUMMINGS..Quartermaster
H. G. KERNODLE...Surgeon
W. A. INSLEY..Chaplain
I. N. JEFFERSON...Officer of the Day
GEORGE W. HAWKINS...Officer of the Guard
GEORGE J. MOSBAUGH...Sergeant Major
L. BELL...Quartermaster Sergeant

Meeting, Second and Fourth Monday.

NAME.	CO.	SERVICE.	ADDRESS.
Abbott E. J..........	C	12th Iowa Inf...................	Garden Grove
Avas John...........	B	47th Ill. Inf...................	Santa Ana
Balcom B. G.........	O	42d Mass. Inf...................	"
Bell L..............	E	36th Mass. Inf...................	"
Berry C. E..........	H	2d Ark. Inf...................	"
	B	2d Kansas Inf...................	
Bowley J. D.........	I	46th Mass. Inf...................	Garden Grove
Buck O. J...........	H	96th Ill. Inf...................	"
Burgess R. F........	A	21st Mich. Inf...................	"
Chase A.............	A	7th Kansas Cav...................	"
Clark J. G..........	F	10th Iowa Inf...................	Orange
Colby L. J..........	E	24th Wis. Inf...................	Santa Ana
Conway D. N.........	G	43d Ind. Inf...................	Orange
Cummings R..........	C	7th Penn. Cav...................	Santa Ana
Doyle G. M..........	B	8th Mo. Inf...................	"
Drips W. H..........	D	6th Ohio Inf...................	"
Eddy E. H...........	F	147th Ill. Inf...................	Pinacate
Edwards E. E........	B	6th Iowa Inf...................	Santa Ana
Everett S. B........	A	4th Ill. Cav...................	Garden Grove
French C. E.........	B	9th Maine Inf...................	Santa Ana
Friend Taylor B....	F	1st Maine Cav...................	Orange
Gardner J. W.......	B	21st Mich. Inf...................	Los Angeles
Halladay M. D.......	D	4th Mich. Inf...................	Santa Ana
Hannah J. Q	F	Mo. State Cav...................	"
Hawkins G. W......	H	1st Col. Inf...................	"

51

NAME.	CO.	SERVICE.	ADDRESS.
Huntington S.......	D	29th Iowa Inf......	Antelope
Insley W. A........	E	72d Ind. Inf......................	Santa Ana
Irish J. M...........	E	8th Ind. Inf......	"
Jefferson I. N.......	A	156th Penn. Inf................	"
Jones E. C..........	F	98th Ill. Inf....................	"
Kernodle H. G......	B	17th Ind. Inf....................	"
	B	116th Ind. Inf..................	
King R.............	B	39th Wis. Inf....	"
Loggins H. B.	G	2d Va. Inf......................	"
Look P. H...........	F	12th Maine Inf..................	"
Mansur C. F	D	8th Wis. Inf....................	"
Matteson S. H......	G	43d Wis. Inf....................	"
Meacham A	L	3d Ky. Cav	Orange
Mosbaugh George J.	D	133d Ind. Inf...................	Santa Ana
Patterson W. A......	D	39th Ill. Inf...................	West Minster
Purcell T. M.......	G	6th Cal. Inf....	Santa Ana
Reynerson J........	D	16th Iowa Inf..	"
Rockwell L. D......	C	7th Ill. Inf.....................	"
Sexton F. L........	K	27th Ill. Inf	Newport
Sheffer F. D........	B	10th Ind. Inf...................	Santa Ana
Smith F. M.	A	35th Mo. Inf...................	"
Smith H. E.........	I	13th Kansas Inf................	"
Stackpole J. E......	F	1st Mass. Cav..................	Lathrop
Sutton S. W.	B	24th Iowa Inf..	Santa Ana
Van Allen B. D.....	A	Nugent's Mo. Battery...........	"
Vanderlip F........	C	20th Ind. Cav..................	Pasadena
Weber J............	G	47th Penn. Inf.................	Orange
West S. B........	M	8th Iowa Cav..................	Santa Ana
White J. A..........	C	40th Ind. Inf..................	Garden Grove
Young H. A.........	A	81st Ill. Inf........	"

HALLECK POST, No. 19.

CHICO, CAL.

OFFICERS, 1886.

I. M. TERILL..Commander
H. T. BATCHELDER.......................................Senior Vice-Commander
O. S. JEWETT...Junior Vice-Commander
JAMES DAVISON...Adjutant
W. R. WILLIAMS...Quartermaster
PHILLIP O'HAIR...Surgeon
J. McC. STILSON........... ....Chaplain
GEORGE S. SNOOK..Officer of the Day
WM. REMLEY......................................Officer of the Guard
DANIEL WINDERS...Sergeant Major
MORRIS RUSSELL.............................Quartermaster Sergeant

Meeting, every Fourth Wednesday.

NAME.	CO.	SERVICE.	ADDRESS.
Batchelder H. T.....	A	22d Maine Inf....................	Chico
Bensley Edwin......	B	119th Ill. Inf......................	"
Bugby S.............	H	27th Mich. Inf....................	"
Davison James......	C	4th Cal. Inf......................	"
Dibble J. S.........	B	22d Ill. Inf......................	"
Eagan James........	E	3d U. S. Cav....	"
Goree M. R..........	D	115th Ill. Inf....................	Durham
Griffith Jonathan...	B	1st U. S. Cav....	Orland
Healey John S......	G	12th Ill. Inf......................	Chico
Hunter J. H.........	B	100th Penn. Inf..................	"
Illig Carl...........	A	2d Cal. Cav......................	Powelton
Jewett Oscar S......	B	7th Mich. Inf....................	Chico
Kelly Joseph M......	I	2d Cal. Cav......................	"
Labish Otto.........	A	8th Cal. Inf.....................	"
Long R. J..........	K	45th Ohio Inf....................	"
Lorton James.......	H	62d N. Y. Inf and D U. S. Eng... .	"
Lowell Geo. A......	A	1st Ill. Light Art.................	"
McConnell James....	F	52d N. Y. Inf....................	"
Morrison James.....	G	12th Wis. Inf....................	"
Nordyke A. T........	A	2d Cal. Cav.....................	"
O'Hair Philip.......	G	13th U. S. Inf...................	"
Remley William....	B	50th Ill. Inf....................	"
Russell Morris......	K	24th N. Y. Inf...................	"
Sherman William P.	D	91st Ill. Inf.....................	"
Smith L. F........	G	27th Iowa Inf....................	"
Snook George S......	C	12th Ind. Inf....................	"
Stevenson Joseph A.	A	3d Mo. Cav......................	"
Stilson J. McC......	A	1st Wis. Cav.....................	"
Swift W. A....... ..	H	1st Col. Inf. and C 1st Col. Cav. ...	"
Terill I. M..........	K	1st Minn. Inf. and A 88th Ill. Inf..	"
Twitchell W. A......	E	12th Mass. Inf...................	"
Watson J. N.........	F	126th Ill. Inf....................	"
Wilder Horace......	H	156th Ill. Inf....................	Paradise
Williams W. R......	D	39th N. J. Inf...................	Chico
Willson James......		U. S. S. "R. R. Cuyler"............	"
Winders Daniel.....	E	75th Ind. Inf....................	"
Woods D. H.........	B	4th Cal. Inf....	Orland

ELLSWORTH POST, No. 20.

SANTA ROSA, CAL.

OFFICERS, 1886.

J. D. BARNETT...Commander
FRANK H. SWETT..Senior Vice-Commander
A. B. STUART..Junior Vice-Commander
J. W. DAVIS...Adjutant
WM. H. VAN DOREN...Quartermaster
WM. F. COOTS..Surgeon
S. M. DODGE..Chaplain
J. S. WILSON...Officer of the Day
J. W. FITTS...Officer of the Guard
J. H. GADDIS...Sergeant Major
DAN HALBERT...Quartermaster Sergeant

Meeting, Second and Fourth Thursday.

NAME.	CO.	SERVICE.	ADDRESS.
Acton Will..........	D	8th Cal. Inf......................	Santa Rosa
Armstrong J. B....		95th Ohio Inf.......	"
Arnold A. W........	A	14th N. Y. Inf.....................	"
Barnett J. D........	A	44th Wis. Inf.....................	"
Barnhardt C. M.....	I	178th Ohio Inf....................	San Bernardino
Bell Stephen S......	D	23d Wis. Inf......................	Santa Rosa
Boswell J. H........	A	116th Ill. Inf.....................	"
Bumbaugh C. M....	B	51st Penn. Inf....	"
Campbell J. T.......	A	3d Mo. Cav. and B 32d Mo. Inf.....	"
Chittenden Wm. I...	E	13th Ill. Inf......................	"
Clemens Geo. W....	H	194th Penn. Inf. and 9th Penn. Cav.	"
Cole E. A....	F	27th Iowa Inf.....	"
Coots Wm. F........	A&E	55th Ill. Inf......................	"
Craig D. N..........		44th Ohio Inf.................	Occidental, Cal.
Dana A. W..........	D	15th Mass. Inf.....................	Santa Rosa
Davis J. W..........	B	7th Del. Inf......................	"
Dibble P. K. Rev...		9th Mo. Cav......................	"
Dodge S. M. Rev....	C	143d Ill. Inf......................	"
Dopp Daniel E......		19th Mich. Inf....................	"
Duffey Thos.........	A	14th Penn. Cav....................	"
Dumbaugh E........	G	5th Mo. S. M. and B 5th Iowa Cav..	"
Duncan Noel........	F	7th Cal. Inf.	San Bernardino
Endicott D. A.......	E	2d Mo. Cav. and I 11th Mo. Cav....	Santa Rosa
Felton Martin.......	E	12th Penn. Cav....................	"
Fisher A. L..........	I	13th Vt. Inf......................	"

54

NAME.	CO.	SERVICE.	ADDRESS.
Fitts Jos. W.........	A	49th Ind. Inf......	Santa Rosa
Fix Joshua..........	A	9th Kansas Cav...................	Sebastopol
Gaddis Jos. H.......	I	9th Ind. Cav.............	Santa Rosa
Gouff J. N..........	K	17th Ohio Inf.............	"
Halbert Daniel......	H	6th Mich. Inf. & H 6th Mich. H. Ar.	"
Hall Albert A..	F	3d Wis. Cav........,............	Forestville
Hathaway Frank....	A	13th Ohio Inf. and 115th Ohio Inf.	Santa Ros v
Hohman Otto.......	A	21st Mo. Inf.....................	Sebastopol
Hornbeck J. H.....	K	21st Ohio Inf. and K 1st Ala. Cav..	Santa Rosa
Johnson Wm........	A	7th Vt. Inf......................	"
Kent Jos. A.........	A	32d Iowa Inf....................	"
Lawson Burd.......	G	6th Mo. S. M..................	"
Linsley Chas. E.....	A	26th Ill. Inf....................	"
Little James W......	B	65th Ind. Inf....................	"
Long Andrew........	D	1st N. Y. Art....................	"
Loring Wm. F......	E	141st Penn. Inf.................	"
Mathisen C. T......		U. S. S. Minnesota..............	Mark West
McCumisky James..		U. S. S. Colorado...............	Santa Rosa
McKoou H. H......	C	44th N. Y. Inf...................	"
Metcalf S. W........	M	2d Wis. Cav......	"
Miller John...	F	3d Mich. Inf. and 6th N Y. Ind Bat	"
Mize F. D...........	D	3d Iowa Cav...	Mark West
Murphy Wyman.....	K	21st Wis. Inf...................	Santa Rosa
Morse J. M..........	K	32d Mass. Inf..................	"
Neilson Bendix.....	K	33d Wis. Inf..................	"
Osborne John W....	H	63d Ind. Inf..................	"
Peck Taylor A......	F	77th N. Y. Inf.................	"
Pflying George......	B	10th N. Y. Inf.................	"
Pierce Calvin.'......	F	11th Wis. Inf..................	"
Poat J. J............		U. S. S. Union...............	"
Rancy Henry........	C	8th Iowa Cav.................	"
Rhinierson G. W....	I	8th Ind. Inf. and 16th Ind. L. Art..	Forestville
Rikert Theo. M.....	I	102d Ill. Inf..................	Santa Rosa
Roach Michael......	D	88th N. Y. Inf......	"
Schenck Henry.....	K	3d U. S. Cav..................	"
Scoville Royal W....	K	3d Mo. Cav...................	"
Shakelford E. A.. ..	H	45th Mo. Inf..................	"
Slater James........	C	2d U. S. Art..................	"
Stevens N...........	G	8th Ill. Inf...................	"
Stuart A. B., M. D...		10th Mo. Inf. and 1st Ala. Cav.....	"
Swett Frank H.....	E & I	10th N. H. Inf................	"
Temple R. A........	F	7th Cal. Inf..................	"
Thayer A. N.........	F	5th Ohio Cav.................	"
Vanderhoof M. H....	M	15th N. Y. Engineers............	"
Van Doren Wm. H..	A	150th Ill. Inf.................	"
Weeks Albert B.....		U S S Sabine & U S S Fort Jackson.	"
Williamson John V..	A	10th Ill. Inf..................	Windsor
Willits Charles M...	O	84th Ind. Inf.................	Santa Rosa
Wilson Camring.....	B	9th Ind. Inf..................	"
Wilson Jos. W......	H	17th Ind. Mounted Inf...........	"

RAWLINS POST, No. 23.

OFFICERS, 1886.

R. S. JOHNSON..Commander
O. N. HITCHCOCK...Senior Vice-Commander
W. S. PETERS..Junior Vice-Commander
O. H. KEAGLE..Adjutant
ED. SCOTT... .....Quartermaster
A. T. HUDSON...Surgeon
R. CONDY...Chaplain
SAM'L REA...Officer of the Day
P. A. DAVIS...Officer of the Guard
SAM'L DASHER...Sergeant Major
EDWARD COURT.. ....Quartermaster Sergeant

Meeting, First and Third Wednesday.

NAME.	CO.	SERVICE.	ADDRESS.
Adams Silas P......		U. S. Navy	Stockton
Alexander B. D.....	E	1st Mass. Inf.....................	"
Alexander W. S......	E	1st Nevada Inf....................	"
Arnold P. B........	E	6th N. Y. Inf.....................	"
Barnes W. R........	F	1st Cal. Cav.....................	Valley Springs
Bateman Emanuel..	I	124th N. Y. Inf....................	Stockton
Beaumont H. E.....	C	45th Ill. Inf.....................	"
Benson Berkley D..	A	7th Cal. Inf......................	"
Bonney J. A........	E	1st Nevada Cav....................	"
Boscher E. S........		Signal Corps, Mass................	"
Brierly M M........	A	5th Mo. Inf.......................	"
Broener John A.....	D	10th Kansas Inf...................	Galt
Brown Charles......	A	5th N. Y. Inf......	Stockton
Bunker Edward S...	C	11th Maine Inf....................	"
Bunn Andrew.......	A	47th Ill. Inf.....................	"
Bywater Wilfred. ..	K	91st Penn. Inf....................	"
Campbell H. R......	H	25th Wis. Inf.....................	"
Cauriure S. S........	A	4th Mich. Inf.....................	"
Cohn Geo..........	H	17th N. J. Inf....................	"
Condell B. M	D	53d Ill. Inf......................	"
Condy Robert.......		3d Cal. Inf.......................	"
Condy Wm..........		3d Cal. Inf.......................	"
Court Edward.......	G	10th Wis. Inf.....................	"
Curry James E......	D	123d Ill. Inf.....................	"
Dasher Samuel......	D	192d Penn. Inf....................	"

56

NAME.	CO.	SERVICE.	ADDRESS.
Davis Bradley S.....	I	50th Ill. Inf......................	Stockton
Davis P. A..........	B	3d Mass. Heavy Art..............	"
Dohrman Julius....	K	2d Mo. Inf........................	"
Drown W. H........	A	61st Mass. Inf....................	"
Dunne M. H.... ...	D	6th Mass. Inf.....................	"
Eaves M. T.........	H	1st Kansas Inf...	"
Edwards N. B.......	E	2d Cal. Cav......................	"
Fann James N.......	I	6th Kansas Cav.................	"
Felton John A......	O	11th N. H. Inf..	"
Fitzgerald E. J......	H	8th Mass. Inf...	"
Fletcher John.......	H	8th Ill. Cav......................	"
Fogg William.......	E	9th Maine Inf....................	"
Fort John B........	A	1st Iowa Cav.....................	"
Foster B. F.........	K	1st Cal. Cav.....................	"
Fry Edward S.......	O	15th Iowa Inf....................	"
Fuller Reuben......	G	1st Wis. Inf.....................	"
Gayotte James......	O	4th Minn. Inf....................	"
Gilabert Joseph.....		U. S. Navy......................	"
Giles Geo. W.......	K	5th Cal. Inf.....................	"
Greer Nathan......	F	21st Ohio Inf.........	"
Haas Jerome........		U. S. Navy......................	"
Hall Frank E........	H	24th Mass. Inf......	"
Hall John A.........	O	37th Mass. Inf...................	"
Harris Benjamin....		10th R. I. Inf...................	"
Hartt Lionel B., M.D		24th Mich. Inf...................	"
Hatch F. R.........	K	16th N. Y. Heavy Art...........	"
Heck Victor V.......	I	6th Cal. Inf....	"
Henery Samuel......		U. S. Navy......................	"
Hickox Gaylord	B	90th N. Y. Bat..............	"
Higgins John..	M	2d U. S. Art....................	"
Hitchcock C. N......	K	48th U. S. Colored Inf..........	"
Hoeffer E...........		U. S. Navy......................	"
Holly F. S...........		1st U. S. Sharpshooters.	"
Holman H. C........	E	7th Cal. Inf.....................	"
Holt Levi B.........	G	6th Cal. Inf.....................	San Joaquin Co.
Hopkins R. W.......	H	14th N. Y. Heavy Art...........	Stockton
Houghton L. E......	G	7th Cal. Inf.....................	"
Hudson A. S., M. D..		34th Ill. Inf.....................	"
Hudson A. T., M. D.		26th Iowa Inf....................	"
Hughes A. P. S......	I	31st Mo. Inf.....................	Lathrop
Hull O. H..........	H	12th Wis. Inf....................	Stockton
Hurd Charles E.....	B	23d Maine Inf....................	"
Hyde Joseph.......		125th N. Y. Inf..................	"
Hyde W. O..........	H	125th N. Y. Inf.	"
Jacobs Emil........	K	8th Mo. Inf......................	"
Johnson R. S........	K	1st Cal. Cav.....................	"
Keagle C. H........	B	20th Iowa Inf....................	"
Kelly Thos. J.......	I	5th Ill. Cav.....................	"
Ketchum Thos. E..	A	3d Cal. Inf......................	"
Kincaide Fred. H...	H	38th Iowa Inf....................	"
Knowlton F. L......	H	14th Maine Inf...................	"
Lamar Charles......	K	43d Wis. Inf.....................	"
Lawrence D. L......	K	22d Maine Inf...................	"
Lehe Eugene........	F	9th U. S. Inf....................	"
Lewthwaite John....	B	77th N. Y. Inf...................	"
Linderwood Thos. S.		22d Wis. Cav....................	"

NAME.	CO.	SERVICE.	ADDRESS.
Lissenden Geo......	M	1st Ill. Art........................	Stockton
Logan J. V. B.......	E	5th Cal. Inf.......................	"
Lonnigan Geo. W...	C	17th Ind. Inf......................	"
Lonnigan Thomas...	C	50th Ind. Inf......................	"
Loomis H. B........		10th Wis. Inf......................	"
Lorrimer W. H......	I	21st Iowa Inf......................	"
Low Frank..........	K	7th Cal. Inf.......................	"
Madison B. J........	B	15th Wis. Inf......	"
Manning C. R.......	E	2d N. H. Inf.................	Merced
Mastin S. A..........	H	11th Mo. Inf......................	Stockton
McCoy Harrison.....	E	4th Cal. Inf.......................	"
McCuen Nelson......	H	16th N. Y. Inf.....................	"
McDonald James....	C	25th N. Y. Cav....................	"
McIntyre H. A.......	A	2d Me. Cav. & 18th Me. Heavy Art.	"
McPherson J. K.	K	6th Wis. Inf.......................	"
Meade John H......	D	4th N. Y. Art.....................	"
Miller Jacob........	G	107th Ill. Inf.....................	French Camp
Moore Simon........	D	103d Ill. Inf......................	Stockton
Moozahn Lewis.	B	48th Ind. Inf......................	"
Nason R. P..........	I	4th Cal. Inf.......................	"
Needham A. T.......		13th Ill. Inf......................	"
Nicewonger L. H. U.		U. S. Signal Corps......	French Camp
Niven Peter.........	I	45th Mass. Inf....................	Stockton
Osborn Joseph S....	C	5th Iowa Inf......................	"
Payne John W......	E	7th Cal. Inf.......................	"
Payne W. H.........	G	8th Cal. Inf.......................	"
Peters W. S....		11th Kansas Cav..................	"
Pickney Robert S...	F	90th Bat. N. Y. Inf...............	"
Piper John A. F.....	G	14th Iowa Inf.....................	"
Rea Samuel.........	C	17th Wis.........................	"
Reid R. K., M. D....		3d Cal. Inf...........	"
Reynolds Myrick....	A	14th Ohio Inf.....	"
Rhodes B. J.........	C	8th Cal. Inf.......................	"
Rolerson D. F.......	I	14th Maine Inf....................	"
Ruhl Fred. A........	B	6th N. Y. Inf.....................	"
Ryan Thomas H.. .	C	9th Conn. Inf.....................	"
Sampson Geo.......	M	11th Ind. Cav.....................	"
Sawyer Charles M...	F	9th Iowa Inf......................	"
Schroeder J. G......	D	18th U. S. Inf.....................	Cressey
Scott Edward.......	H	8th Cal. Inf.......................	Stockton
Scott W. J...........	B	68th Ill. Inf......................	"
Severens J. D.......	H	Veteran Reserve Corps...........	"
Shackleford Samuel.		1st Cal. Cav......................	"
Shine John H........	H	153d Ill. Inf......................	"
Shoemaker J. J.....	F	10th Wis. Inf.....................	"
Simons A............	H	Merrill's Vet. Horse, 2d Mo. Cav..	"
Smith John W.......	I	16th Kansas Cav..................	Galt
Sperry J. A.....	K	25th Mich. Inf....................	Stockton
Spurgeon Felix......	F	2d Ohio Heavy Art...............	"
Starkhouse W. R....	G	10th N. Y. Heavy Art.............	"
Steacy R. E.........	F	30th Maine Inf....................	"
Stowe Alonzo W....	H	5th Cal. Inf.......................	"
Sullivan C..........		U. S. S. Powhattan................	"
Sutherland Henry...	G	14th Kansas Inf...................	"
Swinford Elijah.....	M	2d Colorado Inf...................	"
Teeple W. D.........	H	7th Cal. Inf.......................	"

NAME.	CO.	SERVICE.	ADDRESS.
Thomas David......	C	96th Penn. Inf......	Stockton
Tripp D. D..........	H	41st Mass. Inf....................	"
Vaughn W. W.......	H	8th Cal. Inf................... ...	"
Wagner Michael....	C	7th Penn. Reserve Corps..........	"
Wallam W. B.	D	1st Ohio Art......................	"
Walsh Richard......	K	6th Maine Inf....................	"
Warden R. T.	A	3d Ill. Inf......................	"
Waterman S. D......	I	3d Mass. Inf....................	"
Weaver H. W........	B	13th Ill. Inf....................	"
Weaver L. B........	A	1st Nevada Inf..................	"
West F. M...........	K	13th Mass. Inf..................	"
Wetzell Thos. C.....	C	14th Iowa Inf...................	"
Whitaker D. E......	D	35th Wis. Inf...................	"
Whitney Henry. ...		U. S. S. Wabash...............	"
Williams Henry.....		2d Conn. Inf....................	"
Williams Samuel A..		8th Mo. Cav.....................	"
Wines J. P..........		13th Wis. Battery.......	"
Winser Oscar.	B	23d Ill. Inf.....................	"
Wisdom W. J........	A	1st Cal. Cav....................	"
Wood John E.......	H	1st Wis. Inf....................	"
Woods W. P.........	C	11th Kansas Inf................ ...	"

R. L. McCOOK POST, No.26.

WATSONVILLE, CAL.

OFFICERS, 1886.

B. A. OSBORN...Commander
R. W. EATON..Senior Vice-Commander
C. W. BENJAMIN.......................................Junior Vice-Commander
A. R. ALEXANDER...Adjutant
A. N. JUDD..Quartermaster
J. A BURTON..Surgeon
J. S. KIDDER...Chaplain
A. A. MOREY...Officer of the Day
M. VALENTINE...Officer of the Guard
J. RENFRO..Sergeant Major
L. TRIMBLE..Quartermaster Sergeant

Meeting, Second and Fourth Monday.

NAME.	CO.	SERVICE.	ADDRESS.
Benjamin C. W......	A	13th Ill. Inf......................	Watsonville
Bickmore T.........	A	8th Cal. Inf......................	"
Burton J. A.........	H	25th Wis. Inf.....................	"
Call H.............	C	4th Cal. Inf......................	"
Chapman J. S.......	F	4th Cal. Inf......................	"
Clark F. C..........	I	1st U. S. Engineers...............	"
Cleveland G. S.....	K	2d Maine Cav......................	"
Cox C. P...........	A	72d Ill. Inf......................	"
Crooker Geo........	H	157th N. Y. Inf...................	"
De Hart Wm........	C	1st U. S. Marine..................	"
Eaton R. W........	D	9th Kansas Cav....................	"
Fadden James......	I	10th Minn. Inf....................	Monterey, Cal.
Fantry Geo........	M	1st U. S. Cav.....................	Watsonville
Gilman Joseph C....	F	11th Maine Inf....................	Monterey, Cal.
Hagerman Wm......		7th N. Y. S. M....................	Watsonville
Halleck R..........	I	50th Wis. Inf.....................	"
Hatch I...........	A	8th Cal. Inf......................	"
Hogue J. D.........	E	138th Ill. Inf....................	"
Judd A. N..........	A	6th Iowa Cav......................	"
Kidder J. S.........	A	8th Cal. Inf......................	"
Linscott J. A.......	C	2d Maine Cav......................	"
Lummis J...........	C	25th Ill. Inf.....................	"
McCarty James......	B	11th Conn. Inf....................	"
McCune J...........	A	30th Ill. Inf.....................	"
Monroe E. R........	G	42d Wis. Inf......................	"
Morey A. A.........	G	137th Ill. Inf....................	"
Nelson C. H........	B	3d Ohio Inf......................	"
Osborn B. A........	E	1st Maine Cav.....................	"
Renfro J...........	K	6th Cal. Inf......................	"
Service W. H.......	G	6th Ohio Inf......................	"
Stephens Arthur.....	C	14th Penn. Cav...................	Corralitos, Cal.
Trimble Isaac......	K	2d Cal. Inf.......................	Watsonville
Valentine M........	A	8th Cal. Inf......................	"

60

LANDER POST, No 27.

OFFICERS, 1886.

J. A. MILLER..Commander
I. C. HOOVER..Senior Vice-Commander
E. F. STEPHENS...Junior Vice-Commander
W. A. CLIFFORD...Adjutant
L. RICHARDSON........ ....Quartermaster
M. SOUTHARD............... ....Surgeon
E. B. HEFLIN................... ....Chaplain
W. D. NEWELL...Officer of the Day
——— ———...Officer of the Guard
——— ———...Sergeant Major
——— ———...Quartermaster Surgeon

Meeting, Second and Fourth Wednesday.

NAME.	CO.	SERVICE.	ADDRESS.
Clifford W. A.........	B	8th Mich. Inf................	Austin, Nev.
Farnham A. G......	I	7th Cal. Inf.....	"
Gillman A. D.......	G	31st Iowa Inf.....................	"
Harter Daniel.......	B	19th Iowa Cav..................	"
Heflin E. B..	M	9th Mo. Cav.....................	"
Hickock J. A........	A	5th Iowa Cav.....................	"
Hoover I. C.........	F	3d Cal. Inf	"
Lyng John F.......	I	104th Penn. Inf.....	"
McGlew W. J........	A	84th Penn......................	"
Miller J. A..........	B	5th N. Y. Inf....................	"
Newell W. B	E	7th Mich. Inf....................	"
Parker L. A.........	B	10th N. Y................	Baker City, Or.
Pellin Napoleon	A	2d La. Inf.......................	Austin
Richardson L.......	B	3d Cal. Inf.....	"
Ross R. E...........	E	12th Ill. Cav....................	"
Scott Robert	B	45th Ill. Inf....................	"
Southard M.........	D	9th Maine Inf.....	"
Stephens E. F.....	M	44th Mo. Inf....................	"
Thompson John I...	D	5th Wis........................	Lewis, Nev.
Vincent O. B........	F	148th Ohio Inf..................	Austin

UPTON POST, No. 29.

EUREKA, NEVADA.

—

OFFICERS, 1886.

S. J. BEEBE...Commander
MATT SHATZLEIN. ....Senior Vice-Commander
H. COLE.. ....Junior Vice-Commander
BENJ. C. LEVY...Adjutant
J. S. BURLINGAME...Quartermaster
G. H. THOMA..Surgeon
T. J. BIRD..Chaplain
W. H. TYLER...Officer of the Day
CASPAR PIEL...Officer of the Guard
—— ——...Sergeant Major
—— ——...Quartermaster Sergeant

Meeting, Fourth Saturday.

NAME.	CO.	SERVICE.	ADDRESS.
Alexander F. E......	E	44th Iowa Inf...................	Eureka
Beebe S. J...........	L	2d Mass. Cav...................	"
Bidwell C. B........	E	7th N. H. Inf..................	"
Bird T. J...........	G	2d Cal. Cav...................	"
Broy C. L....	K	6th West Va. Cav...............	"
Burlingame J. S.....	E	1st Maine Heavy Art............	"
Burns E. J	H	2d Col. Cav...................	"
Cole H.............	A	16th U. S. Inf................	"
Davidson Eb........	F	4th Wis. Cav..................	Lake Geneva, Wis.
Dowling Michael...	A	77th N. Y. Inf................	Eureka
Greenup George	G	2d Col. Cav...................	"
Hoadley H. T........	H	15th Conn. Inf....	"
Johnson Chas.......	M	1st Col. Cav..................	"
Jones E. C..........	G	4th Iowa Cav	"
Kehler W. H.......	F	191st Penn. Inf...............	San Francisco, Cal
Leonard Thomas....	E	101st Penn Inf................	Eureka
Levy Benj. C........	A	14th U. S. Inf................	"
Enlisted as Benjamin Constant...			
Longley A. S.........	A	4th Cal. Inf..................	Palisade
Martin J. T.........	B	126th Ill. Inf................	Douglas Is., Alaska
Mathews W. H......	F	4th Wis. Cav..................	Geneva Lake, Wis.
McCullum Edw.	B	37th Ind. Inf....	Eureka
McFarland Chas.....	H	88th Ohio Inf................	San Anton
Müller Fred..	M	4th U. S. Art................	Eureka
Piel Caspar.........	E	13th Mo. Cav..................	"
Rose E. H..........	H	118th Ohio Inf...............	"
Shatzlein Matt......	E	54th N. Y. Inf................	"
Sherman E. L........	K	25th Ill. Inf................	Bay Horse, Idaho
Straudberg J. W. ..	B	28th Mich. Inf...............	Mineral Hill
Taylor W. L........	K	65th Ohio Inf................	Eureka
Thoma G. H., M. D..		2d N. Y. Heavy Art...........	"
Tyler W. H.........	A	56th Mass. Inf...............	"

W. H. L. WALLACE POST, No. 32.

SANTA CRUZ, CAL.

OFFICERS, 1886.

A. L. WEEKS...Commander
C. T. SUTPHEN...Senior Vice-Commander
M. CAMPBELL..Junior Vice-Commander
S. HOHMANN........................ ....Adjutant
GEO. I. HOLT..Quartermaster
U. S. NICHOLS..Surgeon
CHESMAN GOULD...Chaplain
WM. BLACK.. ....Officer of the Day
G. D. LOUCKS.. ....Officer of the Guard
AUGUST MEYER..... ....Sergeant Major
JOHN DELEHANTY.......... ....Quartermaster Sergeant

---

Meeting, Second and Fourth Wednesday.

NAME.	CO.	SERVICE.	ADDRESS.
Abarr J. B...........	I	5th Mo. Inf......	Felton
Aegeter Solomon....	F	77th N. Y. Inf.	Santa Cruz
Armstrong Wm	B	16th Wis. Inf...	"
Bachelder J. A......	G	7th Maine Inf.	"
Barber L. N.........	A	23d Mich. Inf....................	Soquel
Bean W. H..........	H	21st Maine Inf.....	Santa Cruz
Black William	K	27th Penn. Inf....................	"
Butcher John H.....	B	11th Ind. Inf...	"
Campbell Murdock..	B	24th Penn. Inf....................	"
Carroll George H....	F	8th Mass. Inf...	"
Carroll M...........	M	108th Ill. Inf....................	Felton
Chapel Edwin.......	G	9th Iowa Inf.................... ...	"
Coats R. M.........	E	4th Cal. Inf....................	Santa Cruz
Comstock Harvey...		12th Wis. Art....................	"
Craighill Charles....	F	34th Iowa Inf....................	"
Crosby George	E	5th Mass. Art....................	"
Delehanty John.....	H	2d Ky. Inf....................	"
Dinsmore Wm......	D	4th U. S. Art....................	Soquel
Fleckner Wm.......	A	18th U. S. Inf....................	"
George T. C.........	K	7th Kansas Inf....................	Santa Cruz
German J. A........	K	136th N. Y. Inf....................	"
Glass John..........		U. S. S. Sangamon................	Felton
Gould Chesman.....	D	4th Maine Inf.....	Santa Cruz
Green L. K..........		U. S. S. Sangamon................	"
Hart Albert.........	O	55th Penn. Inf......	Soquel

63

NAME.	CO.	SERVICE.	ADDRESS.
Hastings Scott......	B	Ill. Zouaves......................	Santa Cruz
Hobson G. H.		21st Ind. Battery.	"
Hohmann S.........	A	94th Ill. Inf.....................	"
Holt Geo. L.. ...	A	2d Mass. Cav........	"
Hopkins Wm. V......	K	76th N. Y. Inf....................	"
Johnson L..........	K	46th Ind. Inf	Felton
Krider F. L.........	B	127th Penn. Inf..................	Santa Cruz
Latchford Wm	K	1st U. S. Art.....................	"
Loucks G. D........	L	9th Kansas Cav..................	"
Lumbeck J. W......	C	5th Ill. Cav......................	Soquel
Lunt Amos, Jr.....		3d Mass. Inf. (unattached)	Santa Cruz
Mandell Jacob......	K	46th N. Y. Inf....................	"
Marinan M. D.......	D	36th Iowa Inf.....................	Soquel
Martindale A........	H	34th Iowa Inf....................	Santa Cruz
Maynard S	D	13th Ohio Cav....................	"
McAdams J. Y......	C	1st Ohio Art.....................	"
McCalla J. W........	A	10th Iowa Inf............	Soquel
Meyer August.......	I	6th Cal. Inf.....	Santa Cruz
Mills W. F.........	C	62d Ill. Inf......................	Soquel
Molatt Geo. W.......	G	8th N. Y. Cav........... ..	"
Montgomery Joseph.	F	15th Iowa Inf...................	Santa Cruz
Morris Peter	K	77th N. Y. Inf.....	Soquel
Mulligan Dennis....	H	148th U. S. Inf.................	"
Nichols U. S........	B	97th N. Y. Inf..................	Santa Cruz
O'Connor H. A. C...	A	24th Wis. Inf....................	"
Patterson M. S......	D	6th Ohio Cav.....................	"
Peoples Charles		1st N. H. Battery..	Glenwood
Phillips John........	G	2d N. Y. Inf.......	Felton
Pickerell Wm. W....	F	7th Iowa Inf....................	Santa Cruz
Pilger John.........	E	9th Ohio Inf...	"
Plant Wm...........	C	4th Wis. Cav....................	"
Price Ed...........	L	2d Cal. Cav.....................	"
Salsbury J.........	C	141st Penn. Inf..................	"
Schofield Geo. W....	A	8th Cal. Inf..................	Soquel
Sherman W. H......		2d Minn. Inf....................	Santa Cruz
Shrader M. D........	D	70th Ill. Inf....................	Glenwood
Stevenson David....	B	26th Ind. Art...................	"
Stofer J. H..........	I	7th Iowa Inf.......	Santa Cruz
Stowe L. W....	K	1st Minn. Cav.	"
Sutphen Chas. T....		Henshaw's Ill Bat.& 3d N.C.Mt. Inf	"
Sylvester Wm. H....	G	3d Mass. Heavy Art......	"
Waldo B. F..........	A	16th Vt. Inf....................	"
Waldo H. R........		3d Vt. Battery..................	"
Walker C. H........	A	1st Maine Cav....................	Felton
Weeks A. L..........	E	26th Mass. Inf..................	Santa Cruz
Wenger John........	L	1st Iowa Cav ....:......	"
West Geo. O........	C	11th Maine Inf..................	Soquel
West James E......		6th Maine Inf..................	"
White James........	L	6th Iowa Cav....................	Santa Cruz

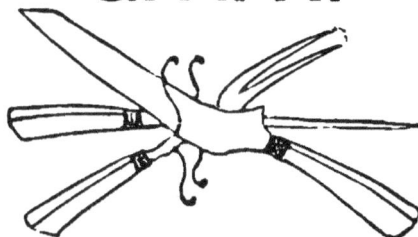

IMPORTING

STATIONERS

AND

PAPER DEALERS

Nos. 215, 217 & 219 BUSH ST.

San Francisco.

★

HEADQUARTERS FOR G. A. R. CARDS.

HEINTZELMAN POST, No. 33.

SAN DIEGO, CAL.

OFFICERS, 1886.

D. F. JONES..Commander
R. M. POWERS..Senior Vice-Commander
J. D. WORKS..Junior Vice-Commander
J. B. BOYD...Adjutant
B. HEALY..Quartermaster
T. L. MAGEE..Surgeon
I. L. PALMER...Chaplain
W. P. HENDERSON...Officer of the Day
A. R. AREY..Officer of the Guard
M. T. GILMORE...Sergeant Major
E. O. LYON...Quartermaster Sergeant

Meeting, Second and Fourth Thursday.

NAME.	CO.	SERVICE.	ADDRESS.
Amick D. B.	E	3d Penn. Heavy Art	San Diego
Arey A. R.		U. S. S. Niphon.	"
Bergman J.	B	1st U. S. Dragoons	Temecula
Blackmer E. T.	A	37th Mass. Inf.	San Diego
Blaisdell S. G.	F	12th N. H. Inf	Poway
Bowers W. W.	I	1st Wis. Cav.	San Diego
Bowne W. S.		Chicago Battery	"
Boyd J. B.	F	139th Ill. Inf.	"
Breedlove R. D.	D	8th Mo. Cav.	Bear Valley
Burbeck L. D.	E	7th Mass. Inf.	San Diego
Burgess Wm.	E	203d Penn. Inf.	National City
Burke C. M.	F	7th Penn. Cav.	San Diego
Carpenter S. H.	C	7th Cal. Inf.	"
Chaney O. F.	K	1st Vt. Cav.	"
Comstock John.	K	45th Ill. Inf.	"
Conklin N. H.	D	2d Ky. Inf.	"
Cook Joseph	B	8th Ill. Inf	"
Crarath I. B.	B	32d Iowa Inf. and U. S. Vols.	"
Crittenden T. T.	A	6th Ind. Inf.	"
Dampf L.	D	7th N. Y. Inf.	"
Daunals G. M.	E	54th N. Y. Inf.	"
Donovan J. W.	H	43d Penn. Inf.	"
Emery H. E.	C	4th Cal. Inf.	"
Emery H. U.	F	1st Nev. Cav.	"
Farley Joseph	I	30th Iowa Inf.	"

65

NAME.	CO.	SERVICE.	ADDRESS.
Fletcher B. F.	A	16th Maine Inf....................	San Diego
Freeman C. H......		U. S. S. Rhode Island.............	National City
Gilmore M. T.	B	15th Maine Inf....................	San Diego
Graham P. A........	A	90th Penn. Inf....................	"
Grant G. W.		U. S. Navy.......................	National City
Green J. A..........	A	8th Cal. Inf......................	San Diego
Hamilton M. D.....	G	17th Ind. Inf.....................	"
Harrall W. H........	B	27th Ind. Inf..........	Arizona
Hartley J. M...	D	44th Iowa Inf....................	San Diego
Hartzel T. B........	C	3d Iowa Cav...............	Poway
Healy B.............	A	8th U. S. Inf	San Diego
Hebbard A. W......	E	28th Wis. Inf....................	Fall Brook
Henderson Wm. P.	I	12th Ill. Inf..............	San Diego
Herrick A. P........	C	1st U. S. Cav....................	Campo
Hicks J. V..........	H	7th Mich. Cav....................	Fall Brook
Holcomb B..........	L	1st Conn. Art....................	Bear Valley
Hooker J. B........	K	2d Minn. Inf.....................	San Dieg
Huntington C.......	H	16th N. Y. Inf. & H 13th N. Y. Cav.	Arizona
Jacobs L. C........	B	36th Wis. Inf....................	Bear Valley
James W. F. C......	E	63d Ohio Inf....	"
Jones D. F..........	D	20th Maine Inf....................	San Diego
Jones J. P..........		U. S. S. Sagamore................	"
Kehoe Wm..........	H	1st Mass. Cav....................	"
King G. V-.........	G	13th N. Y. Heavy Art.............	Los Angeles
Knowles A. P	A	8th Cal. Inf.....................	San Diego
Kooken J. A........	C	152 Penn. Inf....................	"
Langdon J. W......	A	95th Ill. Inf....................	"
Leonard Wm. J.....	K	2d N. J. Inf.....................	"
Lockwood N. S......	A	2d Ind. Inf......................	"
Luce M. A..........	E	4th Mich. Inf....................	"
Lyon E. C..........	E	2d U. S. Cav.....................	"
Magee T. L., M. D...		51st Ill. Inf....................	"
Mandeville F. H....	K	23d N. Y. Inf....................	"
McAuliff Thomas....	L	2d Cal. Inf......................	"
Meriam G. F........	F	3d N. Y. Inf.....................	"
Miles J. F..........		35th Ill. Inf......	"
Mussey A. W........	E	2d Cal. Cav......................	Cajon
Noble John..........	D	5th Cal. Inf.....................	San Diego
Nulton S. D.	G	21st Mo. Inf.......	Bernardo
Ober Wm.	G	93d Penn. Inf....................	Nuevo
Ogden Tully........	C	2d Cal. Inf......................	San Diego
Orcutt H. C........	C	6th Vt. Inf......................	"
Paine J. O. W.......	D	14th Maine Inf......	"
Palmer I. L.	A	36th Ohio Inf....................	"
Pearson M. R.	A	4th Ind. Inf.....................	"
Perigo Wm..........	A	151st Penn. Inf..................	"
Pierce C. O..........	B	7th U. S. Inf....................	"
Pollock S. S.	D	14th Penn. Cav..................	"
Powers R. M....	M	30th U. S. Heavy Art.............	"
Rainbow J. P. M....	E	1st Cal. Inf...	Fall Brook
Reinbach Chas......	A	3d U. S. Inf.....................	San Diego
Remondino P. C....		Medical Dep't U. S. Vols	"
Reupsch Wm........	F	41st N. Y. Inf....................	"
Rice H. B..........	E	14th U. S. Inf....	"
Roberts L. L........	L	18th Ohio Inf....................	"
Root M. S...........	K	103d Ohio Inf....................	"

NAME.	CO.	SERVICE.	ADDRESS.
Sharp W. H.........	K	43d Mo. Inf......................	San Diego
Shaw F. A. T........	H	7th Cal. Inf........................	"
Sherman M..........	G	4th Cal. Inf.......................	"
Sigman M. H........	H	24th Penn. Inf......	"
Smith J. H..........	E	97th N. Y. Inf......................	"
Statler S...	K	1st Ohio Inf.....	"
Stenger W. H........	A	178th Ohio Inf....................	"
Stone Geo. M........	A	2d Mich. Inf....	"
Story H. L..........	C	12th Vt. Inf......................	"
Titus A..............	E	3d Wis. Inf.........................	
Tracey J. F..........	D	189th N. Y. Inf......	Howe
Tyler J. H..........	K	6th Minn. Inf.....................	San Diego
Ward S. L...........	D	39th Ind. Inf.....................	Nuevo
Watson C C.........	D	3d Iowa Inf.......................	Del Mar
Whitney W. J.......	A	57th Penn. Inf....................	
Winder W. A.......		3d U. S. Art.....................	San Diego
Works J. D.........	D	10th Ind. Cav....................	"

SULLIVAN'S

THE LEADING

Cloak and Suit House

120 KEARNY ST.

NEW STYLES

IN

Ladies' Ready-made Ulsters, Jackets, Suits, Wraps, Jersey Waists, etc.

Largest Assortment at very Lowest Prices

A competent person sent to hotels and residences to take measures and fit dresses.

SULLIVAN'S

CLOAK AND SUIT HOUSE

120 Kearny Street, S. F.

Telephone No. 5151

Anheuser-Busch Brewing Ass'n

Celebrated St. Louis Lager Beers are the favorite brands of the G. A. R.

————→Val Blatz Milwaukee Export Wiener Beer ←‹————

For Sale at all the Leading Hotels, Saloons and Restaurants

A. F. EVANS & CO.
Sole Agents
16 Front Street, San Francisco.

DEWEY & CO'S SCIENTIFIC PRESS PAT. AGENCY

Our U. S. and Foreign Patent Agency presents many and important advantages as a Home Agency over all others, by reason of long establishment, great experience, thorough system, intimate acquaintance with the subjects of inventions in our own community, and our most extensive law and reference library, containing official American and foreign reports, files of scientific and mechanical publications, etc. All worthy inventions patented through our Agency will have the benefit of an illustration or a description in the Mining and Scientific Press. We transact every branch of Patent business, and obtain Patents in all countries which grant protection to inventors. The large majority of U. S. and Foreign Patents issued to inventors on the Pacific Coast have been obtained through our Agency. We can give the best and most RELIABLE advice as to the patentability of new inventions." Our prices are as low as any first-class agencies in the Eastern States, while our advantages for

Pacific Coast Inventors are far superior. Advice and Circulars free. Address

DEWEY & CO., Patent Agents, 252 Market Street, San Francisco

A. T. DEWEY   W. B. EWER   GEO. H. STRONG

Veterans! Attention!

DO NOT LEAVE THE CITY WITHOUT SEEING THE

G. A. R.

G. A. R.

COPYRIGHTED.

BATTLE OF WATERLOO PANORAMA!

Open Daily From 9 A. M. to 11 P. M.

Cor. of Eddy and Mason Sts.,   SAN FRANCISCO, CAL.

☞ It is the most wonderful representation ever exhibited of this CELEBRATED BATTLE.

JAMES A. GARFIELD POST, No. 34.

SAN FRANCISCO, CAL.

OFFICERS, 1886.

EDWARD S. SALOMON...Commander
SOLOMON CAHEN...Senior Vice-Commander
JOHN PATTON...Junior Vice-Commander
GEO. A. CRALL..Adjutant
J. H. MORK..Quartermaster
R. A. GRAHAM..Surgeon
W. O. SOUTHWICK..Chaplain
J. H. EUSTICE...Officer of the Day
CHAS. L. BARRY...Officer of the Guard
B. F. HECOX...Sergeant Major
FRANK WADSWORTH...Quartermaster Sergeant

Meeting Second and Fourth Tuesday, at Concord Hall, 114 O'Farrell Street.

NAME.	CO.	SERVICE.	ADDRESS.
Alber John..........	G	2d Cal. Inf.....	903 Kearny
Allen L. D........	G	3d Vt. Inf............	141 East
Allen T. S...........	E	3d Maine Inf..................	218 Eighteenth
Alpers John........		9th U. S. Inf..................	24th & Treat Av.
Anderson Chas......		U. S. S. Cayuga.............	209 Steuart
Anderson John.....	G	7th N. Y Inf................	Alameda
Anson P. F..........	E	35th Iowa Inf............	2011 Hyde
Babbitt John H......	K	90th N. Y. Inf...........	120 Fourth
Bailey Chas. H......	G	13th N. Y. Heavy Art..........	4 Freelon
Barry Chas. L.......	K	11th R. I. Inf....	
	G	3d R. I. Cav............	922 Battery
Bartlett William	C	20th Mass. Inf...............	2 Lawrence
Bauer George........	H	1st R. I. Cav..........	304 Francisco
Bean Wm............	E	3d Maine Inf..............	
	K	1st Maine Art..............	322 Tenth
Beer Jacob	B	42d N. Y. Inf..........	913 Natoma
Berliner Solomon...	K	62d N. Y. Inf............	Nucleus House
Berry John.........		U. S. Vet. Vols	Pt Townsend,W.T.
Biederman Louis....	I	1st Wash. Ter. Inf............	560 Natoma
Bieleck Adam.......	A	3d Mo. Inf........	1007 Harrison
Binder Chas. A......	M	25th N. Y. Cav......	2 Latham
Birch Patrick.......	C	4th U. S. Art...............	16 Dore
Brown Albert........	I	2d Cal. Cav...............	2912 Folsom
Butler Geo. F.......	A	5th U. S. Cav...............	215 Minna
Byrne Thos.........	D	5th Cal. Inf...................	Bush & Buchanan

NAME.	CO.	SERVICE.	ADDRESS.
Oaben Solomon......	C	3d Cal. Inf......................	41 Clay
Cain Edward........	C	1st Oregon Cav...................	214 Hermann
Cauley Wm.........	H	3d Penn. Inf.....................	649½ Folsom
Chapin A. B........	G	8th Cal. Inf.....................	114 Turk
Clynes John.........	F	9th Mass. Inf....................	1012 Columbia
Coffey J. J..........	B	1st Mass. Inf....................	1216 Hampshire
Cohn S. B...........	F	6th Cal. Inf.	961 Market
Cohnheim Max......	F	41st N. Y. Inf...................	P. O. Box 2335
Coulin Owen T......	B	1st R. I. Art....................	24th & Potrero av
Conner Cornelius....		U. S. S. Paul Jones..............	Columbia & 25th
Conners Thos.......	A	23d Ohio Inf....................	1000 Market
Corcoran Thomas....	F	149th Ind. Inf..................	237 Minna
Cox Christ..........	E	10th N. Y. Inf..................	13 Tehama
Crall Geo. A........	F	2d Cal. Cav and U. S. Navy.......	1221 Stockton
Crandall S T. B.....	B	1st R. I. Inf....................	16½ Folsom ave.
Cruse Ferdinand....	K	8th N. Y. Inf...................	
		1st N. Y. Cav...................	2 Regan Pl
Dalmas Wm. W......	H	1st Ohio Light Art..............	25 Potter
Dickenbach Jacob...	A	1st N. J. Art...................	793 Eighteenth
Dill A. F...........	E	43d Mass. Inf. and U. S. Navy. ...	1011 Webster, Oak.
Dorsett G. H........	G	2d Ill. Art.....................	307 Fourth
Eberle Joseph.......	G	14th Maine Inf..................	S Bruno Rd 27 & 28
Eggeling Charles....	O	1st N. J. Cav...................	618½ Post
Ennis Albert........	K	25th N. J. Inf..................	103 Perry
Eustice John H......	G	99th N. Y. Inf..................	252 Tehama
Ewing Alfred B......	A	59th Ohio Inf...................	Pacific and Front
Finnegass Henry....	H	3d Conn. Inf...................	1022 Green
Fisher W. J..........	A	143d N. Y. Inf..................	526 Geary
Frey Alpheus........	F	129th Penn. Inf.................	244 Minna
Frillman H. W......	H	6th Ohio Inf....................	554 Bush
Ganzert Jacob.......		9th U. S. Inf...................	Filbert nr Filmore
Garland Chas. J.....	H	17th Maine Inf..................	217 Linden ave.
Glassford J. R.......		Sturgiss Ill. Rifles..............	1703 Market
Goettig John........	A	1st N. J. Art.................	616 Ellis, rear
Goodman B. F.......	B	57th N. Y. Inf	1002 Powell
Gottschalk M.......	D	39th N. Y. Inf..................	612 Commercial
Graham John T......	C	81st Ohio Inf...................	27th & Presidio av.
Graham Richard	E	1st Bat. Cal. Mountaineers	902 Kearny
Graham Thomas.....	F	2d Mass. Heavy Art.....	Veterans' Home
Grant A. S..........	G	4th Cal. Inf....................	
Graves O. F.........	A	2d Maine Inf...................	728 Seventeenth
Haberlin James.....	F	1st Mass. Cav..................	2 Lombard
Harger John	G	15th Iowa Inf..................	7½ Grand av.
Hatch Frank E......	A	15th Mass. Inf..................	S Bruno Rd 15th av
Hayes Charles H. ..	D	17th Maine Inf..................	
	D	24th Me. Inf....................	407 Main
Heath Leon D.......	A	7th Cal. Inf....................	
Hecox B. Frank.	D	2d N. Y. Art...................	1812½ Geary
Heffernan John......		U. S. S. Brooklyn and Circassian..	142 Hancock
Henry Wm. B........	D	32d Penn Inf...................	
Hochman V. J.......	I	20th N. Y. Inf..................	Dixon, Cal.
Hogue G. W, ...	F	2d Cal. Cav....................	907 Valencia
Holler Anthony......	'	1st Md. Inf....................	518 Jessie
Hollopeter Joseph ..	H	5th Penn. Inf...................	1306 Webster
Holst D.....		U. S. S. Wyoming...............	St. Quentin, Cal.
Hope John..........	K	2d N. Y. Mounted Rifles..........	310 Francisco

NAME.	CO.	SERVICE.	ADDRESS.
Irelan Geo. W.......	K	19th A 20th......................	
	I	49th Penn Inf....................	1015 Howard
Irelan Wm..........	A	29th Penn. Inf....................	334½ Sutter
Isaacs Alfred S.....	H	95th N. Y. Inf	226 Sutter
Iserman Fred W.....	A	1st Bat. Nev. Cav...............	1125 Stockton
Jacobs Simon L......	A	1st Nev. Cav...................	222 Kearny
Johnson Adelbert...	M	12th Penn. Cav....................	161 Clara
Kano Francis J......	I	3d Vt. Inf......................	108 Francisco
Karminsky Jacob....	G	88th Ill. Inf....................	401 Tenth
Kearney Patrick G...	B	2d R. I. Inf,....................	406 Pacific
Keller Charles,......	H	1st N. Y. Light Art...	Roll'g Mills, Potr'o
Kelly Frank A.......		U. S. Marine Corps..............	115 Twenty-fourth
Keyser F. R. II......	F	33d Mass. Inf....................	San Quentin
Krueger Louis.......	F	7th N. Y. Inf....................	1022 Folsom
Kuhn George.........	A	16th Ill. Cav....................	917 Powell
Landis Henry.......	H	107th Penn. Inf..................	New Atlantic Hot'l
Landson Louis......		U. S. Navy......................	272 Tehama, rear
Lardner H. F........	A	7th Conn. Inf.	739 Harrison
Larney N. S........	A	U. S. Engineers..................	25 Downey
Laughton James.....		U. S. S. Colorado.................	18 Russell
Levy Louis..........	B	9th N. Y. Inf....................	905 Folsom
Lewis Ed. M........		51st N. Y. Inf..................	1 Willow
Lovejoy George W,..	B	1st Mass. Art...................	632 Valencia
Lynch Dennis.......	C	79th N. Y. Inf..'...............	Army & Sanchez
Magill James........	B	1st Conn. Art...................	218 Eighth
Mahoney Dennis....	K	61st Mass. Inf..................	Lombard & Sans'm
Mallory A. F........	E	2d Mass. Cav...................	1043 Mission
Mannarick Frank....	C	4th Mo. Cav....................	521 Pacific
Martin John		U. S. S. Ossipee...............	504 Davis
McCarthy Michael...		U. S. S. Vincennes................	17 Vallejo
McChesney Rob't W.	B	36th Ia. Inf....................	
	B	113th U. S Col'd Inf.............	1807 Steiner
McCusker Thomas...	B	78th Ohio Inf..................	119½ Langton
McDermott John....	G	2d Mass. Inf....................	
McDowell Samuel H.	I	19th Ill. Inf...................	620 Merchant
McGovern Robert...	K	91st N. Y. Inf..................	Oakland
McMahon Peter.....		U. S. S. Brooklyn....	Drumm & Comre'l
McMurtry J. F......	D	2d Cal. Cav....................	Sacramento, Cal.
McPeak John........		U. S. S. Fort Donelson	1149 Market
Menges Henry	C	20th N. Y. Inf..................	219 Mission
Meyer C............	C	10th U. S. Inf.................	1157 Folsom
Mork J. H..........	B	28th Ohio Inf..................	Eddy and Powell
Murphy Daniel......		U. S. Navy.....................	2 Eddy Place
Myers Frank E......	I	19th Ohio Inf..................	100 McAllister
Naughton Edward...	F	3d N. J. Cav...................	1717 Leavenworth
Nelson Jacob..	H	56th Mass. Inf..................	St. Charles Place
Newman Leon,......	B	3d Conn Inf....................	31 Garden
Newman Philip......	B	10th N. Y. Inf.................	
		1st N. Y. Engineers.............	24th and York
Nolte Herman.......		3d Mass. Cav...................	803 Montgomery
Norris T. H.........	B	196th Penn. Inf................	118 Eddy
O'Neil Wm.........	H	20th Wis. Inf..................	946 Mission
O'Sullivan Edward..	I	30th N. Y. Inf.................	
Odell Isaac..........		U. S. S. Cossack................	6 Wilson
Page Charle	D	202d Penn. Inf..................	122 Langton
Patton John..........	B	2d Cal. Cav....................	554 Bryant

NAME.	CO.	SERVICE.	ADDRESS.
Paulson Henry......		U. S. Frigate Mississippi..........	1805½ Stockton
Pippey E. W.........	D	36th Mass. Inf.....................	504 Third
Ploeger Peter........	I	73d N. Y. Inf..	Potrero av. & 24th
Porzelt Christopher.	K	8th N. Y. Inf......................	Bavaria Brewery
	G	15th N. Y. Art.....................	
Pulvermuller Otto ..	E	20th N. Y. Inf.....................	734 Montgomery
Quinn David P......	A	25th Iowa Inf.....................	1209 Howard
Quinn Edward......		U. S. S. Ethan Allen..............	407 Main
Quinn Edward Jr....		U. S. S. Dakota.	Lombard & Batt'ry
Reese William.......		U. S. S. South Carolina...........	703½ Davis
Reilley James.......	B	106th Penn. Inf.	
Rise H. G...........	G	5th Penn. Inf......................	Sacramento, Cal.
		93d Penn. Inf.....................	
Robinson Daniel L..	H	16th N. Y. Heavy Art..	419 Stockton
Robinson Harri......	I	1st La. Cav.	Sacramento, Cal.
Roll Francis	E	5th Penn. Cav.....................	San Bruno Road
Russell H. A........	C	63d N. Y. Inf.....................	144 Eighth
Ryan John.........		U. S. S. St. Marys.................	423 Bay
Salomon Edward S..		24th Ill. Inf......................	1420 Post
		82d Ill. Inf.......................	
Sammis Wm. H.		8th Conn. Inf.....................	6 Bay
Sanborn J. H........	B	1st Nev. Inf......................	1109 Mason
Schafer Herman.....		93d U. S. Colored Inf..............	1701 Mission
Schirmeier Fred.....	E	9th Ill. Inf......................	414 Sixth
Schmidt John L.....	A	82d Ill. Inf......................	10 Alemany
Schroeder Albert....	F	45th N. Y. Inf....................	Filbert&Le'v'nw'h
Schultz Louis.......		U. S. S. Union....................	404 Vallejo
Schultz Otto	C	1st N. J. Cav	229 Minna
Schutz Jacob........	I	6th N. Y. Inf.....................	915 Pacific
Segesser Ulrich.....	I	29th Mass. Inf....................	23 John
Shear Abram........	G	127th N. Y. Inf...................	506 Battery
Sherrer John H......	M	1st Cal. Cav......	Milbrae, Cal.
Shevlin James	E	123d N. Y. Inf....................	2439 Greenwich
Smith Charles B.....	F	4th N. Y. Cav....................	627 California
Smith George	E	39th N. Y. Inf....................	Lombard & Batt'ry
Smith Henry........	I	2d Ill. Art.......................	Ritch & Townsend
Smith Henry........		U. S. S. Cumberland.............	1131 Columbia
Smith Joel P........	B	4th Wis. Inf.....................	764 Folsom
Sorensen Andrew,...	F	14th Conn. Inf...................	663 Minna
Southwick W. O.....	E	4th Cal. Inf......................	244 Minna
Spear Chas. J.......	H	15th Ind. Cav....................	1013 Market
Stanley Frederick...	K	2d Cal. Cav.	920 Fell
Stanley James A.....	F	2d Cal. Cav......................	Old City Hall
Stockman Joseph....	D	2d Louisiana Inf..................	407 Pacific
Sullivan John H....		U. S. S. Connecticut	Army & San Br Rd
Sullivan Nash J.....		U. S. S. Cumberland & Brazilear ..	8 Warren av.
Tennihan Michael...		U. S. S. Ohio....................	1929 Fillmore
Thompson J. H......	F	16th U. S. Inf......	1203 Taylor
Toby Edwin L.......	F	34th Mass. Inf....................	512 Mission
Treat Flavius H.....		U. S. S. Cambridge...............	172 Minna
Velbert John.......	D	59th N. Y. Inf....................	418 Hayes
Wadsworth Frank...	I	1st Maine Inf..	1223 York
Wasserman Moses...	G	71st N. Y. Inf....................	526 Fulton
Waterbury Sam'l A..		U. S. S. Cinnamon and Sangamon.	Palace Hotel
Waters W. G....	B	35th Iowa Inf......	26 Turk
Wellendorf Christ...	I	9th N. Y. Inf...............	225 Austin

NAME.	CO.	SERVICE.	ADDRESS.
Wessell Henry......	I	5th Mo. Cav....	13 Clinton
Wetherby Geo. A ...	B	18th Wis. Inf.....................	507 Mission
White Michael		U S S.Niagara & U.S.Marine Corps	1230 York
Wilhelm John......	B	68th N. Y. Inf.	43 Clara
Wilson Chas.........		U. S. S. Cambridge...............	Greenwichnr.Sans
Wilson Henry.......		U. S. S. O. H. Leo and Portsmouth	1028 Battery
Winters Chas........	H	38th N. Y. Inf.........	203 Dolores
Wollner Jacob......	B	23d Ill. Inf......................	922 McAllister
Wuest Wm. F,.......	B	68th N. Y. Inf....................	444 Brannan

NEGLEY POST, No. 35.

TUCSON, A. T.

OFFICERS, 1886.

THOMAS HUGHES..Commander
D. D. HALL...Senior Vice Commander
J. A. ZABRISKIE...Junior Vice Commander
CHAS. J. FREESE...Adjutant
A. B. SAMPSON...., ...Quartermaster
—— - —— ....Surgeon
E. I. MEEKER................. ....Chaplain
ROBERT FRASER...Officer of the Day
FRITZ W. MARTIN..Officer of the Guard
—— —— ....Sergeant Major
—— ,..Quartermaster Sergeant

Meeting, Second and Last Saturday.

NAME.	CO.	SERVICE.	ADDRESS.
Alvord Edwin.......	H	21st Mass. Inf.....	Tucson
Barter Geo. W.......	M	1st Wis. Cav........................	"
Bivins B. F..........	D	24th Iowa Inf.......................	"
Borton Arthur.......	F	23d U. S. Inf......	"
Burrows David J.....	C	5th Cal. Inf........................	"
Crawford B. M.....	I	17th Vt. Inf........................	"
Dobbs E. W.........	B	11th Ky. Inf........................	"
Dobbs John D.......	B	1st Ky. Capitol Guards....	"
Elmer Casper....... ..	G	184th Ohio Inf......................	"
Flynn Matt..........	C	1st Wis. Inf........................	"
Foster Geo. F........	L	1st Cal. Cav	"
Fraser Robert...........		29th Mass. Art............	"
Freese Chas. J.......		U. S. Gunboat "Dragon "........	"
Ganson Theodore....	G	8th Mich Inf.......................	Mesaville
Gibson Henry.......	H	1st Cal. Inf...................	Tucson
Haight Ira G........	C	19th Ohio Inf......................	"
Hall D. D.	G	24th N. Y. Cav.....................	"
Hand Geo. O........	G	1st Cal. Cav.......................	"
Hickock S. B........	B	7th Iowa Inf.......................	"
Horn Chas. H........	B	1st Or. Cav........................	"
Hughes L. C.........	A	101st Penn. Inf....................	"
Hughes Thomas.....	D	17th Kans. Inf.....................	"
Ketchum Myrin. ...	D	44th Ill. Inf.......................	"
Kimball F. E........	B	7th Kans. Inf.....	"
Mahnlz Oscar........	G	15th N. Y. Art.....................	Arivaca

73

NAME.	CO.	SERVICE.	ADDRESS.
Martin F. W.........	G	1st Cal. Inf....................... ..	Tucson
Martin Geo. T......	B	2d Cal. Cav..;....................	"
McCafferty Joseph ..		18th Ohio Battery.	"
Meeker E. I..........	F	3d Wis. Inf..	"
Morgan William.....	C	1st U. S. Cav..................	"
Parker B. C	I	3d Mich. Inf.	"
Patterson J. L.......	D	40th Ill. Inf.	"
Overton James W....	G	1st Cal. Inf.........	"
Riordan D. M........	H	134th Ill. Inf...........	"
Rondepierre Laurent	E	32d Mass. Inf......................	"
Sampson A. B.......	F	1st Cal. Cav......................	"
Skinner Wm....	B	17th U. S. Inf.........	"
Smith H. B..........	F	1st Cal. Cav.....	"
Speedy James......	I	2d Cal. Cav......................	"
Wartamont J. N.....	L	1st Cal. Cav..........	"
Wenk Leopold	F	51st N. Y Inf....................	"
Wilkin Alex.........	B	1st Mass. Art...................	"
Zabriskie James A...		5th Cal. Inf.....................	"

BURNSIDE POST, No. 36.

TOMBSTONE, A. T.

OFFICERS, 1886.

CHAS. D. REPPY..Commander
JOHN P. RAFFERTY.....................................Senior Vice-Commander
ED. A. CLARK...Junior Vice-Commander
GEO. R. WATT..Adjutant
THOS. GREGORY...Quartermaster
I. R. BALDWIN...Surgeon
T. A. ATCHISON...Chaplain
C. E. BARTHOLOMEW...................................Officer of the Day
A. E. HARTMAN..Officer of the Guard
O. S. BLOOMER...Sergeant Major
G. S. BRADSHAW......................................Quartermaster Sergeant

---

Meeting, Second and Fourth Saturday.

NAME.	CO.	SERVICE.	ADDRESS.
Atchison T. A.......	H	157th Ohio Inf.	Tombstone
Bake Oliver.........	G	1st New Mexico Cav..............	"
Baker G. S..........	K	10th Mich. Inf...................	"
Baldwin I. R.... ...	B	87th Ohio Inf. a d A, 13th Kan.Cav.	"
Bartholomew C. E..	E	1st Conn. Cav.	"
Belk John C........	B	5th Mo. Cav.	"
Berner W. J........	H	17th Ind. Inf........	Charleston, A. T.
Bills William.......	A	2d Ohio Cav........................	Tombstone
Blackburn Charles..	C	6th Vt. Inf......................	"
Bloomer O. B.......	D	16th U. S. Art....................	"
Bradley W. F.......	G	1st Cal. Inf.....................	"
Bradshaw G. S.....	E	7th Wis. Inf.....................	"
Branch Wm.........	A	3d Kan. Inf......................	"
Brannon F. M.......	B	27th Mo. Inf.....................	"
Brigham S D... ...	C	15th Mass. Inf...................	"
Brunner L. F.......		22d Ohio Art.....................	"
Bryant S. H.	B	33d Ind. Inf.	"
Bryant S. S.........	B	33d Ind. Inf.....................	"
Calhoun M. L.......	E	111th Mich. Cav.................	"
Campbell J. H......	C	1st La. Cav......................	"
Carter D. J.........	F	4th Cal. Inf.....................	"
Clark Adam........	E	12th Ohio Cav...................	"
Clark Ed A.........		8th Wis. Inf.	"
Clark R B..........		1st Col. Cav.....................	"
Converse M. A......	B	7th Mich. Inf. and 10th Mich. Cav.	"

75

NAME.	CO.	SERVICE.	ADDRESS.
Crowley Daniel.	B	2d Cal. Cav.........................	Tombstone
Diehl William	E	1st Mich. Inf.......................	"
Douglass Wilson....	H	2d N. Y. Inf........................	"
Dyer J. D.......		U. S. Navy.........................	Bisbee, A. T.
Earle F. S..........		4th Mich. Inf. and U. S. Vols..	Tombstone
Elkins James.	A	2d Ky. Cav.........................	"
Fickas B. A.........	A	143d Ind. Inf......................	"
Fleming W. S.......	H	6th Mass. Inf......................	"
Fry Henry..........	D	13th Ill. Cav......................	"
Gage Daniel W......	B	4th Cal. Inf.......................	"
Gilbert J. D.........	H	15th Iowa Inf......................	"
Givens Michael.....	G	59th Mass Inf.....................	"
Gregory Thos.......	D	115th N. Y. Inf....................	"
Grow A. L......		U. S. Navy........................	"
Hart S. L.......	C	10th Wis. Inf. and D 41st Wis. Inf.,	"
Hartman A. E.......	B	7th N. Y. Inf	"
Hatch R. S.........	A	3d Maine Inf.........	"
Hayes F. W.	B	102d Ohio Inf......................	"
Howe H. G.........	C	15th Mass. Inf.....................	"
Keefe Walter.......	A	91st N. Y. Inf.....................	"
Kelso J. W....	A	3d Col. Inf........................	"
Kitt George B.......	K	7th Ind. Inf.......................	Nogales, A. T.
Knight R. S........	H	1st Iowa Cav.......................	Tombstone
Laughlin D.........	A	28th Penn. Inf.....................	"
Lee Howard........	I	109th Ohio Inf.....................	"
Leonard John.......	C	20th Mass. Inf.....................	"
Maher Wm....	M	6th Ky. Cav........................	"
Maynard Ben.......	H	15th Iowa Inf......................	"
McCann J. J	H	7th Cal. Inf.......................	Fairbank, A. T.
McCormack Robert.	I	Wis. Vet. Inf......................	Tombstone
McMahon J. M.....	D	27th Mich. Inf.....................	"
Mehan John........	B	69th N Y. Inf.....................	"
Miller Edw.....	H	46th N. Y. Inf.....................	"
Oaks George W......	I	1st Cal. Inf.......................	"
Rafferty J. P........	C	1st N. Y. Cav......................	"
Reppy Charles D	G	40th Wis. Inf......................	"
Ritter A. J..........	A	21st Ind. Inf......................	"
Shankland D. B	C	12th Ill. Inf.......................	"
Stegler J. F........	H	8th Cal. Inf.......................	"
Spencer W. E.......	B	19th Ohio Inf......................	"
Stebbins A. H.......	D	44th Mass. Inf.....................	"
Tennelly Wm.......	I	78th Ohio Inf......................	"
Tuttle J. H.........	D	125th Ohio Inf.....................	"
Ward J L..........	I	1st Wis. Cav.......................	Phœnix, A. T.
Wardwell D. K.....		5th and 38th Mass. Inf............	Tombstone
Watt George R.....	D	100th Penn. Inf....................	"
Williams George....	C	1st Ky. Art	"
Wiser John.........	M	1st Kan. Cav.......................	"
Wittig Edw........	I	1st Mo. Cav........................	"
Wood S. W.........	F	8th Ill. Cav.......................	Fairbank, A. T.

HOTEL DEL MONTE, MONTEREY, CALIFORNIA.

AMERICA'S FAMOUS SUMMER AND WINTER RESORT.

The most equable temperature in the World. The most elegant Sea side establishment in the World. Elegant and cheerful surroundings for Invalids. Is reached by the Southern Pacific Co., (Northern Division), via San Francisco or San Jose. (Only 3½ hours by Express Train from San Francisco.)

☞ Parks and Drives. Sea Bathing. Warm and Swimming Baths. ☜

➤TERMS FOR BOARD✍

By the Day, $3.00 and upward. Parlors from $1.00 to $2.50 per day extra. Children, $2.00 when accommodated in Children's Dining Room; otherwise full rates will be charged.

E. T. M. SIMMONS, Manager.

Pacific Coast Steamship Co.

STEAMERS of this Company will sail from Broadway Wharf, San Francisco, for ports in California, Oregon, Washington and Idaho Territories, British Columbia and Alaska, as follows :

CALIFORNIA SOUTHERN COAST ROUTE

Steamers will sail about every second day a. m. for the following ports (excepting San Diego, ever fifth day), viz : Santa Cruz, Monterey, San Simeon, Cayucos, Port Harford, San Luis Obispo, Gaviota, Santa Barbara, Ventura, Hueneme, San Pedro, Los Angeles and San Diego.

BRITISH COLUMBIA AND ALASKA ROUTE

Steamship *Idaho*, carrying U. S. mails, sails for Portland, Oregon, on or about the last of each month, for Port Townsend, W. T., Victoria and Nanaimo, B. C., Fort Wrangle, Sitka and Harrisburg, Alaska, connecting at Port Townsend with Victoria and Puget Sound. Steamer leaving San Francisco on or about the first of the same month.

VICTORIA AND PUGET SOUND ROUTE

The steamers *Geo. W. Elder* and *Queen of the Pacific*, carrying Her Brittanic Majesty's and United States mails, sail from Broadway Wharf, San Francisco, at 9 a. m. every Friday for Victoria, B. C., Port Townsend, Seattle, Tacoma, Steilacoom and Olympia, making close connection with steamboats, etc., for Skagit River and Cassiar Mines, Nanaimo, New Westminster, Yale, Sitka, and all other important points. Returning, leave Seattle Friday, at 1 p. m., Port Townsend Friday p. m., and Victoria every Saturday, at 2 p. m.

PORTLAND, OREGON ROUTE

Steamships of the O. R. & N. Co. and P. C. S. S. Co. will sail as follows : Leave Spear-street Wharf, San Francisco, at 10 a. m. for Astoria and Portland, Oregon. *Columbia*, on the 3d and 18th of each month ; *Oregon*, on the 8th and 23d of each month ; *State of California*, on the 13th and 28th of each month. Leave Portland, Oregon, at 12 p. m., for Astoria and San Francisco—*State of California*, on the 4th and 19th of each month ; *Columbia*, on the 9th and 24th of each month ; *Oregon*, on the 14th and 29th of each month.

EUREKA AND HUMBOLDT BAY ROUTE

Steamer *Ancon* sails from San Francisco for Eureka, Arcata, Hookton (Humboldt Bay), every Wednesday at 9 a. m.

POINT ARENA AND MENDOCINO ROUTE

Steamer *Yaquina* sails from Broadway Wharf, San Francisco, at 3 p. m., every Monday for Point Arenas, Cuffey's Cove, Little River and Mendocino.

☞ Members of the Grand Army of the Republic, are entitled to travel over this Company's lines (excepting the Alaska Route), during the encampment on this coast, at two-thirds regular rates.

Ticket Office, 214 Montgomery St.,

(Opposite the Russ House)

GOODALL, PERKINS & CO., Gen'l Agts.

No. 10 Market Street, San Francisco.

KILPATRICK POST, No. 38.

ST. HELENA, CAL.

OFFICERS, 1886.

J. S. HAY..Commander
A. B. SWARTOUT............. ....Senior Vice-Commander
HENRY RAHN..Junior Vice-Commander
M. F. INMAN..Adjutant
W. T. SIMMONS...Quartermaster
DR. ISAAC TABER..Surgeon
REV. W. L. STEPHENS...Chaplain
J. E. LAWSON..Officer of the Day
E. L. STANDIFORD...Officer of the Guard
——— ———..Sergeant Major
——— ———...Quartermaster Sergeant
ADAM KOCH.. ....Color Bearer

Meeting, Second and Fourth Wednesday.

NAME.	CO.	SERVICE.	ADDRESS.
Anderson Gustaff...	E	10th Mich. Cav....................	St. Helena
Bacon Luther.......	M	15th Kan. Cav.	"
Barry James	D	5th U. S. Art.....................	"
Beardsley George D.	G	27th Ill. Inf.....................	"
Carr B. O...........		U. S. Army.......................	"
Chandler W. G......	L	1st Cal. Cav.......	Livermore
Cook Samuel C......	C	1st Nev. Cav.......	St. Helena
Coquillar J..........	C	1st Nev. Inf.....................	"
Dickinson F. M.....	M	1st Conn. Art....................	"
Fisher G. W.........	M	12th Ind. Cav....................	Napa City
Flynn John D.......	G	9th Vt. Inf........	"
Graham J. M........		17th Ill. Inf.....................	St. Helena
Graham John A.....	C	12th Mich. Inf...................	"
Gravatt Wm....	C	9th Ind. Cav....	San Francisco
Haskin A..........	A	73d N. Y. Inf....................	St. Helena
Hay J. S.............		9th Maine Inf....................	"
Henning Fred..	I	17th N. Y. Inf...................	Veterans' Home
Houck Louis........	A	3d Mo. Inf.......................	St. Helena
Inman M. F.........	C	52d U. S. Colored Inf............	"
Kennedy George B..	D	2d Ohio Cav.....................	"
King E. H...........		15th Iowa Inf....................	Napa City
Koch Adam.....	F	2d Cal. Cav.....................	St. Helena
Lawson James E....	H	93d N. Y. Inf....................	"

NAME.	CO.	SERVICE.	ADDRESS.
Lewis A. M.	H	32d Maine Inf	St. Helena
Logan Wm	B	9th Penn. Inf	"
Maguire A. K.	D	21st Maine Inf	"
Medina Theodore	I	3d Cal. Inf	"
Nelson D. W.	F	1st Cal. Cav	Napa City
Parsons A. C.	C	21st Wis. Inf	Veterans' Home
Payne M. H.	F	11th Kan. Cav	St. Helena
Prouty Calvin R.	H	2d Cal. Cav	"
Rahn H.	K	7th N. H. Inf	"
Reeves E. J.		U. S. Navy	"
Ritchie Wm	C	2d Cal. Cav	Veterans' Home
Saulsbury H. P.	H	15th Kan. Cav	St. Helena
Scheffler Wm		U. S. Vols	"
Simmons E. P.	H	81st Ill. Inf	West Oakland
Simmons W. T.	C	11th Mo. Inf	St. Helena
Simpson J. H.		U. S. Vols	San Francisco
Standiford E. L.	C	12th West Va. Inf	St. Helena
Steichelman W. P.	A	22d N. Y. Inf	"
Stephens W. L.	A	24th Iowa Inf	"
Sterling Fred M.		U. S. Navy	"
Swartout A. B.	H	20th Iowa Inf	"
Tabor I., M.D.		Ft. Monroe Medical Dept	"
Thomas D. F.	D	41st Mass. Inf	"
Vanderlip Frank	C	2d Ind. Cav	"
Waller A. W.	K	120th Ill. Inf	"
Wentzell Chas		U. S. Navy	"
White Wm		U. S. Navy	"
Wood E. P.		17th Ill. Inf	Windsor
Wood George H.	K	57th Mass. Inf.	St. Helena

GOV. MORTON POST, No. 41.

CALISTOGA, CAL.

OFFICERS, 1886.

S. W. COLLINS..Commander
C. W. LANE..Senior Vice-Commander
NEWTON CONNER..Junior Vice-Commander
G. W. JOHNSON..Adjutant
W. H. EASLEY..Quartermaster
W. D. SMITH..Surgeon
C. W. WILLIAMS..Chaplain
W. M. CHERRY..Officer of the Day
W. H. REED..Officer of the Guard
D. M. BENTLEY..Sergeant Major
CHAS. TAYLOR..Quartermaster Sergeant

Meeting. First Saturday, in Odd Fellows' Hall.

NAME.	CO.	SERVICE.	ADDRESS.
Bentley D. M........		6th Iowa Inf......................	Calistoga
Cherry W. M........		14th Ill. Inf......................	"
Collins S. W.........		15th Kan. Inf.....................	"
Conner Newton.....		20th Ind. Inf.....................	"
Doe C. H.............		9th Kan. Inf......................	"
Easley W. H.........		2d Col. Inf.......................	"
Flynn Henry........		3d U. S. Art......................	"
Hunt W. T..........		40th Ind. Inf.....................	"
Johnson G. W......	M	3d Iowa Cav.....................	"
Lane C. W...........		2d Minn. Inf.....................	"
Leary J.............		184th N. Y. Inf..................	"
Reed W. H..........		4th Mo. Inf.......................	"
Scott Alva D........	I	8th Cal. Inf......................	"
Smith W. D.		3d Minn. Inf.....................	"
Stratton W. E......		2d U. S. Dragoons...............	"
Towle Augustus.....		18th Mass. Inf...................	"
Veale T. F..........		99th Ill Inf......................	"
Weller H. I........		110th N. Y. Inf..................	"
Williams C. W......		124th Ohio Inf...................	"

79

JOHN A. DIX POST, No. 42.

SAN JOSE, CAL.

OFFICERS 1886.

C. W. GAUSLINE...Commander
ISAAC N. VAN DOREN..........................Senior Vice-Commander
C. M. CURTIS..................................Junior Vice-Commander
S. B. ANDERSON...Adjutant
N. R. CARSON.......................................Quartermaster
J. O. STOUT...Surgeon
S. A. PARKER...Chaplain
M. C. CLOSE.....................................Officer of the Day
G. W. LEE.....................................Officer of the Guard
W. H. THORNHILL..............................Sergeant Major
W. D. FARLEY............................Quartermaster Sergeant
J. W. RAINEY..Organist
J. P. WILBURN....................................Inside Guard
A. V. STOCKWELL..................................Outside Guard

---

Meeting, every Monday.

NAME.	CO.	SERVICE.	ADDRESS.
Ables O. K		1st Conn. Light Battery...........	San Jose
Agan George W......	B	89th Ohio Inf................	"
Allen Charles H....	D	40th Wis. Inf...............	"
Allen Francis M....	B	3d N. Y. Cav..................	"
Allen S. R.........	G	76th N. Y. Inf...............	"
Anderson S. B.......	B	7th Mich. Inf................	"
Archibald J.........	B	41st Ill. Inf. and G, 53d Ill. Inf...	"
Arthur James G.....	D	1st N. Y. Cav and C, 63d N. Y. Inf.	"
Bachhoffer A........	K	65th N. Y. Inf...............	Mountain View
Badger John W......	G	1st N. H. Heavy Art.............	San Jose
Bailey George N.....	L	1st N. H. Cav.................	"
Baker Simeon.......	C	8th Cal. Inf................	"
Bangs Isaac F.......		7th Mass. Light Art...........	"
Barbour J. H........	A	9th Mich.Inf and 16th U.S.Col'd Inf.	"
Barker Silas........	B	10th Minn. Inf..............	"
Beatty George W...	I	58th Penn Inf.....	"
Bell John R........	I	25th Ind. Inf...	San Diego
Bellingall Charles...	B	90th Ill. Inf...............	San Jose
Bennett A. G........	B	81st N Y.Inf.and 91st U.S.Col'd Inf.	"
Bennett D. A........	F	11th Mich.Inf.& 15th U.S.Col'd Inf.	"
Bergin John	I	69th N.Y.S.M.& G,4th N.Y.H'vy Art.	Mountain View

80

NAME.	CO.	SERVICE.	ADDRESS.
Bissell L. R.........	C	17th Iowa Inf.......................	San Jose
Blackman E. S......	H	9th Iowa Inf.........................	"
Bodell L. F..........	H	3d Cal. Inf.: nd 8th Cal. Inf.	"
Borton W. F.........	F	20th Ill.Inf.& gunboat Forest Rose	"
Bowman George M.	D	44th Iowa Inf.....................	"
Breyfogle C. W.....	E	9th Ohio Cav..........	"
Britton John........	F	4th Penn. Inf.....................	"
Britton Robert......		U. S. Marines.............	"
Brown Thomas......		1st Wis. Art......................	San Francisco
Buchele Philip.....	G	9th U. S. Inf.....................	San Jose
Burus B. E..........	L	13th N. Y. Cav....................	Mountain View
Burt Robert.........	E	7th N. H. Inf....................	San Jose
Carson N. R........		U. S. Army	"
Chapin S. F., M.D...		1st Penn. Res. and 139th Penn. Inf.	"
Christonsen C......	G	15th Ill. Inf...........	"
Close Myron C......	D	8th Cal. Inf.....................	"
Coffin F. S..........	B	6th Maine Inf.& 2d U.S.Sharpsh't'rs	"
Coleman J. W......	A	142d Penn. Inf...................	"
Combe L. D........	B	1st Mo. Engineers...............	"
Conterno O. D......	I	12th N. Y. Cav..................	"
Cooper W H........	K	25th Ohio Inf....................	"
Corson S. M........		4th Cal. Inf....................	"
Crichton R. B......		U. S. Navy.....................	Wrights
Crosset F. M.......	C	37th N. Y. Inf..................	San Jose
Curtis C. M........	K	1st Mich. Engineers.............	"
Cutler C. W........	F	40th Wis. Inf...................	"
Daggett George A....	A&K	7th Mo. Cav....................	Santa Clara
Darcey James......	K	30th N. J. Inf. & B 75th N. Y. Inf..	San Jose
Davidson R. M......	I	145th Ill. Inf....................	"
Davis D. D.........	E	15th Iowa Inf...................	"
Drexler H. O........	C	37th N. Y. Inf..................	"
Fancher M. J........	M	8th Ill. Cav....................	"
Farley J. R.........	G C	1st Col. Cav....................	"
Farley W. D........	G H	1st Col. Cav....................	"
Franklin Wm. H....	E	10th N. J. and C 20th Penn. Inf....	"
Fredenburg J........	F	4th Minn. Inf....................	"
Fricke Geo. C.......	H	7th N. Y. Inf....................	"
Fuson Jephta.......	E	9th Iowa Cav...................	"
Gausline C. W......	E	2d Penn. Art...................	"
George T. C.........	H	4 th Iowa Inf...................	"
German Daniel......	F	100th Ind. Inf..................	"
Graham Alexander..	G	19th N. Y. Inf. and 4th Cal. Inf....	"
Green T. H.........	E	1st Minn. Inf. and D, 57th U.S.Inf	"
Gunter H...........	B	27th Mo. Inf. and M. 3d Iowa Cav..	"
Haley W. D.. ......*		17th Mass. Inf., 2d N. C. Inf. and 25th N. Y. Cav..................	"
Hall Sydney........	G	21st N. Y. Inf. and 22d N. Y. Cav..	San Francisco
Hall W. B..........	K	56th N. Y. Inf..................	San Jose
Hanley Michael.....	D	5th Penn. Cav..................	"
Hanson H. W.......	H	11th Iowa Inf..................	"
Harris J. T..........	E	61st Mo. Inf...................	"
Hartman Westley ...	K	13th Iowa Inf..................	Pasadena
Hartzoke John......	A	3d Mo. Inf. and I, 40th Mo. Inf....	San Jose
Haverty John.......		U. S. S. Constellation.............	Mountain View
Hawley Wm.........	A	National Rifles and 4th U. S. Cav..	San Jose
Haynes A. J.........	C	7th Maine Inf..................	"

NAME.	CO.	SERVICE.	ADDRESS.
Hernan B............	A	1st Mass. Heavy Art...............	San Jose
Huencke R..........	I	7th Maine Art.	"
Hume A. J..........	K	43d Ohio Inf.....................	"
Jensen Hans.......	I	1st N. Y. Inf....................	"
Johnson James......	A	9th U. S. Inf...................	"
Kelly Thomas.......	K	41st Ill. Inf...................	"
Kettman B	A	11th Iowa Inf	"
Kivett A. A.........	B	117th Ohio Inf.................	Romeo, Ind
Klink John..........	K	25th Ohio Inf....................	San Jose
Knickerbocker L....	I	138th Ill. Inf..................	"
Knickerbocker M. J.	I	53d Ind. Inf...........	"
Lee George W.......	M	2d Mass. Cav...................	"
Lee G. W...........	D	186th N. Y. Inf................	"
Lieb S. F.......	E	159th Ohio Inf.................	"
Long J. P..........	E	58th Ind. Inf..................	"
Longdon B. C.......	F	30th Ill. Inf..................	"
Maynard A. B.......	C	45th Ohio Inf.................	"
McClellan T. W.....	A	16th Ind. Inf. and Un'n Lt. Guards	"
McDermott W J.....	C	51st Ill. Inf.................	"
Merkel John........	E	14th U. S. Inf..............	Mountain View
Merriman E. R......	K	7th N. Y. Inf.................	San Jose
Messersmith J. G...	B	51st Ind. Inf.................	Milpitas
Mills W. E.........	B	7th Conn. Inf.................	San Jose
Montgomery F. P..	C	3d N. Y. Lt. Art. and 12th U. S. Inf.	"
Murphy J. P.......	C	9th Mass. Inf.................	"
Needham W. C......	H	134th Ill. Inf.................	"
Oeckle Charles......	K	25th Ohio Inf. and Invalid Corps..	"
Owens J. H.........	K	3d N. Y. Light Art.............	"
Parker S. A.........	A	40th N. Y. Inf..........	"
Parsons William....		8th Hancock Veterans...........	"
Peckham J....... ..	F	25th Ill. Inf....	"
Percival Nicholas...	K	59th Ill. Inf.................	Wrights
Percival Richard....	A	1st R. I. Art....................	San Jose
Phipps J. M........	I	132d Ind. Inf.................	"
Potter J. H.........	H	3d Minn. Inf.................	"
Potter John.........	B	41st Ohio Inf.................	"
Prescott B. W........	K	1st Iowa Inf. and 11th Iowa Inf ..	"
Purdy T. V..........	F	1st Mich. Sharpshooters..........	"
Rector Edwin.......	C	95th Ill. Inf.................	"
Rhodes B. J.........	C	8th Cal. Inf.................	"
Rice Judson........	E	45th Wis. Inf.................	"
Rock John..........	H	5th N. Y. Inf.................	"
Rolison L. T........	C	30th Penn. Inf & 15th N.Y.Engin'rs	"
Roper Spencer......	I	37th Ill. Inf.................	"
Ross Marcellus......	A	99th Ill. Inf.................	"
Russell J. H........	F	39th Ill.Inf.& F, 38th U.S.Col'd Inf.	"
Scully John.........	E	2d N. Y. Inf. and B, 2d N. Y. Cav..	"
Secord J. K.........	F	77th Ill. Inf.................	"
Seeber George W....	B	3d Mo. Cav	"
Sigley Henry	K	7th Minn. Inf.................	"
Slaughter L. R......	D	126th Ill. Inf.................	"
Smelser John........	E	10th Iowa Inf.................	"
Smith Wm. H.	I	2d Kan. Cav. & B, 113 U.S. Col'd Inf	Gilroy
Spencer Theodore...	D	63d Ill. Inf. & G, 128th Ill. Inf.....	San Jose
Statler J. S..........	K	14th Iowa & D, 62d U. S. Col'd Inf.	"
Stewart J. J.........	A	61st Mo. Inf.................	"

NAME.	CO.	SERVICE.	ADDRESS.
Stockwell A. V......	H	2d Cal. Cav.........................	San Jose
Stout J. C............	I	91st Ill. Inf...................	"
Taber Orrin.........	A	1st N. H. Art....	"
Thompson Geo. W..	C	25th Iowa Inf.and A,45th Iowa Inf.	"
Thornhill W. H......	D	188th Ohio Inf......................	"
Tufts John..........	B	6th Mass. Inf......................	"
Turner A. P..... ...	F	24th Mich. Inf.and Vet. Res. Corps	"
Umbarger A. F......	K	94th Ill. Inf.......................	'
Valpey C. C..	E	2d Cal.Cav.......	Warm Springs
Van Doren I. N	K	1st Mich. Engineers,...............	San Jose
Watson D. L.........	C	6th Mass. Inf................	"
Wheeler J. M.......	H	14th N. Y. Heavy Art..............	"
Whitney J. D........	I	4th Vt. Inf.........	"
Wilburn J. P........	M	2d Mass. Cav. and 1st Cal. Bat.....	"
Williams B. F.......	E	8th Mass. Inf. and U. S. Navy......	"
Wilmarth P. B......	D	48th N. Y. Inf. and 117th N. Y. Inf.	Firebaughs Ferry
Wilson James.......	K	58th Penn. Inf.....................	San Jose
Winter W. S.	C	10th Ohio Cav.....................	"
Wolcott W. J........	F	7th Mich. Cav.	"
Wright T. F.........	K	1st Vt. Cav	"
Young Frank C......	I	44th Mass. Inf...............	"

CUSHING POST, No. 44.

SAN BUENAVENTURA, CAL.

OFFICERS, 1886.

WM. VANDEVER..Commander
O. R. BEALE..Senior Vice-Commander
J. D. MORGAN...Junior Vice-Commander
NATHAN H. SHAW...Adjutant
IRVIN BARNARD ....Quartermaster
S. L. STUART...Surgeon
STEPHEN BOWERS...Chaplain
JOSIAH KEENE..Officer of the Day
J. B. CHERRY..Officer of the Guard
JUAN DE LA GUERRA..Sergeant Major
F. S. S. BUCKMAN..Quartermaster Sergeant

Meeting, First and Third Friday.

NAME.	CO.	ARM OF SERVICE.	ADDRESS.
Ashley L. W........	F	2d Cal. Cav........................	Los Angeles
Bard C. L............	A	126th Penn. Inf....................	San Buenaventura
Barnard Irvin.......	I	94th Ill. Inf.......................	"
Beale C. R..........	B	Ind'p't Bat., Minn. Cav...........	"
Blackburn D. S.....	F	21st Ill. Inf.......................	"
Bowers Stephen.....	I	67th Ind. Inf......................	"
Buckman F. S. S....	F	65th N. Y. Inf	"
Buker Alpha........	A	4th Maine Inf.....................	Hueneme
Bulûnch Thos. J...		U. S. S. Narragauset.............	San Buenaventura
Cherry J. B	I	25th Ill. Inf.......................	"
De la Guerra Juan...	C	1st Batt. Cal. Native Cav.........	"
Dudley Benj. W	C	1st Wis. Cav.......................	"
Kane J. H...........		U. S. Ship Cyane..................	Springville
Keene Josiah........	H	2d Minn. Inf......................	San Buenaventura
Linn Wm. S.........	C	6th Iowa Inf.......	"
Logue O. R.........	A	103d Penn. Inf....................	"
Morgan J. D	H	62d Ill. Inf.......................	"
Notten John W.....	F	20th Mich. Inf....................	"
Ormsby L. W.......	B	7th Cal. Inf.......................	"
Shaw Jesse A........		U. S. Vols........................	"
Shaw Nathan H....		16th Ind. Inf.....................	"
Shepherd Wm. E....	H	3d Iowa Inf.......	"
Sparks Royal G......	K	101st Ill. Inf......................	Santa Paula
Spencer B. F........	A	16th Ill. Inf.......................	Nordhoff
Stow John T........	D	21st N. Y. Inf....................	San Buenaventura
Stuart S. L.....	K	4th Maine Inf.....................	"
Townsend C. H.....	B	17th Mass. Inf....................	"
Truesdale Geo. K....	B	81st Ohio Inf.....................	San Luis Obispo
Vandever Wm		9th Iowa Inf and U. S. Vols.......	San Buenaventura
Wagner Wm	B	3d Wis. Cav.......................	"
Warner Ed. P........	F	147th N. Y. Inf...................	"
Webster L. F	B	2d Wis. Inf.......................	"

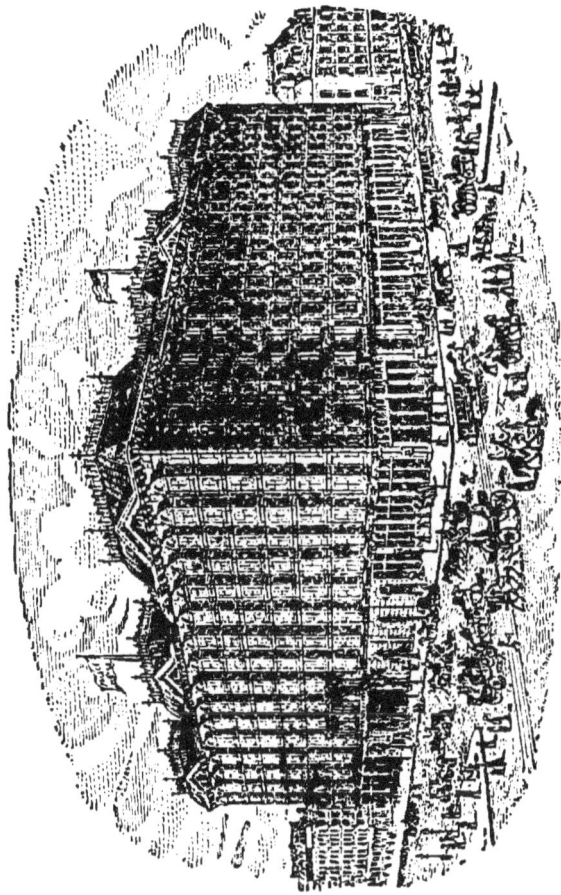

GEO. W. DE LONG POST, No. 45.

HONOLULU, H. I.

OFFICERS, 1886.

R. W. LAINE..Commander
SAM'L McKEAGUE...Senior Vice-Commander
WM. H. PLACE..Junior Vice-Commander
JAMES F. NOBLE.,...Adjutant
R. JAY GREEN...Quartermaster
JOHN S. McGREW...Surgeon
THEO. H. BOEHME..Chaplain
VOLNEY V. ASHFORD...Officer of the Day
J. D. CONN...Officer of the Guard
J. D. ARNOLD...Sergeant Major
—— ——..Quartermaster Sergeant
L. ADLER ....Sentry

Meeting, Second Tuesday.

NAME.	CO.	SERVICE.	ADDRESS.
Adler L...............		6th Cal. Inf.................	Honolulu
Arnol l C. N..........		11th Penn. Vet. Res. Corps........	Hilo Hawaii
Arnold J. D...........		11th Penn. Vet. Res. Corps........	Brisbane, Qu'nsl'd
Ashford Volney V...		21st N. Y. Cav.	Honolulu
Austin Jonathan		78th N. Y. Inf.	"
Boehme Theo. H....		5th U. S. Res. Corps..............	"
Campbell Thos......		U. S. Navy.......................	Huelo Maui
Carey Thomas.		16th Ill. Inf.....................	Honolulu
Clarke F. L..		99th N. Y. Inf....................	"
Conn J. D.......		U. S. Navy.......................	"
Cruzan J. A..........		3d Iowa Inf......................	"
Daly John F....		25th and 91st N. Y. Inf...........	"
Dickey Charles......		4th Ill. Cav......................	Makawao Maui
Eldridge C. H.......		12th Mass. Inf...................	Honolulu
Emerson ι. B.......		1st Mass. Inf	"
Goodale Warren.....		114 U.S.Col'd Inf., 11th Mass.Lt.Art.	Hamakuapoko
Green R. Jay........		26th Conn. Inf...................	Honolulu
James C. P		58th Penn. Inf...................	"
Laine R. W..........		U. S. S. Lancaster and Pensacola..	"
Lawrence W. R.. ...		88th Ill. Inf. and 1st U.S.Engineers	"
Lees George C.......		17th Conn. Inf...................	"
Lovejoy Joseph F....		U. S. Navy.......................	"
McAllister W. B.....		5th Maine Inf....................	"
McCandles W. M ...		2d Iowa Cav.....................	"
McGrew Jno. S.,M.D.		83d Ohio Inf........	"

NAME.	CO.	SERVICE.	ADDRESS.
McKeague Samuel...		38th Penn. Inf................	Honolulu
Merritt W. C........		2d Ill. Light Art..........	"
Noble James F.....		1st Mass. Heavy Art....	"
Overend R..........		2d Mo. Cav......................	Honokaa
Perry W. H.........		25th and 154th Ill. Inf............	Kohala Hawaii
Place Wm. H........		U. S. S. Yeoman and Cyane........	Honolulu
Putnam J. H........		31st Ohio Inf....................	U.S.Con. Honolulu
Ross John..........		U. S. S. Ossipee..................	Honolulu
Schreiber Rudolph..		46th N. Y. Inf....................	Kahului Maui
Simonson J. V.....		18th N. Y. Cav....	Honolulu
Smith George W...		5th N. Y. Inf.....................	"
Smith W. E.........		84th N. Y. Inf....................	San Francisco,Cal.
Webb E. E., M. D....		24th N. Y. Inf....................	Honolulu
White James T.....		1st Ohio Art.....................	Canada
Wilder W. C........		Ill. Inf	Honolulu
Wilkinson W. H. ..		1st N. Y. Mounted Rifles....	Ookala Hawaii
Williams George C..		4th Cal. Inf......................	Kahului Maui
Williams W. F.....		8th Cal. Inf......................	Honolulu
Wright John N.....		22d N. Y. Cav....................	Ookala Hawaii
Yarrick G. W.......		19th Wis. Inf....................	Wailuku Maui

COL. CASS POST, No. 46.

SAN FRANCISCO, CAL.

OFFICERS, 1886.

W. A. WALKER..Commander
JAMES O'CONNELL...Senior Vice-Commander
M. BURNS...Junior Vice-Commander
H. L. CHAMBERS...Adjutant
JOHN GANEY.. ....Quartermaster
J. H. RILEY...Surgeon
BERNARD KENNEY.... ....Chaplain
T CURRAN..Officer of the Day
JOHN HAND..Officer of the Guard
P. B. WHITMARSH...Sergeant Major
JAS. D. BYRNE...Quartermaster Sergeant

Meeting, First and Third Wednesday, Washington Hall, 35 Eddy St.

NAME.	CO.	SERVICE.	ADDRESS.
Birdsall S. T........	G	27th Conn. Inf....................	402 Montgomery
Bonney Joseph......		U. S. Marine Corps...............	414 Clementina
Burke M.............	A	12th U. S. Inf......	821 Vallejo
Butler James........	K	9th Mass. Inf....................	116 Twenty-Sixth
Byrne James D......	F	62d Mass. Inf....................	534 Sixteenth
Chambers H. L......	E	54th Ind. Inf....................	35 Battery
Chaffey John	E	2d Mass. Inf....................	529 Bryant
Clifford T...........	K	9th Mass. Inf....................	114 Twenty-Sixth
Cole George.........	D	5th Wis. Inf....................	Willow ave.
Curran T............	K	3d Mass. Cav....................	1118 Church
Deasy Jerome..	A	70th N. Y. Inf....................	736 Market
Donovan Jeremiah J.	H	25th N. Y. Inf......	4 Elliott Park
Dowdall R. E	H	88th N. Y. Inf....................	324 Eighteenth
Dunn T. D..........	B	12th R. I. Inf....................	1005½ Mason
Eddy David........	I	9th Mass. Inf....................	915 Post
Ford Wm...........	M	2d U. S. Art	Fifth and Howard
Ganey John.........	A	9th N. H. Inf....................	131 Lily ave.
Gartland John	C	12th R. I. Inf....................	247 Clementina
Garvey Patrick......	D	10th U. S. Inf....................	392 Stevenson
Hand John..........	D	37th N. Y. Inf....................	532 Howard
Hart J. J	H	158th N. Y. Inf.....	112 Shipley
Healey Wm........		U. S. S. Nasheau........	1413 Hyde
Holmes Bartlett R...	I	8th Cal. Inf..	10 Verona Place
Jackson William....	B	148th Ill. Inf....................	137 Lily Ave.
Jagoe R. H.........		U. S. S. Colorado......	San Quentin

NAME.	CO.	SERVICE.	ADDRESS.
Johnson Edward....	K	9th Mass. Inf......	1507 Market
Jones Thomas.......	I	2d Cal. Inf....	Oakland
Kelley E.....		U. S. Navy......	748 Howard
Kenney Bernard	E	3d Mass. Inf....................	220 Jackson
Kerrigan Frank.....	G	1st Mass. Cav	500 Bartlett
Kramer Joseph......	A	14th Kansas Cav.............	220 Jackson
Lonergan James	C	1st Nev. Inf...................	7 Sheridan
Massey John........	E	57th N. Y. Inf..............	Mare Isl. N. Yard
McGrath M		U. S. S. Peoria	21 Sherwood Place
Moyle Owen J.......	H	52d Penn. Inf....................	1308 Greenwich
Murray J. E........	A	2d N. Y. Inf.	160 Shipley
Nichuals O. M......	A	52d Penn. Inf..	1058½ Folsom
O'Connell James ...	C	28th Mass. Inf....................	16 Fair Oaks
O'Connor E...	L	1st Ill. Art............	123 Market
O'Donnell John.....		29th Mass. Battery Heavy Art.	500 Bartlett
O'Doyle T..........	F	18th Conn. Inf..................	927½ Folsom
Reid Wm............	I	1st U. S. Cav......	832 Folsom
Reynolds E..........	I	9th U. S. Inf...................	Golden Gate Ho'se
Riley James H......		U. S. S Connecticut..............	556 Stevenson
Sullivan Daniel......		U. S. Marine Corps...............	25 Sansome
Van der Zwaag F....	I	6th Cal. Inf.................	31 Louisa
Wakeley John..	I	15th Kansas Cav..............	
Walker W. A........	A	102d Penn. Inf....................	526 Kearny
Ward P. J...........		U. S. S. North Carolina...........	12 Sherwood Place
Whitmarsh P. B.....		16th Mass. Light Battery..........	509 Sansome

LOU MORRIS POST, No 47.

LIVERMORE, CAL.

OFFICERS, 1883.

C. W. BRADSHAW..Commander
CHARLES MASON............................Senior Vice-Commander
A. J. PALMER...................................Junior Vice-Commander
G. W. LANGAN..Adjutant
DAN. McCAW...Quartermaster
B. C. BELLAMY...Surgeon
W. W. COLESTOCK...Chaplain
P. B. WASHBURN...................................Officer of the Day
S. A. JOHNSON.................................Officer of the Guard
———— ——..Sergeant Major
———— ——.................................Quartermaster Sergeant

Meeting, First Friday.

NAME.	CO.	SERVICE.	ADDRESS.
Barikausky J.......	C	54th N. Y. Inf..........	Livermore
Bellamy B. C........	G	18th Iowa Inf	"
Bradshaw Chas. W..	H	138th Ill. Inf....................	"
Bradshaw R. R......	G	36th Ill. Inf....	"
Brannan B. F.......	F	28th Ind. Inf....................	"
Brown J. N.........	G	24th Mass. Inf....................	"
Campbell John T...	E	2d Mass. Cav....................	"
Carmichael D. L...	C	4th Ohio Cav....................	Pleasanton
Carnduff F. F........	M	7th N. Y. Art......	San Francisco
Clark Alpha.........	F	5th Iowa Cav........	Livermore
Colestock W. W.....	K	16th Mich. Inf....................	"
Connor D. M.......	I	12th Penn. Inf....................	"
Cutler L. H.........	A	32d Ind. Inf....................	"
French E. B.........	L	4th Penn. Cav....................	"
Gayetti John...	B	2d Penn. Art....................	"
Grattan Christopher.	I	13th Penn. Cav..................	Pleasanton
Jacker J. T. H.......	A	9th Ohio Inf....................	Livermore
Johnson S. A........	G	95th Ill. Inf....................	"
Land B. F..........	K	104th Penn. Inf..................	Oakland
Langan G. W........	H	16th U. S. Inf....................	Livermore
London John.......	B	126th Ill. Inf....	East Oakland
Low W. S.....	I	61st Mass. Inf..................	Livermore
Mason Charles	B	1st Cal. Cav....................	"
McBride John.......	F	88th Ind. Inf....................	"
McCaw Daniel	C	4th Cal. Inf....................	Pleasanton
O'Brien James	H	17th U. S. Inf..................	Livermore
Overacker H. T.....	B	9th Iowa Inf....................	"
Palmer A. J..	A	2d Wis. Cav....................	"
Pullen Clark J......	G	11th N. J. Inf..................	Pleasanton
Turner Daniel	C	8th Cal. Inf....................	Livermore
Waltenbaugh P. C...	D	134th Penn. Inf..................	"
Washburn P. B......	C	18th Mass. Inf	"
Winning E. A.......	C	15th Iowa Inf....................	"
Wise John	B	71st Penn. Inf..................	Pleasanton

GEN'L G. G. MEADE POST, No. 48.

SAN FRANCISCO. CAL.

OFFICERS, 1886.

M. L. G. O'BRIEN...Commander
——— ———...... ....Senior Vice Commander
PETER BURK............................ .... Junior Vice-Commander
F. C. MULLER..Adjutant
L. C. STILLEY...Quartermaster
C. A. BAILEY........... ....Surgeon
WM. J. MALLADY..Chaplain
JAMES DANIELS..Officer of the Day
EDWARD BURK...Officer of the Guard
JOSEPH HANNAN...Sergeant Major
GEORGE BEATTY...Quartermaster Sergeant
A. L. OXTON........... ....Inside Sentinel
THOS. M. FRISBEE...Outside Sentinel

Meeting, First and Third Tuesday, in Alcazar Building, 114 O'Farrell.

NAME.	CO.	SERVICE.	ADDRESS.
Allison Edwin C....	D	3d N. J. Cav......................	2229 Filbert
Arents Edward......	D	6th Conn.Inf.....................	616 California
Bailey C. A	F	3d Conn. Inf.....................	286 Stevenson
Barbee C. P..........	G	12th Ohio Inf....................	3½ Larkin
Beatty Charles	K	188th Penn. Inf.................	1221 Folsom
Beatty George.......	G	21st N. Y. Cav...................	119½ Sixth
Belton P. M.........	D	37th N. Y. Inf....................	2627 Harrison
Bennett Wm	D	61st N. Y. Inf....	762 Howard
Bernard Walter.....	B	7th N. Y. Inf.....................	308 Kearny
Blackburn M. S.....	L	5th Ohio Cav....................	521½ O'Farrell
Blankenberger A....	K	15th N. Y. Heavy Art............	
Britton John........	E	22d Mass. Inf	1774 Folsom
Bruger Carl.........	K	51th N. Y. Inf....................	446 Brannan
Burk Edward...		U. S. S. Ohio	86 Brady
Burk Peter..........		U. S. S. Ohio....................	607 Clay
Cahill Thos. J.......	G	Stroud's Penn. Cav..............	225 Fourth
Carolien C.........	B	1st N. Y. Light Art.......	Pt. Bonita Light
Carrahan Patrick....		U. S. S. Lansbee.................	640 Howard
Cashin D. M.........	A	1st Conn. Art..	111 Liberty
Cline Thos		U. S. S. Arkansas................	432 Minna
Cochrane R. W......	E	36th Ind. Inf...................	535 Stevenson
Coffin C. W..........	E	7th Ind. Cav.......	18 Sherman
Colby Francis.......	B	56th Mass. Inf...................	4th St. Bridge

90

NAME.	CO.	SERVICE.	ADDRESS.
Coleman Michael...		U. S. S. Narragansett.............	Vallejo & Front
Costello John.......	B	26th Ohio Inf....................	221 Moultrie
Cousins F. W........	C	13th Maryland Inf...............	36 New Montg'y
Coyle Charles	I	2d Cal. Cav.....................	512 Linden av.
Daniels James	G	1st Cal. Cav....................	662 Harrison
David L N..........	E	18th Penn. Inf..................	cor. Bush & Mason
Deaves Alonzo	C	25th Mass. Inf..................	27½ Fourth
Deutsch Jacob	A	11th N. Y. Inf....., Inf........	1513 Geary
Dolan William.....	E	69th N. Y. Inf..................	47 Ritch
Duffy Chas M.......	H	1st Mo. Inf.....................	5 Cleveland
Eachus F. J.........	F	2d Penn. Inf....................	1228 Market
Egan E. J..........	K	24th Conn. Inf..................	306 Kearny
Elston George......		U. S. S. Narragansett...........	35 Moss
Falconer C. D.......	I	63d Ill. Inf........	
Finch Philetus......	E	6th U. S. Art...................	417 Fourth
Finley Charles......	A	3d U. S. Art....................	64 New Montg'y
Fisher D. F.........		U. S. S. Ohio...................	
Fitzgibbons Patrick.		5th Ohio Independent Battery.....	Harbor View
Fitzpatrick T. B. N..	C	5th Mass. Inf...................	20 Langton
Flood John.........	K	2d Mass. Cav...................	823 Folsom
Foley Michael.......		U. S. S. Home..................	20 Tehama
Frisbee Thos. M.....	C	7th Cal. Inf....................	419 Powell
Gesell John L.......	F	4th U. S. Art..................	
Gilroy Thomas......	K	9th U. S. Inf..................	134 Fourth
Goetsch Ferdinand.	E	69th N. Y. Inf.................	
Graham Robert	E	6th Cal. Inf...................	200 Mission
Grass C. B..........	B	213th Penn. Inf................	Pigeon Pt. Light
Griener Henry.		8th Ohio Independent Battery.....	Siegfried's Hotel
Hagman Charles G..		U. S. S. Niagara................	611 Mason
Haley Morris........	H	17th Mass. Inf..................	Gov. Res. Saucl'to
Hannan Joseph.....	G	11th Ky. Cav...................	Presidio
Hardee Thomas F...	G	1st Oregon Inf..................	McAll'tr & Brod'rk
Harding W. T.......		U. S. S. North Carolina.........	Oceanic S. S. Co.
Horton William.....	H	2d Cal. Inf....................	New City Hall
Hughes John	G	3d U. S. Inf........	6 Bowie ave.
Jenkins A. J........	A	8th Ill. Inf....................	911 Jones
Jenkins E. S	G	12th Mass. Inf....	408 Fourth
Johnson W. H......		U. S. S. Navy..................	48 Fourth
Jordan William.....		U. S. S. Colorado...............	703½ Davis
Kasche William.....	C	22d Conn. Inf..................	38 Hoff av.
Keenan Frank......	K	45th Penn. Inf.................	
Kittle William......		U. S. S. Philadelphia...........	341 Fourth
Knowles S. W.......	B	22d Maine Inf..................	1326 Mission
Kohler John	A	40th Mo. Inf..................	1841 Market
Lane Michael.......		U. S. S. Sabine................	326 Davis
Lane W. W.........		U. S. Navy	504 Davis
Lapsley Thomas.....	K	20th Penn. Inf.................	3 Alabama
Latham Edward.....	A	6th N. Y. Inf..................	425 Pacific
Lauffer J. G........	D	57th Penn. Inf.................	515 Sacramento
Leavitt A. E........	I	26th Mass Inf.................	2217 Howard
Lewis Nelson.......		U. S. S. Niagara...............	
Madigan James......	F	17th Wis. Inf..................	Presidio
Magee John.........	A	1st Mass. Art..................	Virginia City,Nev.
Maherin John.......	A	40th N. Y. Inf.....	1024 Howard
Mallady Wm. J......	G	50th Penn. Inf.............. ..	733 Mission
Mallon Thomas......	H	6th U. S. Inf............... ..	1637 Ellis

NAME.	CO.	SERVICE.	ADDRESS.
Malone L. J........		U. S. S. Gem of the Sea............	48 Zoe
Manning Lawrence..	I	161th N. Y. Inf....................	
McCann John......	H	15th N. Y. Inf......	924 Natoma
McCann P...........	A	69th N. Y. Inf....................	2724 Folsom
McCleery J. F. B....	F	2d Col. Inf.......	Nucleus House
McGuire Patrick....	G	1st Oregon Cav....................	349½ Minna
Miller E. L..........	G	5th N. Y. Heavy Art.	355 Eleventh
Monahan D. M.....		U. S. S. Monongahela.............	560 Stevenson
Montell F. W........		U. S. S. Bienville..................	16¼ De Boom
Moores John........	D	12th N. H. Inf.....................	1031 Mission
Müller F. C.........		30th N. Y. Independent Battery...	1708 Stevenson
Mulvaney Frank....	D	10th N. Y. Inf.....................	1753 Mission
O'Brien M. L. G....	B	53d N. Y. Inf	432 Montgomr'y R 7
O'Grady Patrick.....	E	1st Cal. Inf.......................	111 Sansome
O'Neil John.........	M	10th N. Y. Cav....................	Potrero, S. F
O'Nell Lawrence		U. S. S. North Carolina...........	317 Pacific
Oxton A. L..........	E	20th Maine Inf....................	1635 Eddy
Patten Wm. P.......	G	15th Ill. Inf......................	656 Mission
Prouty Charles......	K	13th Vt. Inf......................	1526 California
Reich Samuel.......	I	10th N. Y. Inf....................	1006 Washington
Reighley J. B........	D	13th N. J. Inf.....................	123 Ridley
Rines Charles H.....	B	25th Maine Inf....................	3013 Mission
Ruddick W. J........	C	2d Col. Cav......................	909 Minna
Savage Patrick	G	11th Mass. Inf....................	433 Clementina
Schander Adolph....		U. S. Navy.........	Angel Island
Schmidt Henry		1st Cal. Inf.......................	835 Cedar, Oakland
Scholz Bruno........		U. S. S. Resacca..................	420 Bush
Simon Isadore.......	G	6th Cal. Inf.............	333 Twenty-sev'th
Small W. S..........	F	19th Maine Inf....................	210 Chattanooga
Stilley L. C.........	D	Mo. Benton Cadets..............	414 Clay
Subers R. S.....	F	114th Penn. Inf...................	109 Van Ness av.
Thompson C. H.....	E	17th Maine Inf....................	105 Stockton
Thorner J. F........	A	6th U. S. Cav....................	1830 Filbert
Tiernan P. J........	E	3d Penn. Cav....................	R 9 Montgom'ry bl
Toothaker W F......	A	24th Maine Inf....	709 Nineteenth
Townsend Joseph...		U. S. Navy	4 Bryant
Van Ness James.....	B	6th N. Y. Inf....................	52 Natoma
Walsh Daniel.......	C	9th Mass. Inf.....................	133 Seventh
Walsh Edward	A	8th U. S. Inf.....................	Geary and Lyon
Wandell N. L........	K	9th Vt. Inf.......................	133 Ninth
Wannemacher G. W.	C	5th N. Y. Inf.....................	263 Jersey
Woerz Henry........	A	1st N. J. Art.....................	5 Hardie Place
Woscho Benj	G	2d U. S. Art.......................	Alaska
Zissig Charles.......	D	8th Cal Inf.....	1611 Baker

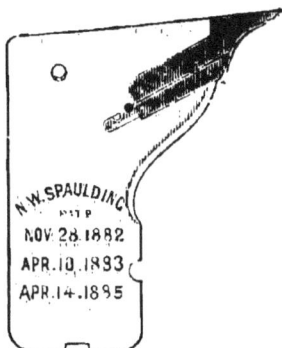

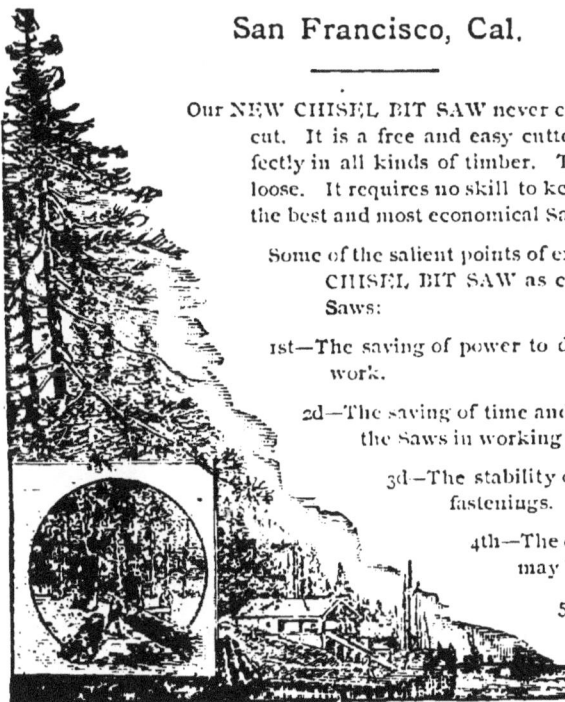

COL. WHIPPLE POST, No. 49.

EUREKA, CAL.

OFFICERS, 1886.

J. H. G. WEAVER	Commander
JOHN QUINN	Senior Vice-Commander
N. D. HULSE	Junior Vice-Commander
W. G. BONNER	Adjutant
C. W. LONG	Quartermaster
—— ——	Surgeon
REV. R. D. CLARK	Chaplain
C. W. RICHARDSON	Officer of the Day
ARCHIBALD McDONALD	Officer of the Guard
N. N. BROWN	Sergeant Major
GEO. C. CARLTON	Quartermaster Sergeant

Meeting, Fourth Monday.

NAME.	CO.	SERVICE.	ADDRESS.
Alexander Wm. R ...	B	39th N. J. Inf	Blue Lake
Armstrong John W..	G	2d Cal. Inf	"
Axe Fred	C	2d Penn. Reserve Corps Inf	Eureka
Barber James B....	D	18th Mich. Inf	Hydesville
Beach Charles E....	B	1st Bat. Cal. Mountaineers	Trinidad
Bennet John F	E	138th Ind. Inf	
Bitterly Oscar A...	H	106th N. Y. Inf	Eureka
Bonner W. G	A	17th Mich. Inf	"
Brown James B....	H	2d Cal. Inf	"
Brown N. N. ...	A	1st Maine Art	"
Bulson H. R	K	1st Mich. Cav	"
Campbell Daniel ...	F	2d Minn. Inf	Kneelands Prairie
Campton Thomas J.	K	12th Ohio Inf	Rhonerville
Carlton George A...	A	6th Kansas Cav	Eureka
Chamberlin John N.	E	2d West Va. Cav	"
Clark R. D....	K	2d Mich. Inf	"
Cole Brackett...	A	31st Maine Inf	"
Douglas Harmon L..	I	22d Maine Inf	"
Ederline Edward....	M	2d U. S. Art	"
Fiebig Charles	1	69th N. Y. Inf	"
Flannigan Patrick...	F	4th U. S. Cav	"
Fresher Thomas.....	A	7th Ohio Inf	"
Geandrot A. J	I	47th N. Y. Inf..	"
Gier Knyphausen A.		1st Bat. Cal. Mountaineers	Bear River
Hulse N. D	D	1st N. Y. Mounted Inf	Eureka

NAME.	CO.	SERVICE.	ADDRESS.
Herrick R. F........	B	1st Bat. Cal. Mountaineers........	Eureka
Hetherington John.		21st Mass. Inf............	"
Hopkins George W..	F	48th Mo. Inf......................	Arcata
Inman Charles J....	G	3d Vt. Inf.......................	Eureka
Kelly Edward.......	A	3d Cal. Inf.....................	"
Leddy Barney.......	D	7th Mo. Inf......................	"
Leppowitz Max.....	B	14th U. S. Inf.....	"
Lingher John..	C	5th Tenn. Cav.....................	Elk River
Long Charles W.....	A	1st Bat. Cal. Mountaineers	Eureka
Lowry J. B..........	B	100th Ohio Inf..	Rohnerville
McDonald A........	E	6th Maine Inf....................	Eureka
McGonegal John	I	7th Iowa Inf.....................	"
Murphy E. B........		3d Maine Art...................	"
Murphy Wm........	E	2d Cal. Inf....	Mad River
Noddin I. J........	F	22d Maine Inf...................	Eureka
Owen James I.......	A	1st Cal, Inf........	"
Paddock W. C.......		1st Wis. Art......	"
Parker B. P...... ...	D	20th Maine Inf	"
Pratt Wm. H........		1st Bat. Cal. Mountaineers........	"
Purser Spencer......	E	23d Penn. Inf......................	SoldiersH'me,N'pa
Quinn John....	D	69th N. Y. Inf.....	Eureka
Rae Thomas...		12th U. S. Inf..................	Rohnerville
Reich Samuel..	I	10th N. Y. Inf...................	Martinez
Richardson C. W ...		1st Maine Art....................	Eurkea
Roberts Charles F...	H	2d Maine Inf....................	"
Ryan James.........	K	3d U. S. Cav....................	"
Schroeder Chris. F..	B	43d Ill. Inf.....................	"
Schuehart Philip....	I	1st Penn. Inf....................	Petrolia
Snow H. O....		13th U. S. Inf........	Eureka
Stanton Edward.....	E	25th Wis. Inf....................	"
Stevens Wm.........	D	88th Ill. Inf....................	"
Stringfield M. W....	A	1st Bat. Cal. Mountaineers........	"
Stuart Alonzo R.....	I	11th Maine Inf....	Arcata
Taylor Charles G....	B	1st Maine Inf....................	Eureka
Taylor Joshua.......	K	23d Mass. Inf...................	"
Thomson James.....	B	U. S. Art......	"
Thurston Charles E.	G	1st District of Columbia Cav..	"
Vanwormer Freland	E	6th Kansas Inf....	"
Walker C. H.........	I	1st District of Columbia Inf.......	"
Weaver J. H. G......	I	11th Mich. Inf..................	"

APPOMATTOX POST, No. 50.

OAKLAND, CAL.

OFFICERS, 1886.

E. K. RUSSELL...Commander
J. J. HAMBRIGHT...Senior Vice-Commander
WM. O'BRIEN..Junior Vice-Commander
J. A. ANDRES...Adjutant
N. S. DOUGLAS..Quartermaster
C. O. PARK..Surgeon
A. T. PRENTISS..Chaplain
GEORGE QUACKENBUSH...Officer of the Day
J. C. ESTEY..Officer of the Guard
M. O. McCLAIN...Sergeant Major
J. S. PETTIT...Quartermaster Sergeant
GEORGE DEAL..Inside Sentinel
D. C. DAVISON...Outside Sentinel

Meeting, every Thursday.

NAME.	CO.	SERVICE.	ADDRESS.
Allen Truman H....	K	22d N. Y. Cav..................	163 Fifth
Andres J. A.........	K	11th N. Y. Cav............	700 Lydia
Barrett Daniel S	F	41st N. Y. Inf...................	773 Sixth
Barrett J. E.	E	150th Ill. Inf.................	Oakland P. O.
Barringer Wm......	B	151st Ill. Inf...................	First and Jefferson
Barry J. E..........	I	5th Mass. Inf.	Alameda
Barton Thomas C..		U. S. Marine Corps..............	Yountville
Beechner Ernest..	B	8th U. S. Inf....................	11th and Franklin
Bodle F. S.........		185th Ohio Inf...............	San Pablo ave.
Bohn J. H..........	H	8th Mich. Inf...................	11th and Franklin
Bortreo David E....	E	U. S. R. R. Service...........	City Hall
Brown David.......	C	2d Iowa Inf..............	1659 William
Burbank L.........	C	30th Wis. Inf	476 Twelfth
Burns Michael.....		U. S. S. Sabine..............	Oakland P. O.
Burns T. R.........	B	22d Conn. Inf..........	75 Valley
Byrnes John B......	D	11th Maine Inf...............	728 Lewis
Cannon E. M.......	F	17th Ill. Inf................	1919 Filbert
Carey L. H.........		12th Wis. Inf..........	916 Eighth
Carpenter Jerome...	C	7th Iowa Cav.................	East Oakland
Canley William......	H	59th Penn. Inf....	Third
Christian Antone....		U. S. S. Cherokee.................	766 Twenty-Seco'd
Collins Geo. H.	E	43d Mass. Inf.................	526 Tenth
Curtis John.........	B	7th Maine Inf.........	1261 Brush
Dakes R. H.........	F	28th Iowa Inf.................	1684 William
Davis Henry........	B	16th Ky. Inf....................	San Quentin

95

NAME.	CO.	SERVICE.	ADDRESS.
Davison D. C........	C	8th Cal. Inf.......................	Grand Armory Hall
Deal George..... ...	K	47th Ind. Inf................... ...	367 Third
Douglas N. R........		1st N. Y. Engineers.....	2015 Chestnut
Duncan J. M........	E	49th N. Y. Inf................	Oakland P. O.
Enos Joseph....		U. S. Navy.......	"
Estey J. C..........	K	4th N. H......................	535 Seventeenth
Enson Jas. H........	M	7th N. Y. Art..., ...	516 Franklin
Farwell F. M.	I	6th Maine Inf..............	378 Twelfth
Fitch Oscar.........	I	7th Cal. Inf.............	483 Plymouth ave.
Fittbogen Paul.....	K	5th Mo. Inf...................	617 Fifteenth
Flynn Timothy......	I	18th Ill. Inf...	Oakland P. O.
Fogg Geo. J........	D	15th N. H. Inf...............	855 Center
French Asa F..	F	11th Ohio Inf...............	827 Franklin
Galvin James.......	H	24th Penn. Inf...............	17th and Tel. ave.
Gee M. C.........	A	103d Ohio Inf...............	362 Tenth
Hall C. D..........	A	124th Ohio Inf...............	1536 Curtis
Hamann August.....	D	1st Cal. Inf..............	1057 Webster
Hambright John J..	O	197th Penn. Inf. & B 79th Penn. Inf	11th and Franklin
Harlow Lloyd.......	B	23d Iowa Inf...............	Oakland P. O.
Hayes E. B........	H	75th Ind. Inf...................	East Oakland
Higham E..........	I	23d Wis. Inf................	Fruit Vale
Hohfeld Edward....	A	5th Penn. Cav..............	1139 Valencia, S. F.
Jacobs W. W........	H	4th N. Y. Heavy Art..............	962 Grove
Johnson Geo. A.....		U. S. Navy	Oakland Pier
Jordan Isaiah......	D	85th Penn. Inf.................	914 Henry
Judell B....	G	47th Ohio Inf.....	Sixth and Castro
Kelly B. J..........	F	26th Penn. Inf...............	216 Minna, S. F.
Koons Geo. B.	B	8th Iowa Inf................	Goat Island
Large W. J. F.		U. S. S. Waterwitch..........	416 Twelfth
Leeds B. F.........		U. S. S. Wabash.................	26th and Cal., S. F.
Little J. R..........	B	5th Penn. Reserve Inf..........	401 Tenth
Lyon J. L...........	A	16th N. Y. Inf...............	9th & Washington
Mackley Fred.	B	14th Penn. Inf...............	Oakland P. O.
Martin G. W........	H	1st Mass. Inf................	677 Fifth
Martin Michael.....		U. S. Navy..................	570 Broadway
Martin T. R........	E	3d Col. Cav...............	935 Pine
Mattingly Joseph...		1st U. S. Cav..	1408 Tenth .
Mauerhan M........	B	8th Kansas Cav............	1665 Atlantic
McClain M. O.	G	6th Ind. Inf. & F 123d Ohio Inf....	16th and Tel. ave.
McDonald T. H.....		U. S. Navy..................	Linden and 28th
Melville Dean......	O	7th Mass. Inf..............	172 Taylor
Montague J. P.....		U. S. Navy	823 Fifth
Mosher Geo.........	I	154th N. Y. Inf.............	919 Thirty-Sixth
Mulvey John........	A	4th R. I. Inf...............	912 Third
Newman Thos.......	L	8th Iowa Cav...............	West Oakland
Norris Wm. E......	E	99th Ill. Inf...............	577 Sixteenth
Nyland H..........	L	1st Conn. Heavy Art..............	Oakland P. O.
O'Brien William....		U. S. Navy..................	869 Henry
O'Connor John......	E	31st U. S. Inf...............	667 Seventh
O'Keefe J....		U. S. Marines.................	1803 Seventh
Osgood S. R........	C	47th Iowa Inf...............	34th and Tel. ave.
Park C. O..........	B	12th Mass. Inf................	623 Seventh
Parritt L S.........	C	29th Maine Inf..............	811 Thirteenth
Patterson Thos......	E	18th Mich. Inf..............	314 Sixth
Pattleton R.....	G	43d N. Y. Inf......	City Hall
Pearce T. J..........	A	33d Ill. Inf...................	Oakland P. O.

NAME.	CO.	SERVICE.	ADDRESS.
Pettit S. S.	D	15th Ohio Inf	367 East Twelfth
Prentiss A. T.	I	49th Ohio Inf	East Oakland
Pritchard B. F.	G	132d Ind. Inf	Market, S. F.
Riggle S. L.	K	30th Ind. Inf	911 Seventh
Riker J. D.	F	1st N. Y. Inf	698 Twenty-Fifth
Russell E. K.		2d and 6th Mass. Light Art	616 Fifth
Santee Henry J	D	1st Wash. Ter. Inf	668 Harrison
Savage Wm. R.	F	1st Cal. Cav	Henry House, 9th
Scranton Ed.	A	33d Ill. Inf	731 Henry
Sebrey Frank.	E	1st Conn. Cav	1455 Third
Sebring D. W.	E	30th N. J. Inf	Oakland P. O.
Seibe Ludwig.	G	133d N. Y. Inf	Shell Mound
Stanley J. W		U. S. S. St. Mary	369 Fourth
Taylor Frank.	A	2d Vt. Inf	Oakland P. O
Thomas W. R.	A	105th Ill. Inf	715 Sixteenth
Thompson T. H.	I	52d Ill. Inf	272 Twenty-Third
Tomaseck Joseph.	E	4th Ohio Cav	East Oakland
Toole Thos	L	69th N. Y. Inf	1329 Thirteenth av
True Geo. H.	B	7th Maine Inf	East Oakland
Tucker J. W.	A	19th Maine Inf	614 Eighteenth
Way Jesse.	G	8th Ind. Inf	944 Pine
Wentzel Frank.	E	1st Kansas Inf	768 Willow
Westover A. E.	H	124th Ill. Inf	692 Twenty-Sixth
Young John.	I	15th N. Y. Engineers	656 Twenty-Seco'd
Zeigler W. O.	H	24th Ind. Inf	474 Thirteenth •

McPHERSON POST, No. 51.

HANFORD, CAL.

———

OFFICERS, 1886.

THEODORE LOVENTHAL................................. ....Commander
GEO. W. CLUTE................. ....Senior Vice-Commander
W. T. BURNETT..Junior Vice-Commander
L. C. HAWLEY........... ....Adjutant
J. V. DODD ....Quartermaster
——— ——.... ....Surgeon
——— ——..Chaplain
C. F. BINGHAM..Officer of the Day
RUDOLPH REY...Officer of the Guard
——— ——..Sergeant Major
——— ——...Quartermaster Sergeant

———

Meeting, Second Saturday.

NAME.	CO.	SERVICE.	ADDRESS,
Althouse Jas. W.....	A	3d Mich. Inf......................	Lemoore
Babcock M S.		U. S. S. Grand Gulf..............	Hanford
Ball Samuel.........	B	6th Kansas Inf.....................	Grangeville
Beckwith C J.......		Coggswell's Battery Ill. Art.......	Hanford
Bingham Charles F..	H	31th Ohio Inf.....................	"
Blakley J. O.........	E	44th N. Y Inf....................	Visalia
Blincoe Thomas.....	I	2d Cal. Cav.......................	"
Brodmer Charles....	M	1st Ohio Art.....	Hanford
Bryan Charles M .		59th Ohio Inf.....................	"
Burnett Wm. T......	A	32d Ill. Inf......................	"
Butler H. M.........	K	1st U. S. Sharpshooters	Visalia
Chambers Thomas	H	2d R. I. Inf......................	Hanford
Clute George W.....	A	1st N. Y. Cav. (Dragoons).........	"
Coon O. E...........		14th Ind. Cav....................	Lemoore
Dodds J. V..........	F	22d Iowa Inf......	Hanford
Dodds Wm. H.	D	3d Cal. Inf......................	"
Dunn Israel........	G	107th N. Y. Inf...................	Lemoore
Durham John A. ...	A	95th Ohio Inf....	Hanford
Dykes Wm. R.......	K	5th Kansas Inf. & A 10th Kansas Inf	"
Friend W. P.........	H	57th Ill. Inf....	"
Hawley L. C.........	C	130th Ill. Inf.....................	"
Hawley W. G........	A	28th Wis. Inf.....................	"
Hayes Albert........	A	6th Maine Inf....................	"

98

NAME.	CO.	SERVICE.	ADDRESS.
House Thomas......	D	Merrill's Horse Ill. Cav............	Hanford
Johnson Oscar S....	E	9th Cal. Inf......................	Visalia
Jones David D.....	C	3d Penn. Heavy Art..............	Hanford
Loventhal Theodore	I	81st Ohio Inf.....................	"
McPhee Francis....	A	5th Maine Inf....................	"
Mitchell J. R........	D	8th Minn. Inf....................	"
Moore William......	I	4th Iowa Inf.............	"
Morgan R. F.......	C	1st Iowa Cav...................	"
Morgan W..........	C	1st Iowa Cav...................	"
Newport W. C......	B	Ohio Heavy Art.................	"
Owens Ephraim.....	K	40th Ind. Inf...................	"
Owens James M....	B	17th Ind. Inf...................	"
Peacock H. F........	I	2d N. Y. Heavy Art.............	"
Pearson Henry......	G	98th Penn. Inf..................	"
Randall John........	C	2d Ohio Inf................	"
Rey Rudolph........	C	111th Ill. Inf...................	"
Schlicht A. E. G.....	G	16th Iowa Inf..................	"
Shipe John H........	G	7th Tenn. Inf.........'.........	"
Smith Amos C.......	B	48th Mo. Inf...................	Kingston
Twining M. J.......	M	1st Penn. Cav..................	Hanford
Wemmer W. R......	D	7th Cal. Int	"
Wilson G. H.........	I	13th Iowa Inf................ ...	"

STARR KING POST, No. 52.

SANTA BARBARA CAL.

OFFICERS, 1886.

O. C. HUNT	Commander
I. B. HARDY	Senior Vice-Commander
GEO. A. NORTON	Junior Vice-Commander
E. M. HOIT	Adjutant
AUG. FLUEHE	Quartermaster
G. W. SOUTHWICK	Surgeon
————————	Chaplain
P. L. MOORE	Officer of the Day
L. W. LEMMON	Officer of the Guard
E. A. HERRICK	Sergeant Major
J. STAPLES	Quartermaster Sergeant

Meeting, First and Third Monday.

NAME.	CO.	SERVICE.	ADDRESS.
Allaire Frank	A	16th Ill. Inf. and B 2d Ill. Art	Santa Barbara
Andrews Jas. H	D	1st Ill. Cav	"
Barker Fred. J	F	47th Mass. Inf	"
Bates Joseph	H	7th Wis. Inf	"
Brobeck Jos	E	75th Penn Inf	"
Chittenden R. H	A	71st N. Y. Inf. and 1st Wis. Cav	"
Cleale J. A	H	23d Mass. Inf	"
Daily Edw	F	38th Ind. Inf	Carpenteria
DuBois L. P	F	128th Penn. Inf	Santa Barbara
Edgar Thos	F	14th Iowa Inf	Santa Ynez
Fluehe August	F	8th Ill. Art. and 5th U. S. Art	Santa Barbara
Forbes J. M	I	92d Ill. Inf	"
Gourley E. T	H	2d Cal. Inf	"
Hardy I. B	A	64th Ill. Inf	"
Harrington John	C	88th Ill. Inf	"
Haverly W. J	B	65th N. Y. Inf	"
Hayman Al	F	57th Ill. Inf	"
Herrick Ezra A	B	127th Ill. Inf. and Vet. Res. Corps.	"
Herrick R. L	B	127th Ill. Inf	"
Hoit Edw. M	D	14th West Va. Inf	"
Hunt Charles C	K	4th Minn. Inf	"
Hunt R. O	B	2d Minn. Cav	"
Keebn Harry	F	1st Maine Inf. and 213th Penn. Inf	"
Klett Julius	A	15th Ill. Inf	"

100

NAME.	CO.	SERVICE.	ADDRESS.
Knighton W. A......	E	1st Bat. Cal. Mountaineers	Santa Barbara
Knox S. B. P., M. D.		49th Penn. Inf.....................	"
Lano Felix..........	F	25th Ind. Inf..........	"
Lemmon Leon W....	H	11th Ind. Inf...............	"
Lucas N. B..........	I	1st Kansas Inf..........	"
Moore P. L		27th N. Y. Battery................	"
Morrill W. H..	A	2d Minn. Cav.....................	"
Muzzall H. W.	A	17th Ind. Inf	"
Myers Sam'l........	H	169th Ohio Inf...................	"
Norton Geo. A......		5th Mass. and U. S. Vols..........	..
Pry J. C.............	A	100th Penn. Inf...................	"
Ross Charles.......	G	84th Ill. Inf.....................	"
Rowe Ben. S........	G	6th Cal. Inf..................... ...	"
Seeley S. S..........	G	38th Iowa Inf...	Goleta
Senteney F. M.	D	60th Ill. Inf......................	Carpenteria
Sheffield E. S.......	D	15th Iowa Inf. and 7th Iowa Cav..	Santa Barbara
Shoup A. L.........	G	7th Ill. Cav......................	"
Smith C. T.........	K	4th Iowa Inf.....................	"
Smith R. D..........	K	8th Vt. Inf......................	"
Smith W. C.........	A	1st Iowa Inf.....................	"
Southwick G.W.,M.D		19th and 85th Ill. Inf............	"
Squier Oliver P......	H	14th Ill. Inf......	"
Stadler John...	A	7th Wis. Inf.....................	"
Staples Joseph......	A	6th Minn. Inf....................	"
Stauffer Henry W....	H	120th Ohio Inf...................	"
Stoddard Henry.....		131st Ohio Inf...................	"
Storko C. A....	G	30th Wis. Inf....................	"
Van Winkle H. W....	G	39th Mass. Inf. & 1st U. S. Col'd Inf	"
Walcott John.......	B	77th Ill. Inf.....................	"
Walker G. H....	D	2d Ill. Cav......................	"
Wallington Wm.	E	3d Iowa Cav.....................	"
Williams H. L.......	A	19th Ohio Inf....................	"
Wyatt Geo. H........	A	17th Ill. Cav....................	"

TOM DOLLARD POST, No. 53.

MENDOCINO CITY, CAL.

OFFICERS, 1886.

M. J. BYRNES..Commander
W. P. SQUIRE.. ....Senior Vice-Commander
M. O'BRIAN..Junior Vice-Commander
R. HILYARD.................. ....Adjutant
C. H. JOY.. ......Quartermaster
W. H. SOMMERS,..Surgeon
W. L. BITLEY ....Chaplain
A. McILREE...................... ....Officer of the Day
J. LANE..Officer of the Guard
PHILIP ACHEY...Sergeant Major
W. A. COALSON.. ....Quartermaster Sergeant

Meeting, Second Saturday.

NAME.	CO.	SERVICE.	ADDRESS.
Achey Philip........	D	2d Col. Cav......................	Pomo
Beard James........	K	38th Iowa Inf.....................	Mendocino
Biley W L........	G	37th Iowa Inf....	Fort Bragg
Byrnes M. J........	E	1st Bat. Mount's Cal & 19th N. Y. Inf	Mendocino
Coalson W. A........	E	3d Cal. Inf.................	Cristine
Hilyard Reuben....	B	47th Penn. Inf.........	Mendocino
Hurst William......		1st Bat. Mountaineers Cal.........	Millers Mills
Joy C. H...........	E	9th N. H. Inf..............	Mendocino
Kell Charles M......	C	1st Cal. Inf.....................	"
Lane Joseph	K	37th Wis. Inf...................	"
McIlree Alex...	E	10th Iowa Inf.....................	"
Nicholson James W.	B	97th Ill. Inf......................	Inglenook
O'Brian Michael.....	A	1st Maine Cav........	Mendocino
Perry Ira C..........	A	Marrion Bat. Mo. Inf............	"
Sommers W. H......	A	53d Ill. Inf	"
Squire W. P........	C	1st Maine Art....	"
Tracy Samuel W.....		1st Minn. Light Art..............	Whitesboro
Tuttle J. T........	B	13th Maine Inf.....	Mendocino

WARREN POST, No. 54.

SACRAMENTO, CAL.

OFFICERS, 1886.

O. M. McLEMORE..Commander
C. W. WALLACE............. ....Senior Vice-Commander
RUDOLPH PEDLAR......................................Junior Vice-Commander
E. B. OSLER...Adjutant
J. N. MOORE...Quartermaster
CHAS. E. PINKHAM...Surgeon
J. E. D. BALDWIN..Chaplain
C. E. PERKINS.........·.... ... .Officer of the Day
HARVEY MOORE...Officer of the Guard
G. L. PARKER..Sergeant Major
J. J. TRARBACH...Quartermaster Sergeant
N. S. MELLUS..Inside Sentinel
M. H. CATLETT..Outside Sentinel

Meeting, Second and Fourth Thursday.

NAME.	CO.	SERVICE.	ADDRESS.
Ames Everett.........	D	2d Cal. Cav......................	Telegraph House
Bachline John.........	G	169th N. Y. Inf..................	614 L
Baldwin J. E. D....	A	5th Kansas Cav..................	411 J
Bartell J. J..........	D	17th Kansas Inf.................	1229 Third
Bowsher Amos L....		63d Ohio Inf. and B 1st U. S. Cav..	1615 Seventh
Brown C. C..........	K	3d Wis. Inf......................	302 K
Carroll J. F.........	D	21st Mo. Inf....................	Seventh bet. D & E
Catlett Milton H....		8th Ind. Art.....................	Thirteenth and J
Copper W. H........	I	11th Mo. Inf.....................	2319 O
Crowell W. H.......	B	92d Ill. Inf.....................	Riverside Road
Doan Wallace.......	E	5th Cal. Inf................	15th bet. N and O
Dougherty Philip...	K	39th Mass........	
Douglas John.......		U. S. Navy	St. George Build'g
Eastabrook J. S.....	F	147th Ill. Inf....	1908 M
Finney Jas....	F	8th Minn. Inf....................	
Gerichten Louis....	A	3d Mo. Inf.......	14th bet. J and K
Girard F. R.........		Ordnance Department U.S.A......	1105 B'way, Oakl'd
Harrington John....	G	6th Ind. Cav.....................	
Harty Alfred........	D	39th Ill. Inf....	Colusa House
Houghton W. A.....	K	17th N. Y. Inf....................	New York City
Humphrey W. O ...	F	103d Ohio Inf....	
Hurlbut S. O........	F	2d Cal. Cav......................	Lewiston, Trinity
Jordon Elmer C.....	E	7th Conn. Inf.....	1111 D

NAME.	CO.	SERVICE.	ADDRESS.
Koester Frederick...	F	2d Minn. Inf......................	719 K
Landers Wm........	E	9th Kansas Cav....................	Seventh and L
Lipowitz Max.......	B	14th U. S. Inf.....................	Sacramento
Lyons Harvey.......	A	15th U.S. Inf.....................	"
Madden Wm. J......	K	1st U. S. Cav. and B 5th U. S. Cav..	"
McCarthy J. M......	H	43d Ohio Inf......................	608 Q
McDonald D. H.....	B	1st Ohio Cav......	
McKearney L........		10th U. S. Cav. and D 71st Penn. Inf	722 L
McLemore C. N.....	C	8th Ill. Cav......................	1315 Fifth
McMahon William.	B	13th N. H. Inf....................	
Mead James A.......	D	141st Ill. Inf...........	821 K
Measure J. H	K	28th Mich. Inf....................	501 O
Mellus N. S.... ...	H	15th U.S.Sappers & Min's & U. S. N'y	Washington, Yolo
Miller Enoch.......	B	48th N. Y. Inf......	St. George Build'g
Mollo John..........	F	1st Cal. Cav......................	Grand Isl., Sac. Co
Moore Harvey.......	F	23d Ohio Inf......................	1223 J
Moore John N.......	D	19th Maine Inf....	2126 J
O'Grady Martin....	I	1st Mich. Engineers...............	719 K
Osler E. B..........		Penn. 100-day Cav................	328 J
Parker G. L.........	A	8th Conn. Inf. and K 1st Conn. Cav	
Pedlar Rudolph....	G	4th Cal. Inf......................	914 Sixth
Pennock John	G	77th Ill. Inf.......	Walsh Station
Perkins C. E........	I	2d R. I. Inf......................	1010 K
Pierrepont J. B.....	K	10th Conn. Inf....	
Pinkham Chas. E....	H	1st Maine Cav....................	820 Eighth
Pogue James........	A	1st Mich. Lancers................	Arcade Building
Rheim Charles.....		U. S. S. Saginaw.................	Mechanics' Exch.
Richards W. H.....	H	80th Ohio Inf....................	1809 J
Ruhl John..........	B	9th U. S. Inf....................	703 Sixth
Smith M. J.........	E	96th Ohio Inf....................	1015 Fourteenth
Spickert Jacob... ..	H	37th Ohio Inf.....................	718 E
Thorne Wm. S......		U. S. Navy......................	Fifth and V
Trarbach J. J.......	F	9th Ohio Inf....	308 M
Tronson Ole		U. S. Navy	831 Nineteenth
Vaughn Edward.....	E	3d N. Y. Inf......................	Washington, Yolo
Vogelgesang Geo...	E	12th Iowa Inf....................	1709 J
Von Meyerhoff Chrs.	I	2d Cal. Inf......................	1122 J
Walker G. A.........	G	10th U. S. Inf....................	L bet. 8th and 9th
Wallace C. W.......	C	93d N. Y. Inf....................	Odd Fellows Tem.
Wallace J. M........	E	7th Ind. Inf.....................	728 K
Ward Phillip.......		U. S. Gunboat Pembrina	Seventh and G
Wheeler F. L.......	A	2d Cal. Cav.	
Williams John......	B	6th N. H. Inf....................	Dixon, Solano Co.
Winchell H. P......	F	141st Ill. Inf.....................	1321 Seventh

STANTON POST, No. 55.

LOS ANGELES, CAL.

OFFICERS, 1886.

J. M. GUINN...Commander
A. M. THORNTON.......................................Senior Vice-Commander
E. P. JOHNSON.......................... ....Junior Vice-Commander
SAM'L C. SYMONDS..Adjutant
A. W. BARRETT...Quartermaster
F. D. BICKNELL....................... ....Surgeon
EDWIN BAXTER...Chaplain
J. C. OLIVER... ....Officer of the Day
DANIEL JONES.................................. ....Officer of the Guard
L. T. PIERCE.... ....Sergeant Major
J. C. BYRAM......... ....Quartermaster Sergeant

Meeting, Second and Fourth Friday.

NAME.	CO.	SERVICE.	ADDRESS.
Adams D. E...........	F	18th Ind. Inf.......	Los Angeles
Adams W. H. H......	K	72d Ind. Inf......................	"
Allen A. J. E........	H	4th Minn. Inf......	"
Atherton Nelson....		....	"
Baker J. S...........	G	3d Iowa Cav.....................	"
Barlow G. H	K	14th N. Y. Art..................	"
Barrett A. M....	D	3d Iowa Inf.	"
Baxter Edwin........	C	1st Mich. Engineers.............	"
Berry M. F..........	E	Independent Minn. Cav.....	"
Bicknell F. D........	A	23d Wis. Inf....................	"
Bixby H. H....:....	K	121st N. Y. Inf.................	"
Blind Philip........	K	8th Ill. Inf..	Savanah, Cal.
Bonebrake Geo. H...		69th Ind. Inf................. ...	Los Angeles
Bourcey Nap'n......	K	12th Vt. Inf.......	"
Bouton E............		U. S Vols.......................	"
Boyce H. H.........	I	45th Ill. Inf.	"
Brown Chas. A......	A	8th Minn. Inf...................	"
Brunson Esty.	I	83d Ill. Inf.....................	"
Butterfield S. H.....	H	193d Penn. Inf.................	"
Byram J. C..........	G	36th Ind. Inf....................	"
Carter J. M.........	B	4th Mich. Inf...................	"
Case C. C.....		8th Maine Inf...................	"
Casterline W. M.....		15th Ind. Inf......	"
Chambers J. S......	A	11th Ill. Inf....................	"
Charnock Chas......	D	5th Wis. Inf....................	"

106

STANTON POST, No. 55.

NAME.	CO.	SERVICE.	ADDRESS.
Clark F. B.	K	21st Conn. Inf.	Los Angeles
Cochran W. G.	K	146th Ill. Inf	"
Collins A. D.	I	85th Ill. Inf.	"
Corker J. R.		8th Kansas Inf.	"
Covey E. H.	D	5th Conn. Inf.	"
Cox E. E.	G	20th Ind. Inf.	"
Crow Geo. R.	G	90th Ohio Inf.	"
Culver F. B	G	123d Ohio Inf.	"
Davis James M.	K	26.h Ill. Inf.	"
Dutton J. B.	H	24th Iowa Inf.	"
Earl C. N.		2d Minn. Battery	"
Field D. W.	B	27th Conn. Inf.	"
Fish L. E.		20th Ind. Battery	"
Fisk John E.	I	39th Mass. Inf.	"
Fitch Ezra	F	3d Iowa Cav.	"
Fitzmier D.	C	9th Mich. Inf.	"
Ford Wm.	L	15th Ill. Cav.	"
Fordham M. C.	A	140th N. Y. Inf	"
Francis J. W.	K	23d Mo. Inf.	"
Frew J. M.		51st Ohio Inf.	"
Furrey W. C.		4th N. Y. Art.	"
Gilbert H.	A	25th Mo. Inf.	"
Gove B. F.	I	11th Ill. Inf.	"
Grisnold L. D.	D	9th N. Y. Cav.	"
Gunn J. M.	C	7th Ohio Inf.	"
Hammett R. H.	G	183d Penn. Inf.	"
Haskins C. H	A	105th Penn. Inf.	"
Hawthorn I. N.	A	8th Minn. Inf.	"
Henderson J. A..e	G	76th Ill. Inf.	"
Hoffman A. P.	A	132d Ill. Inf.	"
Hymer Stewart	H	13th Ind. Inf.	"
James Walter	L	90th Ohio Inf.	"
Johnson E. P.	K	68th Ind Inf.	"
Jones Daniel	H	13th Mich Inf.	"
Jones E. W.		19th Conn. Inf.	"
Jordan Franklin		U. S. S. Macedonian	"
Kelleher D.	D	124th Ind. Inf.	New Mexico
Kelley John.	B	14th N. H. Inf.	Los Angeles
Kittredge Willard	I	3d Cal. Inf.	"
Kittredge W. T.		4th Minn. Inf.	"
Kughen D. A	H	11th Ill. Cav.	"
Lawrence C. W.		22d Mich. Inf.	"
Lawton D. W.	K	7th Cal. Inf.	"
Lenox A. J		74th Ohio Inf.	"
Little Geo. H.	G	11th Minn. Inf.	Pasadena, Cal.
Maltman J. S.	H	2d Mich. Inf.	Los Angeles
Mannon Geo.	F	83d Ill. Inf.	"
Mansfield John.		U. S. Vols.	"
Martin J. H.	F	1st Vt. Cav.	"
Maynard H. H.		2d Ark. Inf.	"
McBratney W. C.	A	193d Penn. Inf.	"
McClure M. D.	G	20th Ohio Inf.	"
McPherson A. S.	F	15th Iowa Inf.	"
Merrill L. O.	K	1st Maine Cav.	"
Mills J. W.	G	2d Neb. Inf.	"
More Ira	G	33d Ill. Inf.	"

NAME.	CO.	SERVICE.	ADDRESS.
Mosher L. E.........	B	9th Kansas Inf........	Los Angeles
Oliver J. C	C	89th Ohio Inf............	"
Osborne H. F.	E	192d N Y. Inf.....	"
Otis H. G..	H	23d Ohio Inf..........................	"
Philips T. F.	A	19th Iowa Inf.......................	"
Pierce L. T..........	K	56th Mass. Inf.....................	"
Plondke Julius......	A	9th N. J. Inf.....................	"
Reed J. W........ ..	B	37th Ill. Inf.....................	San Gabriel
Reese John W.......	G	50th Ill. Inf.....................	Los Angeles
Reynolds A. F.......		Oregon Cav.......................	"
Rhodes W. A. E. ...	D	6th Iowa Inf.....................	Azusa
Rice Geo. S	G	8th Ill. Inf.....................	Los Angeles
Rico Oscar F........		1st Vt. Battery.............	"
Richards D. S.......	B	19th Maine Inf....................	"
Robbins J. S.... .	L	1st Cal. Cav.	"
Roberts Wm. C......	H	2d Ill. Cav.......	"
Robinson N. D.....	B	25th Iowa Inf.....................	Artesia
Schooley E. L...	C	96th Ill. Inf..........	Los Angeles
Scott Wm. H	C	7th Ohio Inf...........	"
Shafer A. C..........	D	92d Ohio Inf.....................	"
Smith Geo. C........	K	1st Minn. Cav....................	"
Spencer J. C. M.....	I	1st Mich. Inf....................	"
Stevens F. D.......	I	12th Penn. Inf.............. ...	"
Stevens L. W.......		U. S. Navy	"
Symonds S. C.......	G	2d District of Columbia Inf.......	"
Tate Chas. M........		100th Ohio Inf....	"
Taylor W. H........	C	3d Md. Inf.......................	San Gabriel
Thomas W. H... ...	G	46th Ill. Inf.....................	Los Angeles
Thornton A. M.....	B	73d Ohio Inf.....................	"
Towner H. C........	G	11th Kansas Inf........	Santa Monica
Van Slyke D........	I	47th Ill. Inf.....................	Los Angeles
Vernon M. R... ...		78th Ill. Inf.....................	"
Wells G. Wiley..		1st N. Y. Cav....	"
West H. S..........	B	20th Iowa Inf.....................	"
Whitcomb M. S.....	I	1st Minn. Inf.....................	"
Woodhead C B.....	G	45th Iowa Inf......................	"
Woodward G. W....	G	2d Vt. Inf.........	"
Young George.......	C	18th Mich. Inf....................	"

GEN. JAS. B. STEEDMAN POST, No. 56.

SALINAS, CAL.

OFFICERS, 1886.

JOHN G. JOY...Commander
HOSEA BREESE..Senior Vice-Commander
J. A. McINTYRE...Junior Vice-Commander
E. K. ABBOTT..Adjutant
J. B. SCOTT...Quartermaster
ELIAS STINEBAUGH.. ....Surgeon
W. R. ELLIS..Chaplain
A. W. ANDERSON...Officer of the Day
D. K. McDOUGALL...Officer of the Guard
——— ———...Sergeant Major
——— ———...Quartermaster Sergeant

Meeting, Last Saturday.

NAME.	CO.	ARM OF SERVICE.	ADDRESS.
Abbott E. K.........	I	9th Ill. Cav........................	Salinas
Anderson A. W,.....	E	144th N. Y. Inf	"
Breese Hosea.......	E	64th N. Y. Inf....................	"
Burrows William....	I	124th Ill. Inf	Chualar
Cayer Ovila.........	G	14th U. S. Inf....................	Salinas
Chamberlin Chas. G.	G	49th Wis. Inf.....................	"
Clark W. H.........	E	92d N. Y. Inf.....................	"
Coffey James........	A	14th U. S. Inf....................	"
Currier Geo. M......	C	6th Cal. Inf......................	"
Eagan Frederick....	I	1st Wash. Ter. Inf...............	"
Ellis W. R..........	C	20th N. Y. Inf....................	"
Fleming W. F.......	K	135th Ind. Inf....................	Jolon
Frasier J. A........		8th N. Y Art.....................	Monterey
Full Michael	C	14th N. Y. Heavy Art	Salinas
Holton Chester.....	K	9th Vt. Inf.	"
Hyler Charles.......	B	4th Cal. Inf......................	"
Joy John G.........	E	2d Maine Inf. and L 31st Maine Inf	"
Kopmann Frank....	G	3d Mo. Inf. and G 43d Ill. Inf......	Castroville
Mantner A..........	M	4th U. S. Art....................	Salinas
McDougall D. K.....	L	2d Mass. Cav....................	"
McIntire John A....	D	8th Cal. Inf....	"
Meller Isaac........	D	24th Iowa Inf....................	Parkfield
Poole Joseph M.....	F	1st Mass. Inf....................	Salinas
Scott J. B..........	E	144th N. Y. Inf..................	"
Soberanes M. G.....	E	6th Cal. Inf.......	Soledad
Stinebaugh Elias...	I	116th Ind. Inf...................	Salinas
Trope F. H.........	E	20th N. Y. Inf...................	"
Tuttle Hiram C.....	H	8th Iowa Inf.....................	"

W. R. CORNMAN POST, No. 57.

SAN BERNARDINO, CAL.

OFFICERS, 1886.

E. C. SEYMOUR	Commander
W. H. WRIGHT	Senior Vice-Commander
TRUMAN REEVES	Junior Vice-Commander
JAMES E. MACK	Adjutant
JOHN FEUDGE	Quartermaster
—— ——	Surgeon
E. A. SMITH	Chaplain
F. T. SINGER	Officer of the Day
E. LANDON	Officer of the Guard
T. H. PALMER	Sergeant Major
W. C. CLARK	Quartermaster Sergeant

Meeting, First and Third Friday.

NAME.	CO.	SERVICE.	ADDRESS.
Ackerman Herman	C	2d Cal. Inf	San Bernardino
Allison H. J.	K	115th Ill. Inf	"
Ashdown Edwin	A	13th Penn. Cav	"
Barnard F. H.	C	6th Mass. Inf. and A 1st Mass. Cav	"
Benner J F.	K	13th Ohio Inf	Colton
Black Sam W.	F	1 6th Penn. Inf	San Bernardino
Brandenberg W M.	K	30th Mo. Inf.	"
Drickett C. H.	E	7th N. H. Inf	"
Callihan Ben. F.	I	12th Ind. Inf	Colton
Carter Luther.	B	26th N. Y. Inf	"
Clark Ward E.	G	11th N. H. Inf	"
Clark W. C	K	11th Minn. Inf	San Bernardino
Damron C N	K	120th Ill. Inf	"
Darlinton C. A		19th Ill. Inf	"
Davidson A. S.	G	36th Mass. Inf	"
Davis M. E	H	11th Wis. Inf	"
Drew Walter	G	96th Ill. Inf	"
Elmer Elliott.	I	4th Mich. Inf	"
Feudge John	H	1st and 10th Tenn. Inf	"
Frederick A	H	2d R. I. Heavy Art	"
Gerner W. B.		56th Ill. Inf	"
Geo Myron		U. S. S. Vandalia	"
Gill U. G.	B	33d Ill. Inf	"
Girard Chas.	I	4th Cal. Inf	"
Guernsey H. A.	K	27th Iowa Inf	"

NAME.	CO.	SERVICE.	ADDRESS.
Hackney John......	C	2d Cal. Cav......................	San Bernardino
Hagens Henry.......	C	5th Md. Inf................	"
Hargrave Joseph P..	F	1st Cal. Inf....................	"
Harrington P........	D	16th Mass. Inf....................	Temescal
Hartley Chas. T.	H	22d Iowa Inf....................	Colton
Hughes H. L..... ..	G	5th Cal. Inf....................	Riverside
Kane John....	D	195th Penn. Inf..................	San Bernardino
Kelley Joseph		U. S. S. Black Hawk........	"
Kendall T. C........	B	21st N.J.Inf. & 46th Vet. Res. Corps	"
La Niece James.....	F	6th Cal. Inf.	"
Landon E...........	A	12th Mich. Inf..................	"
Lawson S. S.........	C	51st Ohio Inf.....................	Colton
Littlepage E. F.....	K	12th Ky. Cav. and 10th Ind. Cav....	San Bernardino
Mack Jas. E.........	E	14th Mass. Inf..................	"
Mannen W. P.......	A	9th Kansas Cav................	"
Markel Peter........	B	65th Ohio Inf...	"
Martin Robert J.....	I	31st Iowa Inf..................	"
Oakes George P.....	E	17th Maine Inf................	"
Osborn John........	A	14th Wis. Inf.................	"
Osterhout J. D......	D	1st Cal. Cav......	"
Otis G. E...........	H	6th Mass. Inf..................	"
Palmer T. H........	B	1st Ill. Light Art...............	"
Pierce E. R........	A	32d Wis. Inf..........	Riverside
Pierce W. H.........	B	12th Mich. Inf..................	San Bernardino
Potter John D......	F	2d Mo. Battery.................	"
Price M. F., M. D....		1st Penn. Light Art..............	Colton
Reeves Truman.. ..	G	6th Ohio Cav,..................	San Bernardino
Remington C. H.....	C	9th Ill. Cav...................	"
Roberts O. P.......	D	17th Kansas Inf.......	"
Rochat Louis	B	10th Kansas Inf.......	"
Rockefeller G. W....	E	108th N. Y. Inf.....	Colton
Sampson Wm........	B	9th N. Y. Cav.................	San Bernardino
Seymour E. O.......	O	76th Penn. Inf..................	"
Simms W. J.........	F	99th Ind. Inf....................	Riverside
Singer F. T......	F	2d N. Y. Cav........	San Bernardino
Smith E. A........ .		2d Kansas Battery.	"
Smith Ed. H.......	I	4th Cal. Inf......	"
Smith Joel...... .		1st Iowa Light Battery............	"
Staples W. P........	O	98th Ill. Inf...................	"
Stevens J. W........	A	9th Kansas Cav................	"
Stone C. M..........		48th N. Y. Inf.........	"
Stone M. J......	I	2d Col. Cav...................	"
Summers A. H......	A	86th Ill Inf....................	"
Summers J. B.......	C	132d N. Y. Inf..	Riverside
Thompson John.....	O	5th Conn. Inf....................	San Bernardino
Thornton P. T......	B	4th Cal. Inf.......	"
Waldron W. R.......	C	7th Mo. Inf. and B 33d Mo Inf....	'
Whitney J. J........	C	5th N. Y. Heavy Art..............	'
Williams Geo........	E	4th Cal. Inf....................	"
Wright W. H........	K	77th N. Y. Inf....................	Colton

JESSE L. RENO POST, No. 58.

HOLLISTER, CAL.

OFFICERS, 1886.

WM. EASTMAN...Commander
HENRY SNIBLEY...Senior Vice Commander
WILBUR McCOBB...Junior Vice Commander
THOMAS YOST...Adjutant
D. K. SANFORD...Quartermaster
WM. CASHMAN...Surgeon
F. W. OLIVER...Chaplain
———...Officer of the Day
JOHN BYER...Officer of the Guard
W. H. KENNEY...Sergeant Major
GEO. W. AUSTIN.....................................Quartermaster Sergeant

---

Meeting, First and Third Saturday.

NAME.	CO.	SERVICE.	ADDRESS.
Austin G. W........	I	137th Ill. Inf.........	Hollister
Blosser W. H.......	F	5th Cal. Inf..............	San Benito
Branch C. H.......		U. S. S. Sonoma....	Sargent
Byer John	E	4th Ohio Cav...............	Emmet
Campbell H. M......	A	7th Kansas Cav....................	"
Cargill C. G.........	H	16th Vermont Inf	San Juan
Cashman Wm.......	B	7th Cal. Inf.....................	Hollister
Chaney H. J.........	F	36th Iowa Inf......................	Emmet
Cleveland L. J......	G	2d Cal. Inf......................	Hollister
Cook C. W.........	I	8th Cal. Inf.....	"
Coyle J. J.	D	9th N. J. Cav., D 52d Wis. Inf., and 38th Wis. Inf....................	"
Cunning F. A.......		32d Ind. Inf.....................	"
Eastman Wm.......	K	56th N. Y. Inf....................	"
Edel Lewis.........	E	1st N. J. Inf....................	San Francisco
Evans R. T.........	D	76th Ohio Inf....................	Hollister
Fredson A. H......	M	1st Maine Heavy Art.	Tres Pinos
Fry Obadiah........	E	54th Ind. Inf....................	Hollister
Gennett John.......	I	2d N. Y. Rifles	"
Goold Horace.......	B	1st Col. Cav....................	"
Gray D. F.........	D	36th Iowa Inf......	"
Hubbard Wm.......	L	1st Col. Cav	"
Ingels W. B.........	D	9th Iowa Inf.........	"
Kehl John...........	K	5th Wis. Inf.....................	"
Kenney W. H......	D	30th Mass. Inf...................	"

111

NAME.	CO.	SERVICE.	ADDRESS.
McCobb Austin.....	B	1st Maine Cav.....................	Hollister
McCobb Wilbur......	B	1st Maine Cav........	"
McIlroy R. H.......	E	1st Cal. Cav.....	Emmet
Moore A. H..........	L	1st Maine Inf	"
Noble F. M..........	F	4th Iowa Cav.....................	Hollister
Oliver F. W.	K	14th Maine Inf...................	"
Purvianco W. H.....	I	9th Ill. Inf.....................	Gilroy
Rohrback G. W.....	M	17th Ill. Cav	Priest Valley
Salter F. F.....	D	2d Cal. Inf.....................	Hollister
Sanford D. K	G	43th Wis. Inf. and E 25th Wis. Inf.	"
Serles Q. V. R.......	F	2d Cal. Cav.....................	"
Shirley Theodore....	H	9th Wis. Inf.....................	Sargent
Snibley Henry......	H	17th Ill. Cav	Hollister
Spider J. W.........	I	9th N. J. Inf......	"
Stephens W. J.......	G	2d Ill. Art...........	Emmet
Taylor J. I......	D	76th Ohio Inf..................	San Benito
White Nathaniel...	D	22d Maine Inf...........	Hollister
Yost Thos.	A	21st Ill. Inf.....................	"
Young J. H	A	3d Wis. Cav.....................	"

GETTYSBURG POST, No. 59.

TULARE, CAL.

___

OFFICERS, 1886.

A. P. MERRITT..Commander
J. F. FAUST...Senior Vice-Commander
JAS. RUNDEL...Junior Vice-Commander
ENOS CHURCHILL...Adjutant
WM SANDERS..Quartermaster
A. W. TYLER...Surgeon
F. H WALES..Chaplain
L. H OWEN...Officer of the Day
GEORGE MURRAY.................................Officer of the Guard
....Sergeant Major
....Quartermaster Sergeant

___

Meeting, First and Third Friday.

NAME.	CO.	SERVICE.	ADDRESS.
Bartholomew Levi..	B	84th Ill. Inf...............	Tulare City
Bolger P. G.........	C	44th Ind. Inf..............	"
Burch John F.......	F	56th N. Y. Inf.............	"
Churchhill Enos....	F	13 h Ill. Inf.............	"
Davis B. A..........	C	12th Mo. Inf..............	"
Dunning Curtis.....	B	41st Ohio Inf.............	"
Faust G. A. W.......	C	182d Ohio Inf.............	"
Faust John F.......	I	42d Ohio Inf..............	"
Flemming John.....	K & B	9th Wis. Inf..............	"
Harmon Chris.......	G	18th U. S. Inf.............	"
Hatfield Wm. R.....	D	140th Ill. Inf.............	"
Hill F..............	D	122d Ind. Inf.............	"
Jackson James......	E	20th Penn. Cav...........	"
Jones Erastus D....	C	4 h Tenn. Inf............	"
Kelms F. O...... ..	B	2d Cal. Cav..............	"
Kerr John...........	K	32d N. Y. Inf.............	"
Main Wm. H ...		3d Iowa Battery..........	"
McCoy John A.......	C	18th U. S. Inf............	"
Merritt Alfred P.....	E	16th Iowa Inf............	"
Murray George......	L	3d Mass. Inf.............	"
Neff A. D........ ..	B	116th N. Y. Inf..........	"
Owen L. H......	B	14th Ind. Inf.............	"
Phillips Christop'r C	F	27th Mo. Inf.............	"
Rundel J. N.........		U. S. Navy...............	"
Sanders Wm. M.....	B	32d Mo. Inf..............	"
Sheppard Wm.......	H	2d Cal. Cav..............	"
Smith W. S. F.......	E	69th Ill. Inf. and B 152d Ill. Inf ...	"
Thurber Chester.	L	2d N. Y. Cav.............	"
Tyler A. W.........	D	1st Ohio Cav.............	"
Wagner F...........	K	2d N. Y. Rifles...........	"
Wales Frederick H..	I	12d Mass. Inf.	"
Wilson Delos E.....	F	10th Wis. Inf............	"
Wilson Richard W...	D	1st Mass. Heavy Art.......	"

113

SHILOH POST, No. 60.

COMPTON, CAL.

OFFICERS, 1886.

MELVIN MUDGE..Commander
MARTIN ELFTMAN...Senior Vice-Commander
S. M. DISE...Junior Vice Commander
C. MEALEY...Adjutant
JOHN R. HANN..Quartermaster
JOSIAH H. SKILLING...Surgeon
DAVID SMITH..Chaplain
HENRY C. KELSEA...Officer of the Day
JOSEPH SANTONGUE...Officer of the Guard
GEO. W. LAZENDY...Sergeant Major
FRANCIS E. BARRON....................................Quartermaster Sergeant

---

Meeting, every Friday.

NAME.	CO.	SERVICE.	ADDRESS.
Barron Francis E. ..	L	2d Mass. Cav.....................	Compton
Dise S. M............	H	39th Mo. Inf............	"
Bowser Lewis W....	H	39th Mo. Inf.........	"
Dunn J. C..........		U S. Navy	Long Branch
Elftman Martin.....	K	14th Wis. Inf..................	Compton
Haizlip John........	I	10th Kansas Inf...............	Los Angeles
Hann John R........	A	20th Ind. Inf.....	Compton
Kelsea Henry C. ...	I	5th N. H. Inf...................	"
Lazenby Geo. W.....	I	7th Iowa Inf.....	"
McComas Asbury.. ..	G	5th Kansas Cav.................	"
McFarland Andrew..	A	14th Ill. Inf.....	"
Medley C............	A	3d Minn. Inf..................	"
Mudge Melvin		11th Mich. Inf................	"
Oman Wm..........	E	1st Cal. Inf..................	Wilmington
Rolfe Geo. W........	C	20th Mich. Inf................	Compton
Santongue Joseph...	F	3d Wis. Cav.....	"
Skilling J. H., M. D..		10th Ill. Cav......	Los Angeles
Smith David.........	E	3d Cal. Inf.....	Compton
Stevens Anson.......	I	28th Iowa Inf....	"
Tripp Wm. H........	I	176th Ohio Inf..................	"

114

VICKSBURG POST, No. 61.

POMONA, CAL.

OFFICERS, 1886.

H. ENO...Commander
C. HOWE..Senior Vice-Commander
L. W. COWLES..Junior Vice-Commander
E. B. SMITH...Adjutant
J E. McCOMAS...Quartermaster
M. NEIERBURG..Surgeon
L. P. CRAWFORD..Chaplain
T. C. THOMAS..Officer of the Day
H. H. WILLIAMS..Officer of the Guard
——— ———...Sergeant Major
————..Quartermaster Sergea..t

Meeting, First Saturday after Full Moon, and each two weeks thereafter.

NAME.	CO.	SERVICE.	ADDRESS.
Bissell H. L.........		U. S. S. Isaac Smith and Sattellite..	Pomona
Bloomer A. C........	K	57th Ill. Inf.....................	"
Bodenhamer W. J...	A	6th Mo. Cav.....	"
Boutell C. H.......		Marine Art.....................	"
Carpenter L. W.	I	82d Ohio Inf....................	"
Clair L. L...........	A	Hachees Minn. Cav.....	"
Cochran R. R........	A	1st N. H. Art..................	"
Cord T. A........	E	14th Ohio Inf..................	"
Corder L. T.	H	61st Ill. Inf...................	"
Cowles Luman.	C	8th Mass. Inf...................	"
Cowles Lyman......	L	4th Mass. Cav.................	"
Crawford L. P......	H	105th Ill. Inf..................	San Pedro
Crowell J. R....... .	D	154th N. Y. Inf................	Pomona
Eccles Jas. S.......	E	14th Ohio Inf..................	Azusa
Eccles W. H........ ...	G	14th Ohio Inf..................	"
Englehardt H. D...	C	83d Ind. Inf.	Pomona
Eno H..............	B	8th Mo. Inf.....................	"
Fuller Wm	H	18th Kansas Cav....	Cucamonga
Germond T. M.. ..	E	35th N. Y. Inf.................	Pomona
Graves L. D.........	C	17th Ohio Inf...	"
Howe Con..........	I	15th Conn. Inf.................	"
Howe Edwin.......	E	9th Minn. Inf..................	"
Hughes P. W........	M	8th Mich. Cav.................	"
Leving J. D.	D	8th U. S. Cav..................	Cucamonga
McComas J. E.	G	5th Kansas Cav	Pomona
Miles E. C..........	E	24th Iowa Inf.....	"
Miller J. T..........	C	2d Iowa Inf.....	"
Miller S. J......	H	1st Mo. Cav....................	Alosta
Mullally Geo. S......	D	7th Ohio Cav..................	Pomona
Neierburg M........	F	12th Ill. Inf...................	"
Scanlon M..........	I	2d U. S. Art	"
Seaver Nelson.	F	5th Kansas Inf.................	"
Sheldon M. M.......	I	142d N. Y. Inf................	"
Smith E. B.........	C	85th N. Y. Inf................	"
Smith John.........	H	4th Cal. Inf....................	"
Thomas Henry......	C	2d U. S. Cav...	"
Thomas T. C........	A	6th Wis. Inf..................	"
Williams H. H......	G	14th Iowa Inf....	"

BARRETT POST, No. 62.

PRESCOTT, A. T.

OFFICERS, 1886.

GEO. H. TINKER...Commander
A. G. RANDAL..Senior Vice-Commander
CHAS. H. ALLABACH....................................Junior Vice-Commander
J. J. GOSPER...Adjutant
GEO. W. SINES..Quartermaster
GEO. D. KENDALL ....Surgeon
N. L. GUTHRIE...Chaplain
R. GRIGSBY...Officer of the Day
JAMES BUTLER..Officer of the Guard
J. W. CLAY..Sergeant Major
JAS. A. GUILD..Quartermaster Sergeant

Meeting, Second and last Tuesday.

NAME.	CO.	SERVICE.	ADDRESS.
Allabach Chas H ...	E	54th Penn. Inf....................	Prescott
Atkinson B..........	K	69th N. Y. Inf................. ...	"
Berry Geo. E........	F	1st Cal. Inf.....................	"
Bisbee E. T.........	E	29th Maine Inf....	"
Bishop Charles......	G	29th Ind. Inf. and F 7th Ind. Cav..	"
Blackburn John	A	16th U. S. Inf.........	"
Butler James.		2d U. S. Inf....................	"
Capelli Carlo.......	L	104th Penn. Inf..................	"
Chandler Isaac......	G	8th Ill. Inf......................	Lynx Creek
Clay J. W..........	C	6th Kansas Cav............. ...	Prescott
Cook James O.......	C	6th Mo. Cav.....................	San Diego
Crapo B. B.........	E	17th Conn. Inf.	Skull Valley
Crellins John.......	C	12th Wis. Inf...................	Prescott
Dake C. P..........	E	5th Mich. Inf...................	"
DeWitt Wm.	H	55th Penn. Inf..............	Whipple Barracks
Donaldson Chas. E..	C	186th N. Y. Inf..........	Ash Fork
Dugan Michael......	A	10th U. S. Inf.........	Agua Fria
Duprez Jos..........	E	4th R. I. Inf..................	Prescott
Ebbett Geo.		U. S. Marine Corps...	"
Fell Timothy........	A	82d Ohio Inf.................	Verde
Ferguson Wm. H....	I	4th Cal. Inf......................	Prescott
Fisher Chas. F.. ...	B	58th Mass. Inf	"
Ford Patrick........	K	3d U. S. Inf.....	"
Fosdick Chas. H.....	K	186th N. Y. Inf..............	"
Gillenwater A. P....	D	29th Iowa Inf.............	"

116

NAME.	CO.	SERVICE.	ADDRESS.
Oonzales Reyes......	F	1st New Mexico Inf.....	Prescott
Gosper J. J.........	I	8.h Ill. Cav.....	"
Grigsby R...........	A	10th Ill. Cav	"
Guild James A......	F	1st Mass. Heavy Art....	"
Guthrie N. L........		.d Independent Ohio Art........	"
Hall J. L............		5th U. S. Inf......	"
Henklo Jacob........	A	20th N. Y. Inf......	"
Herman Michael ...	F	2d Mo. Cav........................	Lynx Creek
Jesson Fritz........		29th Mass. Inf....................	Prescott
Kendall Geo. D......	I	7th Cal. Inf......................	"
King P	B	4th Cal. Inf....................	"
Kirwagen John......	D	9th N. Y. Art....................	Verde
Koch Wm...........	K	164th N. Y. Inf....	Prescott
Marsh J. H. A... ..	B	3d Ind. Cav.....	"
Maxwell James C... ..	B	49th Mo. Inf.....................	"
McCandlessJ.N.,M.D		77th Penn.Inf....................	"
Miller Sam'l J.......		1st N. M. Inf.	"
Murray G. W........	B	1st N. Y. Mounted Rifles	"
O'Boyle Daniel......	I	19th Mich. Inf.	"
O'Neil Wm. J.	E	72d N. Y. Inf....................	"
Otto T.......... ..	I	4th U. S. Art....................	"
Pease R. W	G	4th Cal. Inf.....................	Whipple Barracks
Randal A. G.........	A	4th Cal. Inf.....................	Prescott
Rees S. C...........	G	46th Ohio Inf....................	Chino Valley
Reeso John.........		79th Ohio Inf....................	Prescott
Saunders Chas......	M	2d U. S. Art.....................	"
Schindler W. F. R...	I	2d Cal. Inf......................	"
Sines Geo. W.......	C	214th Penn. Inf..................	"
Taylor Griffith......		1st Cal. Inf.....................	"
Tinker Geo. H		14th U. S. Inf...	"
Wade Chas. A.......	C	3d R. I. Heavy Art...............	"
White Geo. L........	G	6th N. J. Inf......	Agua Fria
Williams P. A.......	C	16th Mo. Cav....................	Prescott
Woods W. A.........		1st East Tenn Inf.............. ...	"

SAN FRANCISCO

ANTIETAM POST, No. 63.

PETALUMA, CAL.

OFFICERS, 1886.

C. MARTIN DRYDEN...Commander
HENRY P. BRAINERD....................................Senior Vice-Commander
ROBERT F. JOHNSON......................................Junior Vice-Commander
JOSEPH B FULMER...Adjutant
CHARLES HETTRICH................................... ....Quartermaster
———— —— ——..Surgeon
JAMES C. HARVEY...... ....Chaplain
BENJ. HAYS...Officer of the Day
JOHN W. WILLIARD...Officer of the Guard
EDWARD B. LEEDS..Sergeant Major
———— ———— ... .Quartermaster Sergeant

Meeting, Second and Fourth Saturday.

NAME.	CO.	SERVICE.	ADDRESS.
Adams Alfred.......	E	12th Ill. Cav........................	Petaluma
Brainerd H. P.......	D	31st Mass. Inf.......	"
Corbett R. S.	D	14th Iowa...........................	"
Dryden C. M........	I	22d Penn. Cav......................	"
Engel J.............	I	8th Ill. Inf	"
Fulmer J. B........	D	9th U. S. Inf......................	"
Graves S. F.		U. S. Navy	"
Hardin Parley.....	C	7th Ohio Inf.......	"
Harvey J. C.........	D	2d Maine Inf	"
Hays B..............	F	9th Mass. Inf....................	"
Hettrich Chas.......	E	12th N. Y. Inf....................	"
Johnson R F.......	E	13th Mass. Inf...............	"
Kuhnle J	M	1st Mich. Cav.....................	"
Leeds E. B.........	F	9th Ohio Inf.....................	"
Murphy A. J........	E	3d Md. Cav.......................	"
Schleicher Fred.....	C	35th N. Y. Inf....................	"
Seiters Henry..	D	15th Ohio Inf...	"
Sloper David.......	A	14th Iowa Inf....................	"
Smith D. A..........	D	20th Ill. Inf.....................	"
Somerville P.......	I	4th Cal. Inf	"
Tally H..............	E	3d and 5th Penn. Cav...........	"
Williard J. W.......	E	58th Ill. Inf.......	·
Winans J. L.	D	100th Ind. Inf....................	"

118

L. H. ROUSSEAU POST, No 64.

KELSEYVILLE, CAL.

OFFICERS, 1886.

JOHN S. MATHER...Commander
JAMES A. HARRIS..Senior Vice-Commander
IRA M. CARPENTER.......................................Junior Vice-Commander
W. G. YOUNG...Adjutant
ALBION DICKINSON..Quartermaster
R. G. REYNOLDS...Surgeon
L. W. SIMMONS..Chaplain
J. A. WILSON..Officer of the Day
T. J. SAGERTY..Officer of the Guard
——— ———..Sergeant Major
——— ———......................................Quartermaster Sergeant

Meeting, Saturday on or after Full of the Moon.

NAME.	CO.	SERVICE.	ADDRESS.
Badgerow Weston...	H	27th Ohio Inf.	Kelseyville
Carpenter Ira M.....	H	2d Vt. Inf.	"
Christie Wm........		U. S. Navy	Upper Lake
Cummings John....	F	23d Ill. Inf.	Lower Lake
Dickinson Albion...		U. S. S. Sabine	Kelseyville
Duffy Henry W......	B	7th Cal. Inf.	"
Evans Luke.	G	22d N. Y. Cav.	Lower Lake
Gillett Charles......	G	1st Ohio Inf.	"
Hampson H. A.....	A	67th Ohio Inf.	Cloverdale
Harding Charles S..	E	203d Penn. Inf.	Kelseyville
Harris James A.....	B	40th Iowa Inf.	Lower Lake
Mather J. S..........	I	9th Iowa Inf.	Kelseyville
McElroy Wm........	K	76th Ohio Inf.	Lakeport
Nutter S. O........	F	2d N. H. Inf.	Kelseyville
Porter Frank H......	B	3d Wis. Inf.	"
Reynolds C. C.......	B	3d Cal. Inf.	"
Reynolds R. G.......	A	193d Penn. Inf.	Upper Lake
Sagerty T. J.........	E	11th U. S. Inf.	Kelseyville
Scudamore G.......		80th Ill. Inf.	Lakeport
Seeley David T......	K	2d Cal. Cav.	Kelseyville
Simmons L. W.......		53d Ill. Inf.	Lower Lake
Sweetser G. W.......	G	8th and 11th Mass. Inf.	Kelseyville
Vickery W. K........	B	4th Minn. Inf.	"
Virgin Thomas......	C	37th Iowa Inf.	Lakeport
Wallen Ezra........	D	2d Cal. Inf.	Kelseyville
Wayne G. W....	F	9th Ky. Cav.	Lower Lake
Wilson J. A........	F	57th Ill. Inf.	Kelseyville
Young W. G........	H	27th Ill. Inf.	"

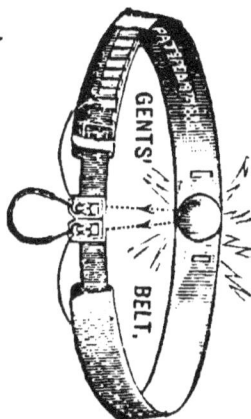

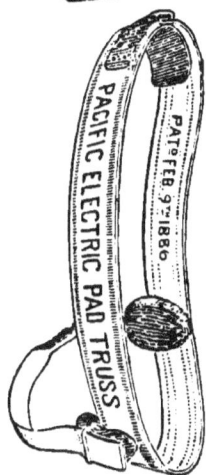

WM. H. SEWARD POST, No. 65.

WOODLAND, CAL.

OFFICERS, 1886.

W. H WINNE. ....Commander
L. W. HILLIKER...Senior Vice-Commander
J. T. WALLIN................................ ... .Junior Vice-Commander
ALLEN T. BIRD..Adjutant
L. G. STONE.............................. ....Quartermaster
A. C. KEATING......... ....Surgeon
W. C. DOUGLAS...Chaplain
W. D. C. HARNISH..Officer of the Day
GEO. W. MYRICK.................................. ....Officer of the Guard
S. M. MONTGOMERY..Sergeant Major
JOHN L. SPONG..Quartermaster Sergeant

Meeting, First and Third Saturday,

NAME.	CO.	SERVICE.	ADDRESS.
Bird Allen T...	E	141st Ill. Inf. and I. 11th Ill. Cav..	Woodland
Brinkman H........	H	4th N. Y. Inf	"
Card W. D..........	K	128th N.Y.Inf.& 2d Bat.Vet.R.Corps	"
Comfort Jos...... .		U. S S. Cowslip...................	"
Condon Elijah......	F	7th Maine Inf......	"
Douglas Wm. C.....	C	39th Mo. Inf..........	"
Farnham E. S........	K	12th Mich. Inf....................	"
Gaynor Patrick.....	F	28th Mass. Inf...................	"
Haines Jacob........	C	84th Ohio Inf....................	"
Harnish W. D. C....	C	11th Ill. Cav....................	"
Henagin David......	F	106th N. Y Inf	"
Henagin John.......	A	92d N. Y. Inf...................	"
Hevel Christopher..	C	8th Ill. Inf.....................	Madison
Hilliker Loron W...	K	16th Mich. Inf...................	Woodland
Holloway John R....	K	134th Ind. Inf...................	"
Keating A. C........	B	1st Mich. Sharpshooters..	"
Kiehl John P........	F	28th Penn. Inf...................	"
Mantaney Henry....	A	3d Wis. Inf......................	"
Mantz John..........	H	58th N. Y. Inf.	"
Mayo Hugh L.......	C	27th Ill. Inf. and 9th Ill. Inf......	Yolo
Miller Charles.......	C	47th Iowa Inf....................	Woodland
Montgomery Sam'l M	C	8th Cal. Inf.....................	"
Myers Daniel........	D	36th Iowa Inf....................	"
Myrick Geo. W......	C	13th Maine Inf..................	"
Nalk Caspar,........,,	G	84th Ill. Inf....................	"

120

NAME.	CO.	SERVICE.	ADDRESS.
Palmer Perry........	G	30th Ill. Inf.................	Woodland
Patterson W. M....	H	25th Wis. Inf.....................	Capay
Pearson J. B........	F	1st Wash.Ter.Inf.& A 2d Mass.H.Art	Woodland
Powers John W......	E	43d Mass. Inf	"
Sebastian R. M......	A	7th Kansas Cav...................	"
Spencer W. F.......	D	8th Cal. Inf.....................	"
Spong John L.......	A	1st Md. Inf..........	"
Stone L. G..........	A	9th Kansas Cav...................	"
Stott Samuel.... ...	E	76th Penn. Inf....	Madison
Thomas Sabin R.....	K	4th U. S. Vet. Res...............	Sacramento
Tully Stephen......	H	90th Ohio Inf.....................	Woodland
Wallin John T......	I	7th Iowa Inf....	"
Ward J. M..........		6th Mich. Inf...........	"
Welch Wm. Thomas.	B	2d Ill. Light Art..................	"
Whittum Stephen C.	H	8th Cal. Inf.....................	"
Wilcox S. J.........	F	1st Nevada Cav...................	"
Williams David.....	H	3d Wis. Inf......................	"
Winne Wm. H.......	B	32d N. Y. Inf., C 15th N. Y. Engineers and B Guard Bat.N.Y.Harbor	"
Wood Wm. E........	E	25th Ill. Inf.....................	"
Woolridge C. C.....	A	107th Ill. Inf....................	Napa

ROBERT ANDERSON POST, No. 66.

LOMPOC, CAL.

OFFICERS, 1886.

C. J. YOUNG. ....Commander
W. II. PECK..Senior Vice-Commander
GEO. INGAMELLS,...Junior Vice-Commander
GEO. S. ELSEMORE...Adjutant
JOHN JOHNSON..Quartermaster
J. W. SAUNDERS..Surgeon
J. B. HIBBETS...Chaplain
H. C. McCABE...Officer of the Day
I. N. DILLE..Officer of the Guard
JOHN T. STEWART...Sergeant Major
JOHN SARGENT...Quartermaster Sergeant

Meeting, Thursday on or before Full Moon.

NAME.	CO.	SERVICE.	ADDRESS.
Dille I. N......	D	192d Ohio Inf. and I. 4th Ill. Cav..	Lompoc
Elsemore Geo. S.....	A	9th Maine Inf.......................	"
Gray W. B.....	K	14th Iowa Inf.......................	"
Harris J. S..........	G	5th Iowa Inf...............	"
Harris J. W.........	G	35th Iowa Inf.......................	"
Henning D. F.	F	76th Ohio Inf.......................	"
Hibbets J. B........	H	82d Ohio Inf..................... ..	"
Ingamells Geo.....	I	27th Iowa Inf...	Santa Rita
Jackson Wm........		3d Mo. Cav.........................	Lompoc
Johnson John.......	G	1st Cal. Cav.......................	"
Kelley E. C.........	A	125th Ohio Inf.....................	"
Mannsell G. W.....		U. S. S. Roanoke..................	"
McCabe H. C........	I	26th Mich. Inf.....................	"
Murray H...........	C	24th Iowa Inf......................	"
Nichols M. S........	B	97th N. Y. Inf............... .	"
Peck W. H..........	E	5th Kansas Cav....................	"
Perry Thomas..... .		U. S. Navy	"
Sargent John........	K	193d Ohio Inf.....................	"
Saunders J. W.......	H	3d Iowa Inf........................	"
Stewart John T.....	I	49th Mo. Inf.......................	"
Warwick H. C.......	D	32d Iowa Inf................	"
Young C. J..........	G	5th Mich. Cav......................	"

GEN. T. E. G. RANSOM POST, No. 67.

FLAGSTAFF, A. T.

OFFICERS, 1886.

LOUIS BURNS...Commander
D. F. HART..Senior Vice-Commander
JOSEPH R. LOCKETT..............................Junior Vice-Commander
WILLIAM GARDNER...Adjutant
GEORGE HOXWORTH ....Quartermaster
——— ———...Surgeon
JAMES W. SPAFFORD...Chaplain
JOHN ROSENBAUGH...Officer of the Day
——— ....Officer of the Guard
ROBERT GREER...Sergeant Major
WM. A. DYER..Quartermaster Sergeant

Meeting, Second and last Saturday.

NAME.	CO.	SERVICE.	ADDRESS.
Burns George.......	I	3d Mass. Heavy Art...............	Flagstaff
Burns Louis........	D	11th Ill. Inf.....................	"
Conrad Adam........	A	32d Ind. Inf.....................	Hackberry
Dyer Wm. A.	B	4th Penn. Cav.	"
Gardner William....	H	102d Penn. Inf..................	Flagstaff
Greer Robert........	G	9th Ill. Cav.	"
Hart D. F...........	I	47th Ill. Inf....................	"
Hill Leonidas.......	A	23d Mo. Inf.....................	"
Hoxworth George....	F	65th Ohio Inf...................	"
Lockett Jos. R......	G	21st Mo. Inf....................	"
Marvin Henry.	I	31st Ill. Inf....................	Belmont
McDonald E. G. ..	A	69th N. Y. Inf..................	Hackberry
Noo an Patrick K...	G	27th Penn. Inf..................	Flagstaff
Rosborough James..	B	1st Ohio Light Art	Hackberry
Rosenbaugh John.	E	3d Col. Cav....................	Flagstaff
Smith J. B..........	I	1st N. Y. Cav..................	"
Spafford James W...	C	5th Iowa Inf....................	"
Taft William........	F	1st Mich. Light Art.............	Hackberry
Wilkerson Horace...	E	28th Wis. Inf....................	Flagstaff

MAJ. E. W. EDDY POST, No. 68.

SANTA PAULA, CAL.

OFFICERS, 1886.

JOHN B. SALTMARSH..Commander
CYRUS KENNEY ....Senior Vice-Commander
HUGH COMFORT.............. ....Junior Vice-Commander
LEONARD SKINNER.. ....Adjutant
ELIJAH BOOR... Quartermaster
M. M. McCULLEY................... . ...Surgeon
J. R. D. SAY.. .....Chaplain
M. ATMORE...Officer of the Day
W. T. SCOTT..Officer of the Guard
—— ——...Sergeant Major
—— ——...Quartermaster Sergeant

Meeting, Thursday on or before Full Moon.

NAME.	CO.	SERVICE.	ADDRESS.
Atmore M............	K	2d Cal. Cav........................	Santa Paula
Bolton J. A..........	G	2d Cal. Inf............	"
Boor Elijah.........	E	120th Ohio Inf....................	"
Comfort H. B..	K	6th Cal. Inf......................	"
Dull W. W...... ..		U. S. Lancers....................	Alma
Jepson I. C..........	B	14th Penn. Inf....	Santa Paula
Kenney Cyrus.......	C	64th Ill. Inf.....................	"
McCulley M. M......	H	4th Penn. Cav....................	"
Rice Lewis	B	43d Penn. Inf......	"
Rowell George W....	G	22d Maine Inf....................	"
Saltmarsh John B...	A	4th Cal. Inf.....................	"
Say J. R. D..........	I	105th Penn. Inf....	"
Scott Wm. T........	G	7th Mo. Inf......................	"
Skinner L...........		9th West Va. Inf.................	"
Warren James R.....	G	13th Kansas Inf..................	"

BYRON HOT SPRINGS.

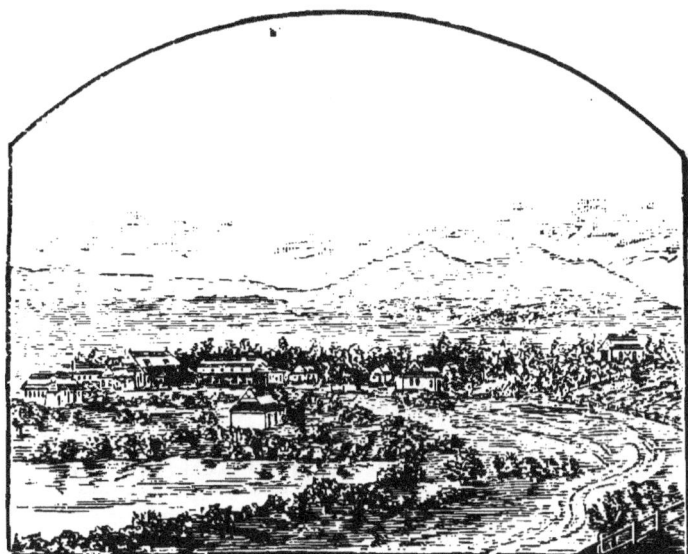

Visitors to California who are suffering from Rheumatism, Neuralgia, Sciatica, Asthma, Catarrh, or any form of blood or skin diseases, should not lose the opportunity of being cured or benefited by using these waters.

Hot Salt, Hot Sulphur, Magnesia and Iron Springs and Baths; also, hot Mud Baths, the best known.

These waters in curative properties are equal to the famous Arkansas Hot Springs, and are only three hours by rail from San Francisco.

Take 9:30 A. M. or 3:30 P. M. train foot of Market street. Hotel carriage meets every train. Hotel accommodations, table, etc., equal to the best in the State.

For Descriptive Circular address:

Manager Byron Springs,

BYRON, CAL.

GEN. O. M. MITCHELL POST, No. 69.

RENO, NEVADA.

———

OFFICERS, 1886.

T. F. LAYCOCK..Commander
A. A. EVANS..Senior Vice-Commander
————..Junior Vice-Commander
N. P. JAQUES..Adjutant
A. FLETCHER..Quartermaster
II. II. HOGAN..Surgeon
WM. LUCAS..Chaplain
D. D. BUTTERFIELD..Officer of the Day
J. C. HAYNES..Officer of the Guard
WM. LONGFIELD..Sergeant Major
C. F. POWELL..Quartermaster Sergeant

———

Meeting, Second Saturday.

NAME.	CO.	SERVICE.	ADDRESS.
Bastian T. H........	O	97th Penn. Inf....................	Wadsworth
Bechtel W. L........	H	21st Penn. Cav........	Reno
Bemis E. P., M. D...		12th Iowa Inf. and 8th Iowa Inf....	"
Bennet John E	B	22d Ohio Inf....................	Quincy, Cal.
Blair J. J........ ...	E	3d Cal. Inf....................	Merrillville, Cal.
Butterfield D. D.....	H	11th Ohio Inf. and I 61st Ohio Inf.	Reno
Clark Chas. W.......	K	119th Ill. Inf....................	"
Cole Wallace W......	F	3d R. I. Inf....................	"
Evans A. A..........		38th Ohio Inf....................	"
Fisher J. J..........	F	2d U. S. Art....................	Greenville, Cal.
Fletcher A..........	B	29th Me. Inf.& E 28th Vet. R.Corps	Reno
Fortimer Theodore..	H	129th Ind. Inf	Greenville, Cal.
Ginnety James......	D	17th Wis. Inf....................	"
Hamlin S. A........	G	5th N. H. Inf. and G. 1st N. H. Inf.	Boca, Cal.
Haynes Wm. H......	A	2d Maine Inf....................	Reno
Hogan H. H., M. D..	G	142d N. Y. Inf....................	"
Hudson Pliny.......	G	9th Ill. Cav....................	Greenville, Cal.
Hussey J. H........	A	16th Maine Inf....................	Reno
Hymers John.......	C	144th N. Y. Inf....................	Pyramid
Jaques N. P........	F	19th Maine Inf....	Reno
Jeffrey A. R........	E	50th Ill. Inf....................	St. Clair
Johnson Charles....	O	26th Iowa Inf....................	Reno
Keating Patrick.....	G	1st N. Y. Inf....................	"
Kemp S. R..........	A	17th Mass. Inf....................	"
Laycock T. F..		U. S. Navy.	"

125

NAME.	CO.	SERVICE.	ADDRESS.
Libbey George......	K	50th Mass. Inf......................	Reno
Lindsey Fulton......	L	1st Cal. Cav.......................	"
Lindsey W. E.......	E	46th Ill. Inf.......................	"
Longfield Wm. M...	D	1st Wis. Cav.......................	"
Lucas Wm., Rev....	B	71st Penn. Inf.....................	"
Mussey N. D........	B	5th Mich. Inf......................	Wadsworth
Palmer W. S........	H	28th Maine Inf.............	Reno
Powell C. F.........	C	7th Penn Cav........	"
Rogers Wm. W.....	C	137th Ohio Inf.....................	Elko
Rood Oliver........	G	8th Vt. Inf ... .·.....	Reno
Runyon B. W.......	F	46th Ill. Inf.......................	Eagleville, Cal.
Sproul James......	L	1st Cal. Cav.........	Reno
Stevens Henry......	H	187th Penn. Inf.....	"
Welch Alex........	B	153d Ill. Inf.......................	"
West Peter..........	F	7th Iowa Cav......................	Lovelocks
Williams W. H. H...	H	19th Iowa Inf. and 7th Iowa Cav...	Reno
Wilson H. C........	F	18th Mo. Inf.............	"
Wormley H. P......	K	23d N. Y. Inf. and G 8th Cal. Inf...	Quincy, Cal.

FRED. STEELE POST, No. 70.

SAN LUIS OBISPO, CAL.

OFFICERS, 1886.

R. B. TREAT...Commander
J. T. WALKER...Senior Vice-Commander
F. E. DARKE...Junior Vice-Commander
JOHN HAMLIN..Adjutant
JOHN LANDELL..Quartermaster
J. H. SEATON ....Surgeon
R. E. JACK..Chaplain
S. D. BALLOU..Officer of the Day
—— ——...Officer of the Guard
WM. GINGERY...Sergeant Major
FRANK CONLEE...Quartermaster Sergeant

Meeting, Third Saturday.

NAME.	CO.	SERVICE.	ADDRESS.
Abbott S. H.........	E	1st Mich. Light Art................	Arroyo Grande
Ballou S. D..........	H	49th N. Y. Inf.....................	San Luis Obispo
Canon W S.........	C	49th Ohio Inf......................	"
Coulee Frank.......	D	65th Ill. Inf...	Creston
Currier J. C.........	I	11th N. H. Inf....................	San Miguel
Darke F. E..........	G	57th Penn. Inf....................	San Luis Obispo
Ferguson James....	H	12th Ill. Inf......................	Arroyo Grande
Fowler James D.....	I	9th Mo. Cav......................	Cayucos
Frick Franklin......	D	111th Ill. Inf,....................	Paso Robles
Gingery W. M.......	A	28th Iowa Inf.....................	San Luis Obispo
Hall H. H...........	B	Penn. Light Art..................	"
Hamlin John........	H	23d Iowa Inf.....................	"
Ide B. C............	C	24th Mich. Inf....................	Arroyo Grande
Jack R. E...........	C	56th N. Y. Inf....,.	San Luis Obispo
Kuhl Wm....	D	5th Mo. Inf.......................	"
Landell John........	A	198th Penn. Inf..................	"
Lane Wm...........	I	24th Iowa Inf....	Arroyo Grande
Martin Charles......	H	56th Penn. Inf..................	San Luis Obispo
Ohms Jos. J.........	G	46th N. Y. Inf..................	Cambria
Orr R. D............	E	10th Mich. Cav..................	San Luis Obispo
Pico Jose R........	A	1st Cal. Native Cav..............	"
Rackliffe Levi.......	B	19th Maine Inf..................	"
Ransom John.......	A	14th N. Y. Cav..................	"
Seaton J. H., M. D..		21st Mo. Inf........... ..	"
Stainford G. B......	A	23d N. Y. Inf..................	"
Treat R. B.		4th Ohio Inf....................	"
Walker J. T........	H	25th Ill. Inf..................	"
Webb Marcus L. D..	G	21st Mo. Inf....................	San Simeon
Webster Geo........	F	10th N. Y. Art.................	San Luis Obispo
Wood Geo P.........	I	29th Mo. Inf....................	Arroyo Grande

127

COL. E. D. BAKER POST, No. 71.

NEWCASTLE, CAL.

OFFICERS, 1886.

M. D. LININGER..Commander
GEO. D. KELLOGG.................... ....Senior Vice-Commander
WM. F. PAYNE.....................................Junior Vice-Commander
JOHN ADAMS................... ....Adjutant
GEO. B. HEWES..Quartermaster
W. S. PATE...Surgeon
A. L. JONES...Chaplain
A. G. ABBOTT...Officer of the Day
BENJ. ALLSPAUGH...Officer of the Guard
WM. H. SCOTT...Sergeant Major
T. S. NASH..Quartermaster Sergeant

Meeting, Monthly.

NAME.	CO.	SERVICE.	ADDRESS.
Abbott A. G.........	K	14th Wis. Inf.....................	Newcastle
Adams John.........	G	45th Ohio Inf......	"
Allspaugh Benj......	D	3d Mich. Inf......................	Lincoln
Ayers Marcellis......	D	15th Mo. Cav....................	Ophir
Fenton H. W...	E	76th Penn. Inf....	Auburn
Fithian Amos.......	A	4th Cal. Inf.....................	Ophir
Guthrie James......	E	3d Iowa Inf.......................	Lincoln
Hewes Geo. B.......	F	8th Ill. Cav.......	Ophir
Johnson Ezra.......	L	3d Ohio Cav.....................	Roseville
Jones A. L..........	L	1st Maine Cav....................	Penryn
Jones J. F.........	A	8th Maine Inf....................	Auburn
Kellogg Geo. D.....	A	23d Wis. Inf.....................	Newcastle
Lininger M. D..	E	28th Iowa Inf....................	Auburn
Malone Robert P....	C	42d Ill. Inf.....................	Lincoln
Martin H. V.........	A	10th N. Y. Inf....................	Alta
Nash T. S...........	H	1st U. S. Sharpshooters...	Anburn
Pate W. S..........	D	35th Ill. Inf.....................	Ophir
Payne Wm. F........	G	2d N. J. Inf......................	Lincoln
Philbrick J. S......	G	4th Ohio Inf.....................	"
Plantz W. A.........	E	46th Ill. Inf.....................	Ophir
Scott Wm. H........	F	22d Mich. Inf....................	Penryn
Sweezy Henry.......	F	86th Ohio Inf...................	"
Taylor H. H........	C	45th Mo. Inf....................	Ophir
White Robert.......	K	45th Iowa Inf...	Newcastle

GEN. GEO. S. EVANS POST, No. 72.

REDWOOD CITY, CAL.

———

OFFICERS, 1886

B. A. RANKIN..Commander
J. H. HALLETT.... ....Senior Vice-Commander
JOHN POOLE...Junior Vice-Commander
E. O. RHODES ....Adjutant
P. P. CHAMBERLAIN...Quartermaster
C. B. SEARS...Surgeon
W. H PASCOE..Chaplain
E. W. THOMPSON.... ....Officer of the Day
L. L. STEVENS..Officer of the Guard
——— ....Sergeant Major
——— ———. ....Quartermaster Sergeant

———

Meeting, Third Friday.

NAME.	CO.	SERVICE.	ADDRESS.
Calhoun J. A........	C	136th Ind.Inf. & M 1st Ind.Hea'y Art	San Francisco
Chamberlain P. P...	A	3d Minn. Inf............	Redwood City
Filkins Geo. E......	I	15th U. S. Colored Inf.............	San Francisco
Hallett Joseph H....		U. S. S. Kingfisher	Woodside
Johnson David M...	B	50th Ill. Inf.....................	Spanishtown
Kelly John..........		U. S. Marine Corps..	San Mateo
Laes Charles........		17th U. S. Inf....................	La Honda
Maese L. D.........		1st Mo. Inf...	San Mateo
McNulty R. J........	A	9th Ind. Inf......................	Woodside
O'Neill John........	I	1st U. S. Art.....................	Menlo Park
Pascoe W. H........		U. S. S. Niagara..................	Redwood City
Poole John..........	D	16th Ill. Cav.....................	"
Randall Chas. D.....	D	3d N. H. Inf......	"
Rankin B. A........	A	1st Cal. Cav....	"
Rhodes Elbert O....		U. S. S. Hunchback.....	"
Stevens L. L........	A	26th Maine Inf.............	"
Thompson E. W.....	K	4th Cal. Inf.....................	"
Waeder Ludwig.....	D	75th N. Y. Inf.....	"
Walker Henry.......	A	28th Ill. Inf.....................	"
Woolf Martin	I	101th Ohio Inf.....	"

129

EDDY LEE POST, No. 73.

FALL RIVER MILLS, CAL.

OFFICERS, 1886.

N. SCHOFIELD...Commander
JAMES I. LANSING ....Senior Vice-Commander
A. J. OPDYK...Junior Vice-Commander
ED. W. LANSING...Adjutant
J. M. MOSS..Quartermaster
A. J. WILSON.. ....Surgeon
F. BENNETT ....Chaplain
J. H. McNAMER..Officer of the Day
M. O. MOOERS...Officer of the Guard
JAMES RAY...Sergeant Major
—— ——...Quartermaster Sergeant

Meeting, First Saturday.

NAME.	CO.	SERVICE.	ADDRESS.
Adams Benj.........	G	1st Oregon Cav..................	Alturas
Bennett F..........	G	4th Iowa Inf....	Burgettville
Buetel H..........	F	43d Ill. Inf.......................	Burney Valley
Carmichael M. A....	F	43d Ill. Inf.......................	Bieber
Lansing Ed. W......	D	6th N. Y. Cav	Fall River Mills
Lansing J. I.........	D	6th N. Y. Cav...	"
McNamer J. H.......	B	1st Oregon Inf........	Pittville
Mooers M. O........	E	22d Maine Inf....................	Burgettville
Moss J. J...........	A	16th Mo. Cav...	Pittville
Moss J M...........	E	1st Ark. Inf....................	Fall River Mills
Opdyk A. J.........	C	85th Ill. Inf.......	Cayton Valley
Ray James..........	F	29th Iowa Inf....................	Fall River Mills
Schofield N..........	E	25th Mich. Inf......	"
Wilson A. J.........	B	47th Ill. Inf......................	Goose Valley
Worley T. J.........	I	21st Iowa Inf....................	Fall River Mills
Young T. B.........	B	97th Ill. Inf.....................	Pittville

130

KIT CARSON POST, No. 74.

NAPA CITY, CAL.

OFFICERS, 1886.

G. M. FRANCIS ....Commander
W. A. SMITH................. ....Senior Vice-Commander
W. E. HARRINGTON.....................................Junior Vice-Commander
O. R. COGHLAN...Adjutant
L. T. HAYMAN..Quartermaster
SAM'L R, SPENCE.. ....Surgeon
ISAAC G. HERRON.................................. ....Chaplain
PHILIP PLASS.................... ....Officer of the Day
J. F. GARWOOD...Officer of the Guard
E. S. GRIDLEY...Sergeant Major
JACOB JAEKLE................................`............Quartermaster Sergeant
JAMES W. HOOVER..Inside Sentinel
H. H. MOFFATT.. ..Outside Sentinel

Meeting, Second and Fourth Friday.

NAME.	CO.	SERVICE.	ADDRESS.
Backus E. H.........	I	20th Mass. Inf....................	Napa City
Coghlan O. R.........	H	29th Mo. Inf.....................	"
Derry Thomas......		3d Wis. Inf......................	"
Francis G. M.......	C	25th Wis. Inf....................	"
Garwood J. F.......	E	82d Ohio Inf....	"
Gridley E. S.........	G	11th Mich. Cav....................	"
Harrington W. E....	I	9th Ind. Inf.....................	"
Harris F. W.........	G	12th Iowa Inf......	"
Hayman L. T........		9th Mo. S. M. Cav...........	"
Herron I. G..........	A	78th Ohio Inf....................	"
Hill F. D.............	C	4th Ind. Battery..................	"
Holden S. E.........	D	16th N. H. Inf...................	"
Hoover Jas. W......	F	Independent Penn. Light Art.....	"
Jackle J.............	F	23d Conn. Inf.......	"
King E. H...........		15th Iowa Inf....................	"
Lasher A. E.........	C	184th N. Y. Inf....	"
Moffat H. H.........	C	39th Iowa Inf....................	"
Mosher R............	A	1st Mich. Engineers.............	"
Peck N. F...........	I	25th Mass. Inf................ ...	"
Peterson Larry......	C	11th Wis. Inf....................	"
Plass P.....	I	5th Cal. Inf.....................	"
Shepard Wm........	D	1st Ohio Cav.....................	"
Smith W. A.........	B	38th Wis. Inf....................	"
Spence S. R..........		2d Penn. Battery.................	"
Stevens J. W........	H	140th Penn. Inf..	"
Van Auken A........	E	21st Conn. Inf...................	"
Wallingford J. N....	I	1st Minn. Inf....................	"
Weaver Henry......	C	28th Wis. Inf....................	"

J. K. MANSFIELD POST, No. 75.

RED BLUFF, CAL

OFFICERS, 1886.

JOHN CLEMENTS..Commander
ANDREW RYAN...Senior Vice-Commander
GEO. W. COLLAMER..Junior Vice-Commander
J. S. DAVENPORT..Adjutant
H. F. RATHJA...Quartermaster
JOHN U. HUFF...Surgeon
E. M. MINOTT...Chaplain
O. E. GRAVES...Officer of the Day
J. M. MILLEURN...Officer of the Guard
J. M. PLYMIRE..Sergeant Major
JOSEPH KNIGHT...Quartermaster Sergeant

Meeting, First and Third Wednesday.

NAME.	CO.	SERVICE.	ADDRESS.
Balls Dan...........	B	146th Ill. Inf......................	Red Bluff
Brummett Wesley..	F	27th Mo. Inf......................	Orland
Bullard G. W......	C	9th Minn. Inf....................	Red Bluff
Champlin Lester....	I	50th N. Y. Eng...................	"
Childs S. M.........	C	12th Kansas Inf..................	"
Chittenden C. C.....	E	8th Vt. Inf..................	Corning
Clements John	K	82d Ill. Inf......................	Red Bluff
Cole John H.........	E	6th Wis. Inf.....................	"
Collamer Geo. W...	H	22d Iowa Inf.....................	"
Commins Job.......		U. S. Gunboat Lexington.......	"
Cooper D. M	I	2d Cal. Cav..................	"
Davenport John S...	D	2d Wis. Cav......................	"
Decker Chas. F.....	C	50th Ill. Inf.....................	"
Dennis Amos........	I	5th Maine Inf....................	"
Doane Scott.........	D	128th Ohio Inf...................	"
Dodd A. N..........	I	6th Iowa Cav....................	"
Emmons F. M.......	I	7th Mo. Cav.....................	"
Fields Anthony......	D	4th Maine Inf....................	"
Galliher Henry......	I	46th Ohio Inf......	"
Glines W. J.........	K	83d Ill. Inf......................	"
Graves Oscar E......	B	4th Vt. Inf......................	"
Green Wm.........	C	10th Wis. Inf....................	"
Henderson I. M.....	B	19th Maine Inf..................	"
Hickman Clement...	C	8th Mich. Inf.................	"
Huff John U.........	K	27th Mich. Inf...................	"

NAME.	CO.	SERVICE.	ADDRESS.
Kamp Albert........	L	1st Cal. Cav.............	Red Bluff
Knight Joseph......	G	10th Maine Inf. & G 29th Maine Inf	"
Loring Abraham....	H	44th Ill. Inf......................	"
Millburn Jos. M....		58th Ind. Inf......................	"
Minott Edwin M....	F	25th Mass. Inf....................	"
Osman James M....	H	8th Ill. Cav.........	"
Phillips Joseph L ..	F	34th Mass. Inf............	"
Plymire Jas. A....	K	8th Penn. Res.	"
Purdy O. W.........	D	18th Wis. Inf.....................	"
Rathja Henry F.	H	2d Cal. Inf.......................	"
Robinson John A....	K	4th Maine Inf..	"
Ryan Andrew.......	A	1st Cal. Inf......................	"
Sawyer T. J........	D	2d Kansas Inf....................	"
Stone Charles.......	C	13th Ill. Inf...................... ,	Corning
Stratton H. L.......	H	7th Cal. Inf.....................	Tehama
Van Gelder Tobias..	G	22d N. Y. Cav......	Red Bluff
Weston Henry......		U. S. S. Dakota..........	"
Whaley A. G	D	2d Cal. Inf......................	"
Wilson John........		U. S. S. John Adams	"
Yager Myron........	K	121st N. Y. Inf....................	"
Zimmerman B.......	F	7th N. Y. Inf.....................	"

CAPT. WM. WALLACE POST, No. 76.

LAKE CITY, CAL.

OFFICERS, 1886.

A. M. HAMLEN...Commander
HORACE WOODS...Senior Vice Commander
GEO. H. PHILBROOK....................................Junior Vice Commander
A. W. CHURCH...Adjutant
HUGH BARCLAY...Quartermaster
J. W. POOR...Surgeon
JULES RUDO...Chaplain
E. SPENCER...Officer of the Day
SAM'L HOOPER...Officer of the Guard
O. A. WILSON...Sergeant Major
SAM'L SEGAR..Quartermaster Sergeant

Meeting, First and Third Saturday.

NAME.	CO.	SERVICE.	ADDRESS.
Barclay Hugh.......	A	5th Iowa Cav.....................	Lake City
Calderwood J. E....	F	2d Cal. Cav........................	Fort Bidwell
Church A. W........	D	2d Cal. Cav........................	Lake City
Hamlen A. M........	B	16th Maine Inf....................	"
Hooper Samuel......	G	10th Mich. Inf....................	"
Johnson G. W.......	A	3d Iowa Cav.......................	Reno, Nevada
Lohrenge Charles...	H	65th N. Y. Inf....................	Fort Bidwell
Miller Sam'l.........	F	5th Iowa Inf......................	Lake City
Peters W. H.........	I	1st Ill. Light Art.................	Burgettville
Philbrook Geo. H....	G	5th N. Y. Heavy Art.............	Lake City
Poor J. W..........	B	1st Maine Cav.....................	Fort Bidwell
Rudo Jules..........	F	51st Ill. Inf......................	Lake City
Segar Sam'l.........	C	33d Penn. Inf.....................	Fort Bidwell
Spencer E..........	B	20th Mich. Inf....................	Lake City
Welcome J. C........	G	73d Ill. Inf	"
Wilson O. A.........	K	2d N. Y. Heavy Art..............	"
Woods Horace......	F	2d Cal. Cav.......................	"

GEN. CANBY POST, No. 77.

OFFICERS, 1886.

G. W. BOWIE..Commander
M. H. BAILHACHE.....................................Senior Vice-Commander
O. L. MARSH...Junior Vice-Commander
A. L. GARTLEY..Adjutant
L. D. MESSIC. ....Quartermaster
H. BURNETT...Surgeon
H. HEINZ..Chaplain
J. B. SMITH..Officer of the Day
ED. HALL..Officer of the Guard
A. WILLIAMS...Sergeant Major
D. GRIFFIN...Quartermaster Sergeant

Meeting, First Saturday.

NAME.	CO.	SERVICE.	ADDRESS.
Bailhache M. H.. ...	I	9th Ill. Inf.......	Martinez
Bennett H , M. D...		U. S. S. Mount Vernon............	"
Bowie G. W........		5th Cal. Inf.......................	"
Brogdon Ed., M. D..	H	27th Maine Inf....	Concord
Doyle R. N		8th Mich Inf	Martinez
Gartley A. L.........	G	11th Ohio Inf.....	"
Griffith D............	H	27th Maine Inf......	
Hall Ed..............	A	2d Cal. Inf.........................	"
Heinz H.............	E	27th Iowa Inf.................	"
Marsh O. L	G	105th Ohio Inf......	"
Messic L. D.	K	12th N. J. Inf.....	"
Smith J. B..	E	2d Cal. Inf.........................	"
Tarwater G..........	B	33d Mo. Inf...	"
Wellington G. W....		U. S. Navy	"
Williams A..........	H	15th N. Y. Inf....................	Walnut Creek

THOMAS AMNER POST, No. 78.

BOULDER CREEK, CAL.

OFFICERS, 1886.

J. R. HOAG..Commander
S. H. RAMBO..Senior Vice-Commander
GEO, BRUCE..Junior Vice-Commander
H. HESSE...Adjutant
W. S. RANDALL..Quartermaster
ANDREW ANDERSON...Surgeon
J. P. STAPLES...Chaplain
G. J. WARD...Officer of the Day
SIMEON RISSONETTE...Officer of the Guard
J. M. JOLLETT..Sergeant Major
JASON CROCKETT...Quartermaster Sergeant

Meeting, Second and Fourth Saturday.

NAME.	CO.	ARM OF SERVICE.	ADDRESS.
Anderson Andrew...	E	2d Minn. Inf........................	Boulder Creek
Bruce George........	H	2d East Tenn. Inf.	"
Claffy John.	D	16th Mass. Inf........	"
Crockett Jason	H	2d Cal. Inf.................	"
Cunningham James.	K	15th Maine Inf. and 1st La. Inf....	"
Ellwood Michael....	C	14th Ill. Inf......................	"
Hesse H.............	G	31st Ohio Inf.....................	"
Hoag J. R......	A	46th N. Y. Inf....................	"
Hossack D..........	K	7th Cal. Inf......................	"
Jollett J. M.........	H	34th Iowa Inf.....	"
Newell F. W.......	F	2d Cal. Inf.......................	"
Rambo S. H........	I	11th Kansas Cav............... ..	"
Randall W. S........	D	1st Maine Cav.......	"
Reed Robert	C	2d Md. Inf	"
Rissonette Simeon..	G	25th Ill. Inf.....................	"
Staples J. P.....	I	115th N. Y. Inf..................	"
Sterrett James......	E	1st Cal. Inf......................	"
Swain R.............		U. S. Navy	"
Walker C. H........	A	1st Maine Cav......	"
Ward G. J...........	E	4th Mich. Inf....................	"

E. F. WINSLOW POST, No. 79.

REDDING, CAL.

OFFICERS, 1886.

LYMAN HOTALING...Commander
JOHN SPELLMAN.....................................Senior Vice-Commander
JOHN FARHNER.....................................Junior Vice-Commander
G. W. HARBINSON...Adjutant
D. N. HONN...Quartermaster
T. B. SMITH...Surgeon
J. H. MILLER...Chaplain
J. P. SMITH...Officer of the Day
H. G. BAKER...Officer of the Guard
—— ——...Sergeant Major
—— ——...Quartermaster Sergeant

Meeting, Third Friday.

NAME.	CO.	SERVICE.	ADDRESS.
Baker G. H.........	H	16th Maine Inf	Redding
Bell J. H............	F	13th Ohio Inf......................	Millville
Butler D. L.........	F	7th Vt. Inf......................	Redding
Castle A. S.........	B	96th Ill. Inf......................	"
Cecil J. M.........	G	2d Tenn. Inf......................	"
Conant J. W.........	H	8th Mo. Inf......................	"
Crosby R. P........	E	5th Kansas Cav...................	"
Deakins Wm	I	4th Mo. Inf.	"
Dirking A. H	G	2d Mo. Cav......................	"
Edge George.......	K	36th N Y. Inf....................	"
Ellis A. C.........	B	5th Minn. Inf....................	"
Farhner J. G........	E	58th Ill. Inf....................	"
Finley W. B........	H	8th Cal. Inf......................	"
Flake J. R.........		29th Iowa Inf...................	"
Green John F.......	C	78th Ill. Inf....................	"
Harbinson G. W.....	C	1st N. Y. Light Art.............	"
Honn D. N..........	B	93d Ill. Inf....................	"
Hotaling L..........		4th Iowa Inf....................	"
Hunter J. H.........	G	179th N. Y. Inf.................	"
Kumiser H. H.......	F	142d Penn. Inf..................	"
Lawry J. B........:	C	5th Iowa Inf....................	"
Lee W. W...........	D	2d Cal. Cav....................	"
Miller J. H.........	A	22d Mich. Inf..................	"
Palmer G. W........	A	71st Ill. Inf..................	"
Paul C. C..........	H	2d Minn. Inf..................	"
Sandy Wm.........	C	41st Ill. Inf..................	"
Smith J. P.....	C	49th Penn. Inf..................	"
Smith T. B.........	I	7th Cal. Inf....................	Shasta
Spellman John......		U. S. Marine Corps..............	Redding
Thomas Henry......	H	3d Ohio Inf.	"
Thompson D. S......	F	10th Ohio Inf..................	"
Tilson J. R.........		11th Mo. Cav..................	"
Woodman H. C......	E	2d Cal. Cav....................	"

CORINTH POST, No. 80.

MARYSVILLE, CAL.

OFFICERS, 1886.

W. T. McLEAN...Commander
J. D. FULLER...Senior Vice-Commander
CHARLES E. COBB..Junior Vice-Commander
W. L. CAMPBELL...Adjutant
J. K. HARE..Quartermaster
N. S. HAMLIN..Surgeon
J. P. SWIFT... ....Chaplain
JOHN COLFORD...Officer of the Day
W. A. McHENRY..Officer of the Guard
J. W. HICKS..Sergeant Major
J. C. KINGSBURY...................................Quartermaster Sergeant
PETER ERICKSON...Inside Sentinel
J. M. TAYLOR...Outside Sentinel

Meeting, every Tuesday.

NAME.	CO.	SERVICE.	ADDRESS.
Albert James W.....	B	7th Cal. Inf........................	Brownsville
Bailey George W....		Fremont's Scouts.................	Yuba City
Beesley Thomas		17th Iowa Inf	Marysville
Bennett James	C	193d Ohio Inf	"
Berkenmeyer Alois..	G	103d N. Y. Inf....................	Moore's Station
Berry James R......	G	125th Ind. Inf....................	Wheatland
Boomer Herman K..		51st Ill. Inf. and A 8th Ill. Cav....	Marysville
Bossart John........	D	1st Ill. Cav........	Wheatland
Bradford Caleb,.....	I	2d Cal. Cav......................	Yuba City
Brainard David H...	I	40th Mass. Inf...................	"
Brockleman Ernest	A	72d N. Y. Inf....................	Meridian
Brown Asher P.....		26th Conn. Inf..........	Smartsville
Brown C. C..........	B	7th Cal. Inf.....................	Yuba City
Brown William.....	B	7th Cal. Inf.....................	Gridley
Bruce Horace.......	F	3d N. Y. Art........	Yuba City
Burns James........	F	2d Cal. Inf	Smartsville
Byers John	I	96th Ill. Inf.....................	Marysville
Campbell W. L......	C	54th Ind. Inf. and G 139th Ind. Inf.	"
Carter E. J	G	2d Cal. Cav......................	"
Chambers E. W.....	B	7th Cal. Inf	"
Christine A....	B	7th Cal. Inf	"
Clay Henry S........	C	6.d U. S. Col'd Inf...............	"
Cobb Charles E.....	K	1st N.Y.Mtd.Rifles & C 8th N.Y.Cav.	"
Colebaker Samuel...		7th Ind. Battery.................	'
Colford John		U. S. S. Nipsic and Hope and U. S.	"
		Submarine Corps.................	
Colville J. O.......	A	7th E. Tenn. Inf.............	Yuba City
Cook H. H.........	H	2d Penn. Inf......	Marysville
Cooley Allen........	C	3d Mass. Cav.....................	"
Cotter Patrick......	A	11th Conn. Inf...................	"
Courtney Martin L..	F	1st Nev. Cav.......	"

138

NAME.	CO.	SERVICE.	ADDRESS.
Cudderback D. C....	G	12th Ill. Cav......................	Marysvlile
Davis E. A.........	G	27th N. Y. Inf.	"
Day Henry.........		1st Iowa Battery................	"
Dean Thomas	A	1st Cal. Cav...................	Yuba City
Doman Alex S......	B	157th Penn. Inf...	Marysville
Doty Jacob.........	C	U. S. Sharpshooters............	Meridian
Duston C. M.......	B	16th N. Y. Inf., B 25th N. Y. Inf. &	
	A	6th Vet. Res. Corps..........	Gridley
Earl John A........	D	Mass. Independent Cav. Bat......	Marysville
Ellington Ed. E.....	C	143d Ill. Inf..................	Yuba City
English S. C........	I	44th Wis. Inf...........	Gridley
Erick J. H....	K	2d Cal. Cav...................	Marysville
Erickson Peter......	G	5th Md. Inf....................	"
Field Charles W....	C	9th Maine Inf................	West Butte
Finley J. B.........	H	12th Mo. Cav.................	Marysvllle
Fogelman Fritz.....	D	71st Ill. Inf................	"
Fuller J. B.........		1st Mich. Battery, 4th Mich. Battery and D 1st Mich. Res. Art.....	"
Gardner John.......	K	7th N. Y. Inf.............	Live Oak
Gilbert John........	F	7th Mo. Inf........	Marysville
Hamlin N. S., M. D..		18th Mo. Inf..	"
Hankins A. J.......	A	15th Maine Inf.............	Brownsville
Hanley T. M........	C	8th Ill. Cav.................	"
Hare J. K..........	G	8th Cal. Inf..................	Marysville
Haynes James.......	M	——Ohio Heavy Art............	Yuba City
Heintzen George....	I	4th Mich. Inf...............	Browns Valley
Hendricks E. J......	D	67th N. Y. Inf..........	Livo Oak
Hendrickson W. M..		4th N. Y. Inf..............	Wheatland
Hicks J. W.........	F	29th Iowa Inf.............	Yuba City
Hilliard J. P	B	136th Ill. Inf.............	Wheatland
Hoard Luther......	C	Nevada Inf.................	Marysville
Hoffman Josiah.....	D	1st Cal. Cav................	Sheridan
Holland W. W.......	A	22d Penn. Cav.............	Marysville
Hollen Ed........ ...	F	50th Penn. Inf.............	"
Hopkins T. B.......	E	107th N. Y. Inf	South Butte
Hughes W. D........	I	1st Nevada Cav............	Marysville
Humphrey Arthur..	K	27th N. Y. Inf.............	"
Ingersoll Albert T	K	1st Ohio Art....	"
Jasper R. L.........	C	9th Mo. Cav..............	Wheatland
Jones Charles F.....	E	19th Maine Inf...	Oregon House,Cal.
Jones Joshua H.....	C	36th Iowa Inf............	Marysville
Jones Thomas C.....	B	7th Cal. Inf.............	Nicolaus
Kelser Chris........	F	23d Ohio Inf......	Wheatland
Kingsberry J. C.....	B	7th Cal. Inf.............	Marysville
Larsen Michael	F	15th Wis. Inf......	"
Lewis A. W....... ...	B	7th Cal. Inf......	"
Liening John H.....	D	1st Cal. Cav................	Colusa
Little David S..	G	23d Iowa Inf.............	Wheatland
Luke Isaiah..	I	8th Iowa Cav....	Marysville
Mangles Peter......	A	9th Ill. Inf................	Camptonville
Martindale Kellogg	B	7th Mich. Cav.............	Gridley
McClanahan Allen C.	I	7th Cal. Inf......	Tehama
McHenry W. A......	D	Penn. 100-day Inf., Capt. J. K. Weaver's Indep't Mt. Penn. Inf. and D 135th Penn. Inf........	Marysville
McKenney George ..	B	4th Ohio Independent Battery	"

NAME.	CO.	SERVICE.	ADDRESS.
McLean W. T........	L	8th N.Y.State Mil.& 4th N.Y.In't B'y	Marysville
Morris Francis......		3d Vt. Battery................	Pike City, Cal.
Mumby William	C	35th Wis. Inf.....	Gridley
Nellis William H....	D	11th Iowa Inf......	Marysville
Nye George W.......	G	8th Cal. Inf...................	Yuba City
Overmeyer E. H.....	G	7th Cal. Inf...................	Marysville
Owens Henry	D	128th Ind. Inf.................	"
Palmer John W....	K	6th Cal. Inf...................	Yuba City
Parker Daniel S.	D	1st Frontier Cav. (or 26th N.Y.Cav.)	
		and 11th Mass. Battery...........	Marysville
Parks W. H....... ..		Provost Marshal Northern Cal....	"
Peck W. F...........	F	33d Mass. Inf.....	Yuba City
Pegg Henry R......	E	17th Ind. Inf...................	"
Perry Fred M......		U. S. Gunboat Silver Cloud......	Marysville
Reilly J. J.........	I	2d N. Y. Mounted Rifles.........	"
Richardson A. M....	C	30th Mich. Inf.................	Moore's Station
Riggs S. B..........	K	8th Penn. Inf.................	Meridian
Ripholt Thomas.....	L	1st N. Y. Light Art........... .	Marysville
Ripley Charles J....	G	12th N. Y. Inf.................	"
Robinson J. C......	G	12th Ill. Cav..................	Yuba City
Robinson N.........	A	118th Ill. Inf.....	"
Roche Thomas......	G	8th Cal. Inf...................	Camptonville
Rumery Thomas J..	B	7th Cal. Inf...................	Brownsville
Schenck Andrew....	E	86th Ill. Inf..................	Yuba City
Searle E. J.........	A	148th Ill. Inf.................	Marysville
Shaefer Eusebius...	I	24th Ill. Inf..................	Browns Valley
Siebert J...........		8th Cal. Inf..................	Marysville
Skidmore T. B.....	G	5th Ill. Cav..................	Live Oak
Slatterly Patrick....	A	98th N. Y. Inf................	Marysville
Smallwood John W.	E	21st Mo. Inf..................	"
Smith Hardin......	C	23d Iowa Inf.....	"
Somers Obediah.....	A	18th U. S. Colored Inf...........	"
Sowell William C...	B	78th Ill. Inf..................	Wheatland
Spinner William....	I	73d Ind. Inf..................	Marysville
Sutliffe George W..	C	76th Ohio Inf....	Wheatland
Swift J. P..........	B	6th N. H.Inf.................	Marysville
Taber L. H..........	I	9th Ind. Inf.................	"
Taylor James.......	K	12th Ind. Cav.................	
Taylor J. M........	B	7th Cal. Inf..................	Marysville
Taylor R. E.........	H	23d Maine Inf................	Gridley
Thorpe Arnold.....	I	34th Ky. Inf.................	Yuba City
Thurman Elijah....	E	21st Mo. Inf.................	Nicolaus
Trunnell John W...	E	21st Mo. Inf.................	Biggs
Tucker W. E.... .	K	1st N. Y. Engineers	South Butte
Van Buskirk George	K	6th Ohio Inf.................	Marysville
Van Buskirk James.	K	27th Ohio Inf.................	"
Vaughn James H....	D	7th Cal. Inf....	"
Waistell Robinson ..	K	6th Cal. Inf..................	Smartsville
Wakefield Ray.......	A	16th Iowa Inf. and 8th Cal. Inf...	Marysville
Welsh Barney.......	E	27th Iowa Inf................	Meridian
White A. W.... ...		2d Maine Inf.................	Marysville
White J. C.... ,....	G	8th Cal. Inf..................	Yuba City
Wissel H. C.........		105th Penn. Inf................	Marysville
Woods W. B..... ...	H	30th Ill. Inf.................	Wheatland
Young George H....	H	13th Maine Inf. & H 30th Maine Inf	South Butte

J. W. MOREY POST, No. 81.

OFFICERS, 1886.

SAMUEL VARNER... ....Commander
DAVID HETZEL...Senior Vice-Commander
G. L. COBB........................ ....Junior Vice-Commander
G. DIETZ...Adjutant
W. V. CARR..Quartermaster
J. J. ANTHONY...Surgeon
JOSEPH SMITH................................ ....Chaplain
J. J. KEATON..Officer of the Day
J. A. CROSBY............................... ....Officer of the Guard
JAMES NEAL........ ....Sergeant Major
W. V. COLE...Quartermaster Sergeant

Meeting, First Monday

NAME.	CO.	SERVICE.	ADDRESS.
Anthony Matthew J.	K	8th Cal. Inf.......................	Guerneville
Bigelow Z. M........		16th Mich. Inf....................	"
Burke J. M..........	O	29th N. Y. Inf....................	"
Carr W. M..........	H	2d Mass. Inf........	"
Cobb G. L...........	O	1st Wis. Inf..............	"
Cole M. V...........	C	38th Iowa Inf....................	"
Cook George........	K	5th U. S. Inf....................	"
Crosby J. A.........	L	8th Ill. Cav.....	"
Hetzel D............	O	74th N.Y.Inf. & K 7th U. S. Vet. Inf	"
Hull Z. F...........	I	21st Maine Inf...................	"
Jewell Andrew.....	H	141st Ill. Inf....................	"
Keaton John J......	G	16th Ind. Mounted Inf.......	"
Lawler Ph. G.......	F	21st Maine Inf...................	"
Neal James H.......	E	25th Iowa Inf...... ..	"
Smith Joseph.......	O	5th Ill. Cav.....................	"
Springer David.....	B	11th Ill. Inf....................	"
Squibb Samuel......	C	7th Ind. Inf....................	"
Stoffel Phil.....	D	27th Ohio Inf....................	"
Thompson E G. C...	F	1st Maine Inf....................	"
Varner Samuel......	H	1st West Va. Inf.................	"
Wallace Charles.....	M	192d Penn. Inf..................	"
Whitney Chester V..	I	3d Wis. Inf....................	"
Wood J. K..........	F	6th Minn. Inf..	"

E. O. C. ORD POST No 82.

LOS GATOS, CAL.

OFFICERS, 1886.

EBEN C. FARLEY..Commander
JACOB C. MANSUR................... ....Senior Vice-Commander
OWEN E. GAFFANY.......................................Junior Vice-Commander
GAIUS WEBSTER.............. ....Adjutant
JAMES H. LYNDON...Quartermaster
JOHN F. TOBIN...Surgeon
DANIEL PARKS...Chaplain
SAMUEL NOTT... ....Officer of the Day
A. C. COVERT...Officer of the Guard
——— ——...Sergeant Major
——— ——.............................. ....Quartermaster Sergeant

---

Meeting, Second and Fourth Friday.

NAME.	CO.	SERVICE.	ADDRESS.
Coffey H. R...........	H	132d Ill. Inf........................	Los Gatos
Covert A. C..........	H	88th Ind. Inf......................	"
Crane Levi.	C	124th Ill. Inf.......	"
Deno William.......	A	98th N. Y. Inf.................. ..	"
Farley Eben C.......	B	8th Cal. Inf.....	"
French Chas. A.....		U. S. Navy	Saratoga
Gaffany Owen E.....		2d Vt. Art.........................	Los Gatos
Hamilton L. E......	O	86th Ohio Inf.....................	"
Hinman R. W.......	A	2d Ill. Light Art.............	"
Irwin Stuart...	I	132d Ill. Inf.....................	"
Jewett David........	C	1st Oregon Inf.......	"
Lyndon James H....	H	21st Mass. Inf....................	"
Mansur Jacob C.....	K	10th Vt. Inf......................	"
Nott Samuel.........	A	148th N. Y. Inf...................	"
Parks Daniel........	A	123d N. Y. Inf....................	"
Schrepfer Fred......	A	22d Ill. Inf......................	"
Shannon Thomas....	B	7th Cal. Inf.....	"
Sutton Charles......	C	1st Wis. Inf......................	"
Tobin John F.......	F	26th Ind. Inf.....................	"
Webster Gaius......	A	144th N. Y. Inf...................	"
Wilson James H.....	A	15th Maine Inf....................	"
Woodard James L....	F	42d Ohio Inf.....................	"

142

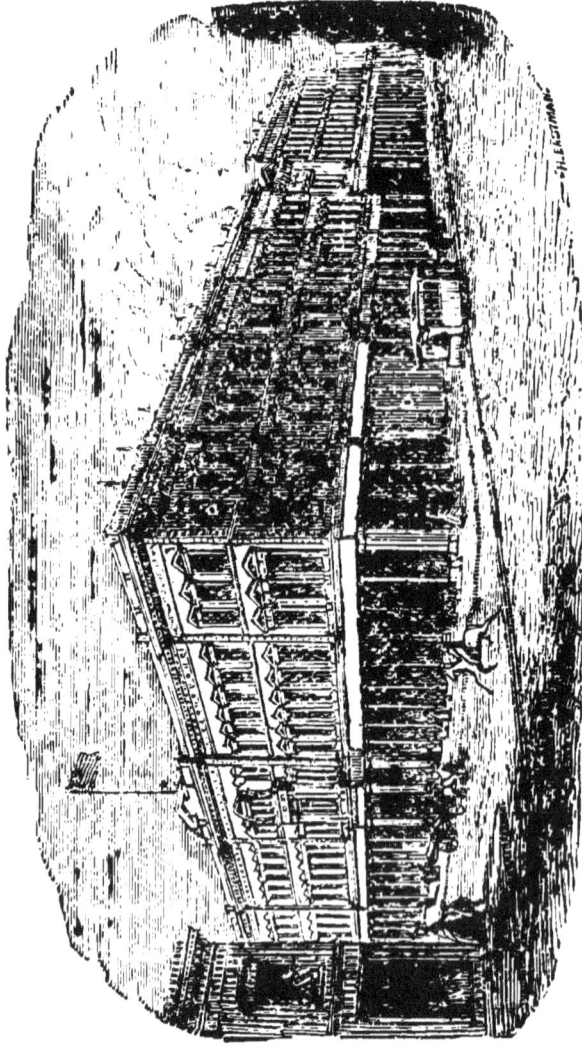

LICK HOUSE

AMERICAN AND EUROPEAN PLAN.

The Dining Room the Finest in the World.

Sutter and Montgomery Sts.

San Francisco. Cal.

Charles Claffey,

Proprietor.

J. W. OWENS POST, No. 83.

PHŒNIX, A. T.

OFFICERS, 1886.

CHAS. H. KNAPP...Commander
GEO. F. COATS...Senior Vice-Commander
R. J. CARTWRIGHT...Junior Vice-Commander
JOS. B. CREAMAR..Adjutant
JOHN KING...Quartermaster
J. E. WHARTON..Surgeon
H. B. LIGHTHIZER ....Chaplain
L. H. TIFFANY..Officer of the Day
JOHN M. MULLIN..Officer of the Guard
ANTHONY HEGERUP..Sergeant Major
JOHN R. SILSBEE.......... ....Quartermaster Sergeant

---

Meeting, First Tuesday.

NAME.	CO.	SERVICE.	ADDRESS.
Buck Theodore......	F	2d Ill. Art.........................	Phœnix, A. T.
Calderwood M. H....	D	7th Cal. Inf.	"
Cartwright R. J......	K	123d Ill. Inf......................	"
Coats G. F..........	E	1st Iowa Cav....	"
Creamar Jos. B......	H	142d Ill. Inf......................	"
Grable Henry.......	K	12th Ind. Inf......................	"
Hancock W. A.......	K	7th Cal. Inf. and C 1st Oregon Cav.	"
Hegerup Anthony...		U. S. Navy	"
King John..........	H	34th N. Y. Inf. and C 188th N.Y. Inf	"
Kingman Geo. W....	D	3d N. Y. Inf. and C 22d N. Y. Cav..	"
Knapp Charles H....	I	11th Ind. Inf......................	"
Lighthizer H. B.....	E	4th Wis. Cav......................	"
McCann Wm........	K	13th Conn. Inf. and F 1st La. Cav..	"
Mills J. K..........		2d Maine Art.....................	Los Angeles, Cal.
Mullin John	A	1st Cal. Cav......................	Phœnix
Schwartz Edward....	H	8th N. Y. Inf. and 9th N. Y. Cav...	"
Silsbee John R......	A	10th N. Y. Art....................	"
Stearns C. W.......	A	26th Mass. Inf................. . .	Maricopa
Tiffany L. H........	C	18th Ind. Inf.....................	Phœnix
Veil Charles H......	G	9th Penn. Res. and C 1st U.S. Cav..	"
Wharton J. E........	D	2d Iowa Cav. and 1st Col. Militia..	"
Woods W. T.........	B	7th Cal. Inf......................	"

143

GEN. GEO. B. McCLELLAN POST, No. 84.

ETNA, CAL.

OFFICERS, 1886.

H. B. MATHEWSON...Commander
THOMAS J. KIST..Senior Vice-Commander
JACOB ELLER...Junior Vice-Commander
MARTIN MARX..Adjutant
JOHN F. SKELTON...Quartermaster
ELISHA DE WITT...Surgeon
FRANK MARKEY...Chaplain
MICHAEL LIGHTHILL..Officer of the Day
ABRAM ERNO...Officer of the Guard
W. W. EASTLICK...Sergeant Major
JACOB CONNER...Quartermaster Sergeant

Meeting, Third Saturday

NAME.	CO.	SERVICE.	ADDRESS.
Burrows A. H......		136th Penn. Inf..................	Yreka
Conner Jacob.......	A	118th Ill. Inf......	Oro Fino
DeWitt Elisha.......	K	7th Mo. Inf.........................	Yreka
Eastlick W. W......	E	53d Ind. Inf.......................	Oro Fino
Eller Jacob.........	I	34th Iowa Inf......................	Etna
Erno Abram.........	H	16th U. S. Inf.....................	Mugginsville
Kist T. J...........	C	5th Ohio Inf.......................	Etna
Lighthill Michael...	A	17th Iowa Inf..................	Fort Jones
Markey Frank.......	F	1st Cal. Cav.......	"
Marx Martin........	B	7th N. J. Inf......................	Etna
Mathewson H. B....	F	1st Cal. Cav......................	McAdams
Skelton J. F.........	B	1st Iowa Inf. and U. S. Vols.......	Etna
Sovey Leon..........	E	3d Cal. Inf.......................	"

144

GEN. BERRY POST, No. 85.

TRUCKEE, CAL.

OFFICERS. 1886.

PIERCE LAFFAN..Commander
O. H. BARTON...Senior Vice-Commander
DENIS BURCKHALTER...............................Junior Vice-Commander
B. F. TACKABERRY..Adjutant
J. G. BOOTH...Quartermaster
D. W. THORNDYKE..Surgeon
A. O. CAMPBELL..Chaplain
J. N. DURNEY...Officer of the Day
THOS. SMITH...Officer of the Guard
SAM'L SMITH..Sergeant Major
W. G. CASE.................................Quartermaster Sergeant
J. LAMBRECHT...Inside Sentinel
O. J. CHAMBERLIN.................................Outside Sentinel

---

Meeting, Second and Fourth Monday.

NAME.	CO.	SERVICE.	ADDRESS.
Barton C. H.........	A	1st Bat. Maine Sharpshooters	Truckee
Booth J. G.........	K	153d N. Y. Inf.....................	"
Burckhalter Denis..		11th N. Y. Battery.................	"
Campbell A. C......		U. S. S. Gen. Price	"
Case Walter G.......	E	31st Ohio Inf.....................	"
Chamberlin Clark J.		3d Vt. Light Art..................	"
Conners John.......	K	18th Wis. Inf.....................	"
Dunn Henry G......	E	6th Wis Inf......................	"
Durney J. N.........		26th Maine Inf...................	"
Hellwig Jacob.......	H	2d Wis. Inf......................	"
Hubbard John N....	K	19th Ind. Inf....................	"
Laffan Pierce........	D	11th Maine Inf....	"
Lambrecht Jacob...	E	144th N. Y. Inf..................	"
McPheeters Dan....	B	22d Maine Inf...................	"
Smith Samuel.......	A	2d Mass. Cav....................	"
Smith T. J.........	I	19th Iowa Inf..............	"
Tackaberry Ben. F..	O	6th Cal. Inf....................	"
Thorndyke D. W....	F	2d Cal. Cav....................	"
Weed Abner.........	G	8th Maine Inf..................	"

DUNHAM POST, No. 86.

KINGSBURG, CAL.

———

OFFICERS, 1886.

JOHN D. BUTLER..Commander
WILLIAM COX...Senior Vice-Commander
JOHN C. McDERMID................... ....Junior Vice-Commander
JOHN A. BROWN................................... ....Adjutant
SAMUEL A. CLINE.. ... Quartermaster
EDWARD RUSSELL..Surgeon
SOLOMON A. LOOMIS..Chaplain
JOHN DELBRIDGE...Officer of the Day
GEORGE BOYER..Officer of the Guard
——— ———..Sergeant Major
——— ———..Quartermaster Sergeant

———

Meeting, Second and Fourth Friday.

NAME.	CO.	SERVICE.	ADDRESS.
Boyer George.......	D	46th Ill. Inf.......	Kingsburg
Brown John A......	K	26th Iowa Inf......................	"
Butler John D......	D	41st Ohio Inf. & 7th U.S. Engineers	"
Cline Samuel A.....	C	2d Mich. Inf.	"
Cline William V....	K	13th N. Y. Inf.....................	"
Cox Francis M......	K	23d Mo. Inf.........	"
Cramer William.....	C	61st N. Y. Inf.....................	San Francisco
Delbridge John C...	D	1st Iowa Cav.......................	Kingsburg
Fowler Laman D....	I	3d Ohio Inf........................	"
Loomis Salmon H...	F	4th Cal. Inf.......................	"
McDermid John C...	I	2d Mich. Cav......................	"
Rea Francis.........	H	59th Ill. Inf.....................	Traver
Russell Ezra M......	B	13th U. S. Inf....................	Kingsburg

146

VIENNA GARDENS,

The Established Family Resort.

A Legitimate Entertainment,

Conducted on Business Principles.

J. A. BROWN, PROPRIETOR.

Camp Fire Every Night.   Late Lieut. 5th N. Y. Art'y.

R. ROEMER.   C. ROEMER.

⟶VIENNA⟵

MODEL BAKERY AND CAFE

From The Centennial Exposition.

205 KEARNY ST., SAN FRANCISCO.

In addition to our Specialties, we also Serve Regular Dinners from 5 to 8 P. M.

ROEMER BROS., Proprietors and Caterers.

CUNNINGHAM, CURTISS & WELCH,

STATIONERS

Blank Book Manufacturers and Dealers in School Books

327-329-331 SANSOME ST., SAN FRANCISCO.

Represented by   Geo. H. Thomas Post No. 2.
J. B. AMERMAN.   Dept. Cal. G. A. R.

UNION—BREWERY—UNION

UNION BEER, THE BEST IN THE CITY.

For Sale in all the Principal Places.⟶

⟶ Special Attention Paid to Country Orders.

HENNING THODE, PROPRIETOR,

326 Clementina Street,   Between Fourth and Fifth.

McDERMIT POST, No 87.

WINNEMUCCA, NEV.

OFFICERS, 1886.

J. H. SACKETT........ ....,......Commander
W. L. RUSE.......... ....Senior Vice-Commander
B. F. WOODS ....Junior Vice-Commander
WM. PERKINS...Adjutant
M. B. STAUNTON....... ....Quartermaster
——— ————..Surgeon
THOS. SOARS... ....Chaplain
PAT O'DONNELL...Officer of the Day
J. A. ROBINSON...Officer of the Guard
J. B. McGONAGLE..Sergeant Major
——— ————...Quartermaster Sergeant

Meeting, First Friday.

NAME.	CO.	SERVICE.	ADDRESS.
Andrews Walter.....		U. S. S. Wabash...................	Winnemucca
Bigelow R. R........		53d Wis. Inf.....................	Elko
Cole Nicholas.......		13th Md. Inf....	Wadsworth
Curschmann George		5th Mo. Reserve Corps...........	Winnemucca
Grannis D. D........		21st Iowa Inf.....................	Lovelock
Jackson J. W........		39th Iowa Inf......	Winnemucca
McGonagle Jos. B...		1st Nevada Cav....................	"
Nelson V. H........		62d Ohio Inf....	Dun Glen, Nev.
O'Donnell Patrick..		9th Md. Inf......................	Winnemucca
Perkins William....		1st Mo. Light Art................	"
Robinson James A..		3d U. S. Heavy Art...............	"
Ruse L. W..........		81st Ohio Inf.....................	"
Sackett James H....		1st Nevada Cav. and 1st Cal. Inf....	"
Soars Thomas... ...		11th Kansas Inf. and 9th Mass. Inf.	"
Staunton Michael B.		1st Nevada Cav...................	"
Woods B. F.........		31st Iowa Inf.....................	"

LOOKOUT MOUNTAIN POST, No. 88.

BERKELEY, CAL.

OFFICERS, 1886.

O. R. LORD...Commander
WM. M. HILTON...Senior Vice-Commander
GILBERT SMITH...Junior Vice-Commander
F. L. PALMER...Adjutant
JOHN M. CREED...Quartermaster
A. KSCHIESCHANG...Surgeon
REV. W. F. BICKFORD..Chaplain
W. R. BATTEN...Officer of the Day
A. B. COLE...Officer of the Guard
——— ———...Sergeant Major
——— ———..................................Quartermaster Sergeant
J S. PARLET...Sentinel

Meeting, every Monday.

NAME.	CO.	SERVICE.	ADDRESS.
Acton M. J...........	K	2d Mass. Cav....................	Berkeley
Ayer Henry.........	D	20th N. Y. Cav....................	"
Batten W. R........	O	88th Ill. Inf....................	"
Bickford W. F.....	L	1st Dist. of Col. Cav.& L 1st Me. Cav	Lorin
Boswell Benj. D.....	A	4th West Va. Inf. & 2d West Va. Inf.	Berkeley
Boyd John E........		U. S. S. Sumpter................	"
Brown Conrad.....	C	124th Ill. Inf......................	Lorin
Colby Edw. L.......	E	2d Mass. Art.......................	West Berkeley
Cole A. B...........	I	15th Ind. Inf	Berkeley
Creed John M......	F	17th Ohio Inf......................	"
Culver O. B.......	G	7th Cal. Inf.......................	533 Market St., S.F.
Frick Christian.....	D	4th Del. Inf......................	Berkeley
Gast Frederick.....	D	193d Penn. Inf....	West Berkeley
Grubelstein J........	A	11th N. Y. State Militia...........	Berkeley
Higgins Jas.........	F	6th Cal. Inf.......................	West Berkeley
Hilton Wm. M.......	O	11th Ind. Cav.....................	Berkeley
Kschieschang A....	G	55th Penn. Inf.....................	"
Lord C. R...........	G	1st Mo. State Militia..............	"
McCleave Wm.......	A	1st Cal. Cav.......................	"
Norwood Wm. H....	H	2d Maine Inf.......................	"
Palmer F. L.........	E	9th U. S. Inf......................	"
Parlet J. S..........	O	1st Oregon Cav.....................	"
Polhamus David....	O	25th N. J. Inf.....................	"
Smith Gilbert.......	E	6th N. Y. Cav......................	"

FOOTE POST, No. 89,

SANTA MARIA, CAL.

OFFICERS, 1886.

L. K. MORTON...Commander
W. V. POWELL...Senior Vice-Commander
JAS. ELLIOTT ....Junior Vice-Commander
W. W. AYRES..Adjutant
B. F. BELL...Quartermaster
H. BARTRON............. ....Surgeon
D. N. KELSEY,...Chaplain
O. D. KINCAID ....Officer of the Day
M. WHITFORD ....Officer of the Guard
F. F. FIELD..Sergeant Major
THOS. MORAN............:...............................Quartermaster Sergeant

---

Meeting, Saturday after Full Moon.

NAME.	CO.	SERVICE.	ADDRESS.
Ayres W. W.........		39th Mo. Inf.......................	Santa Maria
Bartron H....	K	149th Penn. Inf...................	"
Pell B. F.......	E	11th Penn. Inf..	"
Elliott James.......	A	46th N. Y. Inf..	"
Field F. F...........	A	15th Conn. Inf......................	"
Foster David........	E	14th Kansas Cav...................	"
Gale S. M............	O	2d Mo. Inf.........................	"
Goudy G. M.........	K	7th Cal. Inf.......................	"
Kelsey D. N.........	F	1st Mass. Bat...............	"
Kincaid O. D........	E	1st Iowa Cav......................	"
Montgomery D. O...	A	17th Ohio Inf......................	"
Moran Thomas......	D	34th Wis. Inf......................	"
Morton L. K........	B	Penn. Bucktails and F Vet. Res....	"
Powell W. V........	I	99th Ind. Inf......................	"
Smith John.........	H	2d Conn. Inf.......................	"
Stilwell W. W.......	D	16th Mo. Inf.......................	"
Van Husen H. S.....		....	"
Whitford M.........	C	9th Minn.Inf. & C 67th U.S.Col'd Inf	"
Winters Nathaniel F.	G	2d Cal. Cav	"
Yelken R............	O	2d Kansas Cav....................	"

GEN. McDOWELL POST, No. 90.

SAN RAFAEL, CAL.

———

OFFICERS, 1896.

JOSEPH B. LAUCK..Commander
IL A. GORLEY...Senior Vice-Commander
HENRY HARRISON...Junior Vice-Commander
EDWIN KURKUP...Adjutant
THOMAS CURREY...Quartermaster
——— ———...Surgeon
GEORGE KALER..Chaplain
PETER CLANCEY..Officer of the Day
HARRY C. DEAN..Officer of the Guard
——— ———...Sergeant Major
——— ———...Quartermaster Sergeant

———

Meeting, First and Third Monday.

NAME.	CO.	SERVICE.	ADDRESS.
Allison John W.....	H	65th Ohio Inf......................	San Rafael
Atchley George W...	D	1st Oregon Inf....................	"
Beedle W. H.........		2d Battery Maine Light Art.........	"
Clancey Peter.......	F	59th Mass. Inf..	"
Currey Thomas.....	A	6th Penn. Cav.....................	"
Day Timothy........	B	3d U. S. Inf......................	"
Dean Harry C..		11th Mass. Inf....................	"
Farrell Domnick....	H	3d Mass. Inf. and B 99th N. Y. Inf.,	"
Gorley H. A.........	D	1st Cal. Inf...........	"
Harrison Henry.....	K	158th N. Y. Inf........	"
Kaler George........	A	18th Mo. Inf.....................	"
Kurkup Edwin......	D	38th Iowa........................	"
Lauck Joseph B.....	L	1st Ohio Heavy Art................	"
Miller Charles N....	H	132d Ill. Inf......................	Ono, Shasta Co.
O'Reilly J. J........	M	2d U. S. Art......................	San Rafael
Roslat John.........	B	71st N. Y. Inf....................	"

150

MODOC POST, No. 91.

ADIN, CAL.

———

OFFICERS, 1886.

C. C. AUBLE..Commander
L. A. NASH..Senior Vice-Commander
C. PHILLIBER..Junior Vice-Commander
C. A. McCASH...................... ....Adjutant
SAM. WATSON..Quartermaster
JERRY ROSE..Surgeon
JOHN DRISCOLL..Chaplain
M. AUBLE...Officer of the Day
JOHN MARCUS..Officer of the Guard
——— ———...Sergeant Major
——— ———...Quartermaster Sergeant

———

Meeting, First and Third Thursday.

NAME.	CO.	SERVICE.	ADDRESS.
Auble C. C...........	B	141st Ill. Inf......................	Adin
Auble Montgomery..	B	141st Ill. Inf......................	"
Campbell Geo. A ...	I	2d Ohio Art.....	Canby
Dibble Samuel C....	A	3d Cal. Inf.......................	Adin
Driscoll John S.....	D	2d Neb. Cav.....................	"
Fuller Henry H.....	H	1"th Ill. Cav......................	"
Marcus John........	E	1st Nevada Cav..................	Lookout
McCash C. A.........	F	45th Iowa Inf...................	Adin
Nash L. A...........	D	37th Wis. Inf....................	"
Philliber Clinton...	D	14th Mo. Cav....................	Bieber
Rose Jerry..........	C	2d Wis. Cav.....................	Hayden Hill
Watson Samuel......	E	26th Ohio Inf...................	Bieber

ATLANTA POST, No. 92.

FRESNO, CAL

OFFICERS, 1886.

FRED. BANTA..Commander
J. S. M. FOSTER...Senior Vice-Commander
AMOS HUSSEY...Junior Vice-Commander
R. P. CHAPIN..Adjutant
HENRY BANTA..Quartermaster
JOHN DENNIS..Surgeon
REV. J. O. JORDON...Chaplain
WALTER N. BISHOP...Officer of the Day
JOY NICHOLS...Officer of the Guard
V. T. WARD...Sergeant Major
RAY WHITE..Quartermaster Sergeant

Meeting, First and Third Thursday

NAME.	CO.	SERVICE.	ADDRESS.
Bancroft Jerome....	D	5th Wis. Inf......................	Fresno
Banta Fred..........	E	44th Ind. Inf. and D 102d Penn. Inf.	"
Banta Henry........	E	17th Ind. Inf......................	"
Bishop Walter N....	M	5th N. Y. Cav.....................	"
Caldwell D. V.......	F	76th N. Y. Inf....................	"
Cardwell William...	L	11th Mo. State Militia Cav.........	"
Chapin R. P.........		Gunboat Cincinnati...............	Reno
Combs Eli	H	31st Ind. Inf.....................	Fresno
Covin John..........	A	30th Ill. Inf.....................	"
Dennis John........	G	13th and 56th Ill. Inf.............	"
Donahoo Wm........	H	24th Iowa Inf....................	"
Donohoo M. J.......	F	13th Iowa Inf....................	"
Dougherty Joseph T.	O	1st Ark. Cav.....................	"
Ewing James A......	B	11th Mo. State Militia Cav.......	"
Ferrel Marion.......	B	10th Iowa Inf....................	"
Foster John S. M....	M	15th N. Y. Cav....................	"
Fouts D. P	C	1st Ohio Cav.....................	"
Fuller C. A.........	C	2d R. I. Inf.....................	"
Gilson J. H.........	H	3d N. Y. Cav.....................	"
Halbert Joel........	K	80th Ind. Inf....................	"
Harris William......	A	81st Ill. Inf.....................	"
Harvey William.....	K	19th Mich. Inf...................	"
Hunting W. H.....	F	6th Kansas Cav...	"
Hussey Amos........	F	2d Ky. Inf.......................	"
Jordon J. C.........	O	11th Mich. Inf...................	"

152

NAME.	CO.	SERVICE.
Kelly D. O	B	100th Ohio Inf
Knepper Hugh	A	2d Cal. Cav
Kramer Fred	M	2d Mo. Art
Lawson Geo	I	9th Ill. Inf
Love Frank P	H	13th Mich. Inf
Madden Liberty T.	H	29th Iowa Inf
Mahoney Michael	E	57th Ill. Inf
Miller Frank	B	19th Conn. Inf
Newton William G.	C	8th Cal. Inf
Nichols D. E	H	8th N. H. Inf
Nichols Ivy	B	9th Mo. Cav
Redfield A. N	C	126th N. Y. Inf
Reeves Geo. J	H	1st Neb. Cav
Renfro Erastus	A	48th Iowa Inf
Roemer Henry	F	45th Penn. Inf
Sharp M. B	K	15th Ind. Inf
Smith O. C	O	68th N. Y. Inf
Smith John W	O	95th Ill. Inf
Stevens N. J	M	3d Iowa Cav
Truworthy H. E.	E	2d Cal. Cav
Tucker E. H	K	1st Wash. Ter
Walter O. L	C	11th Ill. Cav
Ward Vernon T	A	67th Ill. Inf
Watson V. O	F	40th Wis. Inf
Wharton James F.	A	11th Mo. State Militia Cav
White Ray A	D	1st Vt. Cav
Williams John B	E	2d N. Y. Cav

JOHN F. GODFREY POST, No. 93.

PASADENA, CAL.

OFFICERS, 1886.

J. D. GILCHRIST...Commander
E. S. FROST...Senior Vice-Commander
A. K. McQUILLING...Junior Vice-Commander
WESLEY BUNNELL..Adjutant
JOHN ELLIS...Quartermaster
LYMAN ALLIN..Surgeon
W. J. F. BARCUS..Chaplain
C. C. BROWN..Officer of the Day
GEORGE A. BLACK..Officer of the Guard
A. WAKELEY...Sergeant Major
MILES J. GREEN...Quartermaster Sergeant

Meeting, Alternate Saturdays.

NAME.	CO.	SERVICE.	ADDRESS.
Allin Lyman........	A	40th Ohio Inf......................	Pasadena
Barcus W. J. F......		33d Ind. Inf......................	"
Barnhardt G. W;....	G	16th Ill. Inf......................	"
Black Geo. A........	G	102d Ohio Inf.....................	"
Brown C. C..........		2d Ill. Inf.......................	"
Bunnell Wesley.....	K	143d Penn. Inf....................	"
Croft Thomas F.....		U. S. Navy	"
Ellis John..........	L	9th Iowa Cav......................	"
Frost E. S..........	E	1st Maine Cav.....................	"
Gilchrist J. D......	A	11th Kansas Inf...................	"
Green Miles J.......	O	86th N. Y. Inf....................	"
Hill John B........		U. S. S. Gazelle..................	"
Kent Horatio J.....		2d Mass. Art......................	"
Lorden W. H........		U. S. S. Saratoga	"
McQuilling A. K....	A	30th Ill. Inf....................	"
Newlan L. J........		25th N. Y. Cav....................	"
Turner E...........	O	86th Ill. Inf....................	"
Wakeley A..........	I	98th N. Y. Inf....................	"
Woodbury F. J......	K	23d Iowa Inf......................	"
Youngclaus John...	F	5th Ohio Inf.....................	"

DONELSON POST, No. 94.

TAYLOR, NEV.

OFFICERS, 1886.

ISRAEL C. MOON...Commander
JOSEPH LIDDLE...Senior Vice-Commander
SAMUEL SNYDER..Junior Vice-Commander
THOMAS H. SILLYMAN...Adjutant
JAMES MEE ....Quartermaster
JOHN COWAN,...Surgeon
ALLISON R. WATSON..Chaplain
HENRY M. GOODRICH......... ....Officer of the Day
AUGUSTUS S. PULSIPHER....................................Officer of the Guard
JOSEPH LANDER..Sergeant Major
WILLIAM ALLEN..Quartermaster Sergeant

Meeting, every Saturday.

NAME.	CO.	SERVICE.	ADDRESS.
Allen Wm...........	G	4th Wis. Inf......................	Taylor
Bishop Levi T......	I	5th Wis. Inf......................	"
Burris Wm. H.......	E	45th Mo. Inf......................	"
Cowan John.........	G	2d Cal. Cav......................	"
Dunton M. B........	H	8th Maine Inf....................	"
Goodrich Henry M..	M	2d Mass. Cav.....................	".
Lander Joseph......	D	10th Vt. Inf.....................	"
Leavitt Levi	G	3d Ill. Cav......................	Ward
Liddle Joseph.......	C	15th Ill. Inf....................	Taylor
McQuaig John.......	I	106th N. Y. Inf..................	"
Mee James..........	H	3d N. Y. Art.....................	"
Montgomery Rob't..	E	1st Mo. Inf......................	"
Moon Israel C.......	K	22d Wis. Inf.....................	"
Pulsipher A. C......	I	1st N. Y. Mounted Rifles.........	"
Rutherford Daniel...	A	140th N. Y. Inf..................	Shoshone
Shimp T. E..........	A	46th Penn. Inf...................	Taylor
Sillyman Thos. H...	H	48th Penn. Inf...................	Ward
Snyder Samuel......	C	75th Ill. Inf....................	Taylor
Somelott Carl......	B	28th Wis. Inf....................	"
Thomson Joseph....	B	16th Wis. Inf....................	"
Travis George.......	I	10th Wis. Inf....................	Ward
Watson Allison R...		2d Col. Cav......................	Ely
Williams Geo. W....	I	195th Ohio Inf...................	Taylor
Williams Rodham ..	F	31st Ohio Inf....................	"

COL. J. W. S. ALEXANDER POST, No. 95.

OFFICERS, 1886.

HAMPTON ELLIS..Commander
JOHN H. EATON..Senior Vice-Commander
B. F. PASCOE...Junior Vice-Commander
GEO. A. ALLEN..Adjutant
ALEX. A. LOVE...Quartermaster
——— ———..Surgeon
WM. H. BEARD...Chaplain
W. H. HARRELL..Officer of the Day
GEO. C. STRONG...Officer of the Guard
JAMES WILEY...Sergeant Major
CLARENCE WEST...Quartermaster Sergeant

Meeting, Second and Fourth Saturday.

NAME.	CO.	SERVICE.	ADDRESS.
Allen Geo. A.........	A	76th N. Y. Inf......................	Globe
Beard Wm. H.......	E	111th Ill. Inf........................	"
Colvig Clark S......	A	21st Ill. Inf........................	Armer
Eaton John H.......	D	190th Ohio Inf......................	Globe
Ellis Hampton......	K	8th Ind. Inf........................	"
Harrell W. H........	B	27th Ind. Inf........................	"
Love A. E...........	G	2d Col. Cav........................	"
Montgomery F. C...		2d N. Y Cav........................	"
Pascoe B. F...........	I	1st Cal. Cav.	"
Schulze Charles.....		1st Kansas Inf......................	"
Shanley Patrick.....		2d U. S. Inf........................	"
Strong George C....	B	1st New Mexico Cav...............	"
West Clarence.......	E	3d N. Y. Inf........................	"
Wiley James........	F	15th N. Y. Heavy Art.............	"

T. W. SHERMAN POST, No. 96.

OROVILLE, CAL.

OFFICERS, 1886.

H. O. BELL..Commander
D. F. FRYER...Senior Vice-Commander
J. H. KARSNER...Junior Vice-Commander
R. De LANCIE..Adjutant
D. R. PERKINS..Quartermaster
F. W. BENJAMIN..Surgeon
T. J. WILKERSON..Chaplain
J. T. CRESS...Officer of the Day
S. C. CHAMBERLIN...Officer of the Guard
W. Y. BLISS..Sergeant Major
J. H. MARTIN..Quartermaster Sergeant

Meeting, Second Tuesday and Fourth Saturday.

NAME.	CO.	SERVICE.	ADDRESS.
Bell H. O............		Signal Corps.......................	Oroville
Benjamin F. W......		3d Mass. Art....	"
Bierce Jas. O........		....	
Bliss W. Y..........	A	1st Cal. Cav......................	"
Bringham F. J.......	B	44th Iowa Inf.....................	"
Calmes M. B.........	M	1st Ark. Inf......................	"
Chamberlin S. O....	O	26th Mich. Inf....................	"
Chase E. O..........	L	2d Cal. Cav.......................	Pentz
Cress Thos....... .	O	9th Iowa Inf......................	Oroville
Davis W. J..........	A	1st Cal. Cav......................	"
De Lancie R.........	A	1st Cal. Cav......................	"
Doyle Thos..........	O	82d N. Y. Inf.....................	"
Edwards John.......	G	6th Cal. Inf......................	"
Ellis I. N...........	F	15th Kansas Cav...................	"
Frost Andrew J.....	B	47th Iowa Inf.....................	"
Fryer D. F..........	H	55th Ill. Inf.....................	"
Gable George........	D	7th Iowa Inf.........	"
Gibbs David........	G	6th Cal. Inf......................	"
Glazier J. E.........	F	23d Mass. Inf.....................	"
Green Robert M	A	Ohio Inf..........................	"
Haycock M. S. B.....	A	5th Ill. Inf......................	Berry Creek
Heckert Wm........	D	3d Iowa Inf.......................	Pentz
Humphrey W. H....	A	1st Cal. Cav......................	Enterprise
Karsner J. H.... ..	O	1st Del. Inf......................	Oroville
Keene Asa H........	B	8th Maine Inf.....................	"

157

NAME.	CO.	SERVICE.	ADDRESS.
Langenecker G. H..	M	16th Penn. Cav.....................	Nelson
Leech Wm...........	D	157th Ill. Inf......................	Oroville
Lewis A. H..	H	3d Minn. Inf......	Bidwell's Bar
Maley John..........	C	3d Iowa Cav......................	Magalia
Mansfield I. Le Roy..		2d N. J. Inf......................	Wyandotte
Marcovich John.....	A	1st Cal. Cav......	Cherokee
Martin J. H.........	G	2d Cal. Cav......................	Oroville
Maxon John........	A	1st Cal. Cav......................	Bidwell's Bar
Merrifield Wm......	D	63d Ill. Inf......	Clear Creek
Patten Henry.......		4th Maine Light Art............. ..	Oroville
Perkins D. K........		Maine............................	"
Perry Alvin A..		2d Maine Battery.................	Magalia
Plaskett Wm........		144th N. Y. Inf...................	Forbestown
Ratrey John........		....	Wyandotte
Rebscher J..........	F	52d N. Y. Inf	Oroville
Richards R. B......	A	9th Kansas Cav...................	"
Riley G. W..........	I	27th Ill. Inf.....................	"
Rowe Edwin........	C	37th Wis. Inf...........	Cherokee
Rowe James.........	C	31st Wis. Inf.....................	"
Scott N. B...........	A	11th Maine Cav...................	Nelson
Strover Lewis.......	A	28th Ohio Inf....................	Lovelock
Turner J. C.........		2d Battery Maine Res. Corps	Bangor
Voorhees William...	C	7th Cal. Inf......................	Oroville
Wagner John.......		....	Merrimac
Wilkinson T. J......	B	122d Ill. Inf.....................	Oroville
Williams David......	A	1st Cal. Cav.....................	Berry Creek
Woodman E. M......	K	2d Cal. Cav.....................	Enterprise
Wright Andrew.....	A	5th Cal. Inf.....................	Oroville
Wyckoff Charles.....	,	....	Brush Creek

FREDERICKSBURG POST, No. 97.

POINT ARENA, CAL.

OFFICERS, 1886.

RICHARD BOURNES............. ....Commander
J. A. MADDOX...Senior Vice-Commander
ETHAN ALLEN. ....Junior Vice-Commander
DANIEL SULLIVAN...Adjutant
LEWIS PARRISH...Quartermaster
——— ———..Surgeon
DRURY SHOEMAKE...Chaplain
JOHN MAYER...Officer of the Day
J. M. KNAPP..Officer of the Guard
G. P. YOUNG...Sergeant Major
D. L. MADDOX..Quartermaster Sergeant

Meeting, Monday on or before Full Moon.

NAME.	CO.	SERVICE.	ADDRESS.
Allen Ethan..	A	14th Ill. Cav......................	Point Arena
Bedell A. M.........	H	1st N. H. Art................... ...	"
Bournes Richard....	O	4th Penn. Res. Inf......	"
Drew C. N..........	K	6th Maine Inf....................	"
Ketcham Levi.......	F	10th Ill. Cav....................	Manchester
Knapp J. M........	C	7th Iowa Cav....................	Point Arena
Maddox D. L........	L	13th Mo. Cav....................	Miller
Maddox J. A........	M	2d Mo. Cav.......	Point Arena
Mayer John.........	K	103d N. Y. Inf.	"
Parrish Lewis.......	C	6th Mich. Heavy Art....	"
Shoemake Drury....	A	8th Cal. Inf......................	Manchester
Sullivan Daniel......		U. S. S. Iva.................	Point Arena
Wilson G. I.........	G	6th Maine Inf......	Gualala
Young G. P..........	E	22d Penn. Inf....................	Petaluma

159

J. F. REYNOLDS POST, No. 98.

SANTA CRUZ, CAL

OFFICERS, 1886.

HORACE WANZER...Commander
HAMILTON FAY...Senior Vice Commander
A. H. KANE.. Junior Vice Commander
O. J. LINCOLN...... ....Adjutant
I. L. BLAISDELL.. ....Quartermaster
J. M. GROVER...Surgeon
ROGER CONANT....................................... ....Chaplain
W. P. ENGLAND...Officer of the Day
H. C. VEATCH...Officer of the Guard
H. F. WRIGHT..Sergeant Major
J. C. TOLL...Quartermaster Sergeant

Meeting, Second and Fourth Friday.

NAME.	CO.	SERVICE.	ADDRESS.
Blaisdell I. L........		U. S. Navy	Santa Cruz
Burke Bart..........	I	67th Ind. Inf......	"
Conant Roger........	O	14th N. Y. State Militia...........	"
Emery W. E.........		7th Cal. Inf.......................	Laurel
England W. S.......	F	47th Iowa Inf......	Santa Cruz
Fay Hamilton......	D	35th Iowa Inf.....................	"
Fitzsimmons Chas..		2d Minn. Sharpshooters..........	"
Fresham J. T........	A	8th Cal. Inf.......	Soquel
Goldsby Z. N.......	D	12th Mo. Cav...........	Santa Cruz
Grover J. M.........	G	86th Ind. Inf......	"
Halstead Samuel H..	I	8th Mo. Inf.......................	"
Hamlin O. L.........		U. S. S. Sabine and 19th Maine Inf..	"
Houck F. L..........	B	95th Ill. Inf......	"
Kane A. H...........	A	59th Ind. Inf.....................	"
Knight Benjamin...	I	1st Mass. Cav....................	"
Lincoln O. J........	F	21st Maine Inf....................	"
Littlefield G. B......		U. S. S. Niagara.................	"
Peaks J. B..........	A	1st Maine Cav.................	"
Perry E. D..........	O	153d Ill. Inf...............	"
Reynolds J. A..	M	9th Iowa Cav.....................	"
Spalsbury Edgar....	I	35th N. Y. Inf....................	"
Sullivan J. T........	E	1st Mass. Cav....................	"
Toll John C..........		9th Wis. Art.....................	"
Veatch H. C.........	C	5th Ind. Cav.....................	"
Wanzer Horace......	G	22d N. Y. Inf....................	"
Wright H. F........		U. S. S. Ohio....................	"

UNION POST, No. 99.

LEMOORE, CAL.

OFFICERS, 1888.

ALFRED S. CUNINGHAM.................................. ....Commander
AARON MOONEY...Senior Vice-Commander
WM. T. SPRAGUE...Junior Vice-Commander
J. H. FOX...Adjutant
ISRAEL DUNN...Quartermaster
OSCAR E. COON..Surgeon
THOMAS F. HENRY...Chaplain
PETER STOLZ..Officer of the Day
R. GRAINGER..Officer of the Guard
JAMES AULTHOUSE...Sergeant Major
———— ————...Quartermaster Sergeant

Meeting, Second and Fourth Thursday.

NAME.	CO.	SERVICE.	ADDRESS.
Aulthouse James....	A	3d Mich. Inf........................	Lemoore
Coon Oscar E........	K	4th Ind. Cav.........................	"
Cuningham Alfred S.	E	1st Ohio Inf.........................	"
Dunn Israel.........	G	107th N. Y. Inf.	"
Fox Julius H........	E	11th Mich. Inf.......................	"
Grainger Robert....	H	78th Ill. Inf...................... ..	"
Henry Thos. F......	B	4th Iowa Inf.................	"
Hill Robert M. C....	E	10th Kansas Cav....................	"
Jacobs Justin.......	C	16th Wis. Inf........................	"
Mooney Aaron......	A	26th Mich. Inf.......................	"
Rhoads Andrew J....	H	2d Cal. Cav..................... ...	"
Sprague Wm. T.. ...	D	10th Iowa Inf........................	"
Stolz Peter..........	I	9th Ohio Inf........................	"
Taylor Jonathan....	D	4th Tenn. Inf.......................	"

CHAMPION HILL POST, No. 100.

PLYMOUTH, CAL.

OFFICERS, 1886.

W. T. JONES..Commander
—— ——..Senior Vice-Commander
JOHN MILLER...Junior Vice-Commander
E. W. THOMAS..Adjutant
WALTER H. SARGENT...Quartermaster
—— ——...Surgeon
ELI WITHROW...Chaplain
B. A. DOWNEY..Officer of the Day
PHILLIP KHERES...Officer of the Guard
—— ——...Sergeant Major
—— ——...Quartermaster Sergeant

Meeting, Second and Fourth Tuesday.

NAME.	CO.	SERVICE.	ADDRESS.
Corrilla Bisento.....	K	2d Cal. Cav......................	Plymouth
Downey B. A........	K	6th Cal. Inf......................	"
Ellis F. H..........	F	2d Mounted Rifles...............	Amador City
Jones W. T..........	H	173d Penn. Inf..................	Plymouth
Kheres Phillip......	A	3d U. S. Inf....................	"
McMillin W. M....	D	21st Mo. Inf....................	"
Miller John.........	M	1st Cal. Cav....................	"
Moon H. B..........	O	7th Cal. Inf....................	"
Phelps George......	O	1st Cal. Inf....................	"
Phillips John.......	A	105th Ohio Inf.................	"
Sargent Walter H....	O	35th Mass. Inf.................	"
Thomas E. W........	G	77th Penn. Inf.................	"
Way Wm. G.........	B	3d Cal. Inf....................	"
Withrow Eli,.......	F	15th Iowa Inf..................	"

BELMONT POST, No 101.

AUBURN, CAL.

OFFICERS, 1886.

J. W. McCULLOUGH..Commander
LOUIS RABE..Senior Vice-Commander
W. H. CURTIS..Junior Vice-Commander
L. S. NEWCOMB..Adjutant
A. S. LOWER..Quartermaster
T. M. TODD..Surgeon
H. H. RICHMOND..Chaplain
W. J. ROBINSON..Officer of the Day
JOHN McCOY..Officer of the Guard
F. J. FOLSOM..Sergeant Major
J. H. RITTINGER..Quartermaster Sergeant

Meeting, First Friday on or before Full Moon.

NAME.	CO.	SERVICE.	ADDRESS.
Ackerman Truman..	E	19th Wis. Inf.	Auburn
Arnold Isaac........	H	51st Ill. Inf.	"
Ashburn Joseph....	A	4th Cal. Inf.	Cisco
Atkins E. S.........	C	61st Ill. Inf.	Auburn
Austin James........	B	4th Cal. Inf.	Iowa Hill
Baker Ira D.........	H	2d Bat. U. S. Inf.	Auburn
Beecher B. B........	C	193d Penn. Inf.	"
Birce F. A...........	O	2d Maine Inf.	Towles Station
Blaisdell A. G......	K	4th Cal. Inf.	Gold Run
Bonham J. S........	K	1st Cal. Inf.	Iowa Hill
Copelin George......	I	6th Kansas Inf.	Clipper Gap
Curtis W. H.........	I	11th Ind. Inf.	Auburn
Davis Walter S.....	F	22d Mass. Inf.	Mammoth Bar
Dean J. S...........	G	24th Ind. Inf.	Auburn
Earskine A. E.......	D	12th Maine Inf.	Towles Station
Folsom F. J.........	L	7th Maine Cav.	Auburn
Gattiker John.......	D	1st Cal. Inf.	"
Haines G. W........	I	1st Md. Inf.	"
Hateky Frederick....	I	1st Mass. Inf.	Iowa Hill
Hawkins F. S	D	19th Maine Inf.	Auburn
Higgins Chas. O.....	A	1st Nevada Inf.	Blue Canyon
Hill Frank W........	A	1st Mass. Heavy Art.	Auburn
Kelley Andrew......	D	3d N. Y. Art.	"
Logan Samuel.......	E	5th Cal. Inf.	"
Lower O. S..........	K	4th Cal. Inf.	Newcastle

163

NAME.	CO.	SERVICE.	ADDRESS.
Lyman Walter......	C	42d Wis. Inf.............	Auburn
Mallory Ogden......	I	133d Ohio Inf......................	"
Martin P. J..........	D	7th Cal. Inf........................	New Eng. Mills
McCoy John.........	G	18th U. S. Inf......................	Yankee Jim
McCullough J. W....	D	1..!st Ohio Inf. and 20th Ohio Inf..	Auburn
Myer John M........		27th Mich. Inf.....................	"
Newcomb L. S......	L	3d N.Y.Art.& 24th Ind't N.Y.Battery	"
Ogle D. W...........	G	39th Ill. Inf.......................	"
Ogle John...........	H	72d Ind. Inf.......................	"
Perry Wm...........	M	10th Mich. Inf....	Lincoln
Rabe Louis..........		2d Wis. Bat.......................	Blue Canyon
Rea John............	K	23d Mich. Inf.....................	Lincoln
Richardson W. H....	E	3d Cal. Inf........................	Auburn
Richmond H. H.....	C	21st N. Y. Inf.....................	"
Rittinger J. H.......	D	7th Cal. Inf.......................	"
Robbins J. B.,......	B	1st Maine Heavy Art.	Colfax
Robinson W. J......	E	3d N. Y. Cav..	Auburn
Sparhawk Jared.....	L	2d Mass. Inf......................	Iowa Hill
Spoor G. L.,........	A	160th N. Y. Inf.	Blue Canyon
Storrs O. D..........	A	2d Berdan Sharpshooters..........	Auburn
Todd T. M......... .	G	Independent Penn. Bat...........	"
Towle A.............	I	1st Mass. Inf.....................	"
Tyler Levi..........	D	186th N. Y. Inf....	Hotaling
Whittier Geo. G.....	I	2d Iowa Inf....	Spanish Dry Dig's.
Yoder Enoch E......	L	2d Cal. Cav......................	Iowa Hill
Zuver Levi..........	C	13th U. S. Inf....................	Auburn

JAMES KEHOE POST, No. 102.

BISBEE, A. T

OFFICERS, 1886.

J. F. DUNCAN..Commander
J. W. HOWELL..Senior Vice-Commander
E. G. NORTON. ....Junior Vice-Commander
J. RENNARD..Adjutant
H. C. PURCELL...Quartermaster
G. H. EDDLEMAN..Surgeon
J. LONG...Chaplain
T. M. SHEARER ....Officer of the Day
J. W. GRANT...Officer of the Guard
CHAS. FELDMAN...Sergeant Major
R. J. LOWTHER......................................Quartermaster Sergeant

---

Meeting, First and Third Tuesday.

NAME.	CO.	SERVICE.	ADDRESS.
Duncan James F....		46th Penn. Inf..................	Bisbee
Eddleman G. H......	K	6th West Va. Cav..................	"
Ellickson J..........	H	27th Wis. Inf......................	"
Feldman Charles....	G	84th Ill. Inf......................	"
Fetterman L. T......	E	101st Penn. Inf...................	"
Grant J. W..........	D	7th Cal. Inf......................	"
Herring M. F........	G	5th Cal Inf......................	"
Howell J. W........	M	6th West Va. Cav..................	"
Kline Louis.........	G	14th Ill. Inf.....................	"
Lemunyan C........	I	6th Mich. Inf.....................	"
Long J. H...........	G	8th Mich. Inf.....................	"
Lowther R. J.......	K	1st Cal. Inf......................	"
Maloney Phil......	F	6th Kansas. Cav..................	"
McMartin John.....	E	7th Cal. Inf......................	"
Moore J. L.........	H	7th Cal. Inf......................	"
Norton E. G........	D	2d Maine Cav..................	"
Purcell H. C........	M	1st Cal. Cav......................	"
Rennard J. R........	I	47th N. Y. Inf......	"
Shearer T. M........	F	1st Col. Cav.....................	"
Wood A. E..........	F	13th Iowa Inf....................	"

T. B. STEVENS POST, No. 103.

ELSINORE, CAL.

OFFICERS, 1886.

H. I. GRUWELL..Commander
WILLIAM COLLIER...Senior Vice-Commander
GEO. R. FEZLER...Junior Vice-Commander
L. B. PECK..Adjutant
SAMUEL J. SHAW.. Quartermaster
BENJ. A. RICE...Surgeon
JESSE T. COBB..Chaplain
T. C. GULLIVER..Officer of the Day
L. N. DIKE..Officer of the Guard
B. J. LEE..Sergeant Major
W. W. CAMPBELL...Quartermaster Sergeant

Meeting, every other Saturday.

NAME.	CO.	SERVICE.	ADDRESS.
Campbell W. W.....	A	7th Ill. Inf........................	Elsinore
Cobb Jesse T........	D	1st N. H. Inf......................	"
Collier William.....	C	45th Iowa Inf.....................	"
Dike Latimer N....	G	67th Ohio Inf.....................	"
Fezler Geo. R.......	B	33d Ill. Inf.......................	Murietta
Gruwell H. I.	B	14th Iowa Inf.....................	Elsinore
Gulliver T. C........	C	50th Penn. Inf....................	"
Lee B. J.............	B	1st Nevada Cav...................	Temescal
McCanna J. H.......		30th Iowa Inf.....................	Perris
Peck L. B...........	H	14th Ill. Inf......................	Elsinore
Rice Benjamin A....	C	9th Kansas Cav..........	"
Schelling Jacob.....	F	64th Ill. Inf......................	"
Shaw Samuel J......	L	7th Iowa Cav.....................	"

HANCOCK POST, No. 104.

MERCED, CAL.

OFFICERS, 1886.

GEO. B. COOK ....Commander
CLARK RALSTON....................... ....Senior Vice-Commander
W. J. QUIGLEY...Junior Vice-Commander
J. O. BLACKBURN............... ....Adjutant
E. A. PACKER...Quartermaster
GEO. P LEE...Surgeon
A. L. WELLMAN...Chaplain
W. W. GRAY...... ....Officer of the Day
L. A. MANCHESTER..Officer of the Guard
A. N. AMES...Sergeant Major
H. N. MARTIN...Quartermaster Sergeant

Meeting, Second and Fourth Wednesday.

NAME.	CO.	SERVICE.	ADDRESS.
Abbott W. W........	F	17th Mass. Inf.....................	Merced
Ames A. N..........	C	13th Maine Inf. and K 30th Me. Inf	"
Blackburn J. O.....		U. S. S. Avenger..................	"
Conant Sumner F....	F	26th Maine Inf..	"
Cook Geo. B........	D	4th Conn. Inf. and 1st Conn. Art..	"
Eastabrooks A.......	M	1st Cal. Cav.	"
French H. W........	K	21st Maine Inf....	"
Gray W. W........ .		....	"
Lee Geo. P..........		....	"
Manchester L. A....	E	2d Mass. Cav.....................	"
Marks Chas. H......	G	80th Ind. Inf.	"
Martin H N.........	H	100th N. Y. Inf...	"
Packer E. A.........	E	26th Conn. Inf...................	"
Quigley W. J........	A	23d Penn. Inf....................	"
Ralston Clark.......	A	125th Ill. Inf.....................	"
Smith H. A		....	"
Smith James........	E	4th Cal. Inf.....................	"
Stevens Abram......		....	"
Wellman A. L.......	F	48th Ill. Inf.....	"

WINCHESTER POST, No. 105.

ANDERSON, CAL.

OFFICERS, 1886.

```
J. H. BEECHER.....................................................Commander
CHAS. M. PALMER......................................Senior Vice-Commander
THEODORE PLEISCH..............  ......................Junior Vice-Commander
R. B. KEELEY...............................................................Adjutant
P. H. COLE..............................  .....  .........................Quartermaster
H. C. WALKER................................................................Surgeon
JOS. CROGHAN...............................................................Chaplain
E. K. BRIGHTMAN...............................................Officer of the Day
J L. DAVIS........................................................Officer of the Guard
W. I. DAVIS.............................................  .....................Sergeant Major
GEO. O. ENGLISH............  .............................Quartermaster Sergeant
```

Meeting, Tuesday on or before the full moon.

NAME.	CO.	ARM OF SERVICE.	ADDRESS.
Beecher Jas. H......	C	129th Ind. Inf.....	Anderson
Brightman E. K.....	F	126th Ill. Inf......................	"
Cole Peter H........	E	1st Mich. Cav.......................	"
Croghan Jos.........	H	44th Ind. Inf......	"
Davis John L........	I	5th Cal. Inf......	"
Davis Wash I........	H	10th Ill. Inf....	"
English Geo. O.....		1st Battery Kansas Art............	"
Himes W. H	K	3d Iowa Cav.......................	"
Keeley Richard B....	G	2d Iowa Inf........	"
Palmer C. M........	G	1st Ill. Cav.......................	"
Pleisch Theodore....	A	60th Ind. Inf.......	"
Walker Henry C.....	I	8th N. Y. Cav.....................	"

168

GELCICH POST, No. 106.

EAST LOS ANGELES, CAL.

OFFICERS, 1886.

W. H. McKEAG..Commander
F. W. TYLER..Senior Vice-Commander
A. SAUNDERS..Junior Vice-Commander
WINSLOW MALY...Adjutant
SYLVANUS SMITH...Quartermaster
O. A. MOORE...Surgeon
J. C. MILLER...Chaplain
W. H. HARRISON...Officer of the Day
E. W. RUSSELL..Officer of the Guard
O. R. STEAVENS.. ..Sergeant Major
W. S. HURLBUT...Quartermaster Sergeant

Meeting, First and Third Friday.

NAME.	CO.	SERVICE.	ADDRESS.
Barroclough H. O....	D	1st Conn. Inf......................	East Los Angeles
Ells Charles O.......	E	8th Minn. Inf....................	"
Hamilton E. M......	B	1st Minn. Inf....................	"
Harrison W. H......	E	51st Ill. Inf.....................	"
Hurlbut W. S........		U. S. Signal Corps.............	"
Maley Winslow	E	Independent Bat. Minn. Cav.....	"
McKeag W. H......	I	25th N. J. Inf. and A 3d N. J. Cav..	"
Miller J. C..........	H	7th Ill. Cav. and G 115th Ill. Inf...	"
Moore O. A..........		11th Veteran Res. Corps..........	"
Richards D. S.......	B	19th Maine Inf.................	"
Robb Charles.......	G	97th N. Y. Inf. and A 79th N. Y. Inf	"
Russell E. W........	A	4th Minn. Inf..................	"
Saunders A..........	H	17th Maine Inf.........	"
Smith Sylvanus.....	F	12th N. H. Inf..................	"
Steavens O. R.......	H	2d Iowa Cav.....................	"
Tyler F. W..........	K	52d Ill. Inf.......	"
Vogan J. D..........	E	100th Penn. Inf.................	"
Vosburgh Herman..	I	49th Mass. Inf.................	"
White J. J..........	B	33d N. J. Inf....	"

GOV. DICK YATES POST; No. 107.

TRAVER, CAL.

—

OFFICERS, 1886.

ROBERT L. FREEMAN..Commander
E. W. HOLMES..Senior Vice-Commander
T. L. REED..Junior Vice-Commander
P. Y. BAKER..Adjutant
THOS. HOUSE.. ....Quartermaster
D. TURNER..Surgeon
L. S. SPROAT...Chaplain
J. A. ELLERT.. ....Officer of the Day
THOMAS PHILLIPS..Officer of the Guard
—— —— ....Sergeant Major
W. D. HAYNES............ ....Quartermaster Sergeant

———

Meeting, First and Third Saturday.

NAME.	CO.	SERVICE.	ADDRESS.
Baker P. Y..........	O	2d Cal. Inf.........................	Traver
Bates John T........	E	7th Ky. Inf.........................	King's River
Brush Peter.	E	7th Ky. Cav.....	Traver
Campbell Nathan....	M	12th Mo. Cav....	"
Clark Thomas N....	K	23d Mo. Inf.......................	"
Ellert John A........	B	1st Bat. Cal. Mountaineers........	"
Freeman Robert L..	K	1st Iowa Cav......................	"
Haynes W. D........	E	14th Ohio Inf.....................	"
Holmes E. W........	D	14th Iowa Inf.....................	"
House Thomas......	D	2d Mo. Cav.......................	"
Kerr John...........	K	32d N. Y. Inf......................	"
Metcalf Geo. N......	D	2d Mo. Cav.......................	"
Phillips Thomas....	G	4th N. Y. Cav.....................	"
Reed T. L....	A	66th Ohio Inf.....................	"
Ross William E......	F	10th Ind. Cav......	"
Sproat L. S..........	G	28th Ill. Inf......................	"
Turner D............	H	1st Cal. Inf.....	"
Vose Warren........	E	3d Cal. Inf.....	"

170

PLACERVILLE POST, No. 108.

PLACERVILLE, CAL.

OFFICERS, 1886.

ANDREW CULBERTSON ....'...Commander
CHARLES H. WEATHERWAX...........................Senior Vice-Commander
M. O'KEEFFE. ....Junior Vice-Commander
H. B. TURMAN... ....Adjutant
H. S. MOREY.. ... Quartermaster
WARREN M. FALES........................... ....Surgeon
JAMES CURRY..Chaplain
W. H. H. FELLOWS...Officer of the Day
A. A. GIGNAC...Officer of the Guard
R. O. WATKINS...Sergeant Major
DAVID W. MACOMBER...................................Quartermaster Sergeant

---

Meeting, First Monday.

NAME.	CO.	SERVICE.	ADDRESS.
Baldwin Julius A....	L	9th Iowa Cav.....................	Placerville
Bayles J. W.........	B	3d Iowa Inf......................	"
Bruce George.......	K	8th Cal. Inf.....................	"
Burlingham N. D...	H	1st N. Y. Dragoons...............	Garden Valley
Chapman Joseph....	L	2d Cal. Cav.....................	Diamond Springs
Chapman N.........	K	2d Cal. Cav.....................	"
Crawford J. J......	H	100th Penn. Inf.................	Placerville
Culbertson A. T.....	H	5th Wis. Inf.....................	"
Curry James........	B	187th Ohio Inf..................	"
Dean S. C...........	I	2d Cal. Cav.....................	El Dorado, Cal.
Dixon Wm. H.......	E	5 th Ill. Inf.....	Placerville
Fales Warren M....	I	6th Iowa Inf....................	"
Fellows W. H. H....	D	7th Cal. Inf.....................	"
Gignac A. A.........	D	6th Cal. Inf.....................	"
Jewett J. R.........	A	1st Ohio Art....................	Diamond Springs
Lewis D. C	E	11th Mass. Inf..................	Garden Valley
Macomber David W..		U. S. Navy..............	Placerville
McGregor W. H. ..	A	7th Cal. Inf.....................	"
Morey Henry S		6th Maine Inf...................	"
O'Keeffe Michael....	I	2d Cal. Cav.....................	"
Turman H. B........	K	8th Cal. Inf.	"
Watkins James M....	E	85th Penn. Inf.	"
Watkins R. O.......	E	1st Ohio Art....................	"
Weatherwax Chas. H.	K	2d Cal. Cav.....................	"
Whitbeck W. H......	K	17th Ill. Cav...................	"
Worth Thomas G....	G	7th Cal. Inf.....................	El Dorado

ISLAND No. 10 POST, No. 109.

SELMA, OAL.

OFFICERS, 1886.

W. L. DEMONBRON...Commander
MARION SIDES..Senior Vice-Commander
JACOB E. WHITSON..Junior Vice-Commander
JOHN MALTRY..Adjutant
CHAS. H. ROBINSON...Quartermaster
JOHN ALL...Surgeon
O. H. VAN HORN...Chaplain
WALTER HOBBS...Officer of the Day
ALEX H. GRAVES...................................... ....Officer of the Guard
—— ——...Sergeant Major
—— ——...Quartermaster Sergeant

Meeting, Second and last Tuesday.

NAME.	CO.	SERVICE.	ADDRESS.
All John.............	F	85th Ind. Inf......................	Selma
Demonbron W. L...	E	11th Ky. Inf...................	"
Diedrick W. H......	I	3d Mass Heavy Art...	"
Gilbert Julius L....	C	40th Wis. Inf.........	"
Graves Alex. H......	F	22d Wis. Inf......................	"
Hobbs Walter.......	G	1st Cal. Cav......................	"
Maltry John........	A	40th N. J. Inf.........	"
McClanahan Chas...	C	1st Mo. Cav......................	"
Robinson Chas. H...	I	47th Ill. Inf......................	"
Royal Ben..........	L	1st Cal. Cav......................	"
Sides Marion........	D	18th Mo. Inf.....	"
Van Horn O. H......	E	5th Iowa Cav................... ..	"
Whitson Jacob E....	E	13th Iowa Inf...................	"

GEN. JOHN F. MILLER POST, No. 110.

COLUSA, CAL.

OFFICERS, 1886.

C. M. BALLANTINE...Commander
E. DE ST. MAURICE ....Senior Vice Commander
ADELBERT E. POTTER................................. Junior Vice Commander
JOHN E. HAYMAN..Adjutant
A. B. HOOPER...................... ....Quartermaster
FRANK Z. SMITH.. Surgeon
J. B. GEORGE................... ....Chaplain
F. J. CALMES...Officer of the Day
D. B. McCOLLUM...Officer of the Guard
——— ——— ....Sergeant Major
——— ———...Quartermaster Sergeant

Meeting, Second and Fourth Wednesday.

NAME.	CO.	ARM OF SERVICE.	ADDRESS.
Ballantine Chas. M..		153d N. Y. Inf.....................	Colusa
Hauning W. W......	D	25th Ohio Inf. & 12th Ohio Battery.	Grimes, Cal.
Bows John..........	B	39th Ill. Inf........................	Colusa
Calmes F. J.........	G	2d Cal. Cav......................	"
Cooper A. B........	I	14th Mo. Cav................... ..	"
De St. Maurice E....		170th N. Y. Inf....	"
Garden L. B.........	F	8th Ill. Cav.......................	"
George J. B.........	A	6th Mo. Cav..........	Grimes, Cal.
Graham George......	B	1st Ky. Inf......................	Colusa
Harpham John H....	M	1st Col. Cav......................	College City
Hathaway Wm.......	E	5th Mass. Battery.	Colusa
Hayman John E..	I	134th Ind. Inf......	"
Keffer S.............	B	Cass Co. Mo. Home Guards........	"
Liening John H....	D	1st Cal. Cav.....................	"
McCollum D. B......	K	7th Mo. Cav....	"
Miller Isaac.........	G	129th Penn. Inf................	Butte City Cal.
Potter A. E.........	H	160th N. Y. Inf.....	Colusa
Richter H...........	B	23d N. Y. Cav....	Maxwell
Riley Edward.......	I	9th Ill. Cav.......................	Grimes, Cal.
Smith F. Z.......	A	14th N. Y. Inf....................	Colusa
Stone Philander.....	E	84th Ill. Inf.......................	Butte City

GEN'L GEO. WRIGHT POST, No. 111.

VISALIA, CAL.

OFFICERS, 1886.

JACOB L. ASAY.. ....Commander
HARRISON WHITE..Senior Vice-Commander
JAMES O. BLAKELEY.....................................Junior Vice-Commander
CLAUDE J. GIDDINGS...Adjutant
JOHN EDWARDS...Quartermaster
WILLIAM H. HARRIS...Surgeon
W. G. PENNEBAKER...Chaplain
AUGUSTUS WEISHAR.................................Officer of the Day
HARVEY N. DENNY.................................Officer of the Guard
GEORGE R. ANDERSON.................................Sergeant Major
....Quartermaster Sergeant

Meeting, every Wednesday, Good Templar Hall.

NAME.	CO.	SERVICE.	ADDRESS.
Adams David M.....	K	88th Ill. Inf......................	Visalia
Anderson Benj. C...		2d Ohio Battery...................	Farmersville
Anderson George R..		Tenney's Kansas Battery..........	Visalia
Asay Jacob L........		142d and 208th Penn. Inf.........	"
Beard John	A	2d Cal. Cav......................	"
Blakeley James O...	E	44th N.Y.Inf. & D 19th U.S.Col'd Inf	"
Butz M. Chris........	H	46th Ill. Inf....................	"
Butz William A......	B	2d Ill. Light Art................	"
Clark John	I	155th and 152d Ill. Inf..........	Farmersville
Dailey James R......	E	2d Cal. Cav......................	Visalia
Denny Harvey N....	E	51st Ind. Inf....................	"
East Thomas.........	G	3d Mo. Cav	"
Edwards John.......	B	76th Ill. Inf....................	"
Eltel George	B	4th Cal. Inf.....................	"
Giddings Claude J ..	C	84th Ohio Inf....................	"
Griffin Asa T........	A	6th Ill. Inf.....................	"
Harris Rufus R......	B	55th Ohio Inf....................	"
Harris William H....	K	65th N. Y. Inf...................	"
Hummason Lewis A.	K	3d Minn. Inf.....................	"
James William D....	D	29th Mass. Inf.	"
Kline James S.......	H	11th Kansas Inf..................	Grangeville
Lacey David M......	E	89th Ill. Inf....................	Visalia
Lemmon W. B.......	I	71st Ohio Inf....................	"
Loos Thomas F......	K	61st Ill. Inf....................	"
Palmer Joseph C....	I	2d Cal. Cav......................	"
Pennebaker W. G....	I	4th Iowa Inf.	Farmersville
Pratt Daniel...	K	78th N. Y. Inf. and C 28th Mich Inf.	Visalia
Speise Frederick....	A	200th Penn. Inf..................	"
Thompson H. R.....	D	3d Mich. Cav....................	"
Weishar Augustus ..		U. S. S. Saginaw................	"
White Harrison......	B	4th Ill. Cav.....................	"
Wild William E......	K	141st Ill. Inf...................	"

SOUTHERN PACIFIC COMPANY.
(PACIFIC SYSTEM.)
Trains leave and are due to arrive at San Francisco.

Lve. for, }	FROM JUNE 1st, 1886,	{ Arr. from.
‡ 8.00 A.	....Byron...	‡ 6.10 P.
8 00 A.	....Calistoga and Napa....................................	10.10 A.
4.00 P.	.... " "	6.10 P.
7.30 A.	....Colfax..	5.40 P.
7.30 A.	....Delta, Redding and Portland...........................	6 40 P.
* 3.30 P.	....Galt via Martinez......................................	*10.40 A.
8.30 A.	....Ione via Livermore....................................	5.40 P.
4.00 P.	....Knights Landing.......................................	10.10 A.
* 5.00 P.	....Livermore and Pleasanton..............................	* 8.40 A.
8.00 A.	....Martinez..	6.10 P.
* 8.30 A.	....Milton..	* 7.40 P.
3.30 P.	Mojave, Deming, El Paso & East, Express & Emigrant	10.40 A.
10.00 A.	....Niles and Haywards....................................	3.40 P.
3.00 P.	....Ogden and East, Express & Emigrant....................	11 10 A.
7.30 A.	....Red Bluff via Marysville..............................	5.40 P.
7.30 A.	....Sacramento via Benicia................................	6.40 P.
8.30 A.	.... " via Livermore	5.40 P.
3.00 P.	.... " via Benicia	11.10 A.
4.00 P.	.... " via Benicia..............................	10.10 A.
* 4.00 P.	....Sacramento River Steamers............................	* 6.00 A.
8 30 A.	....San Jose..	* 3.40 P.
†10.00 A.	.... "	‡ 3.40 P.
3.00 P.	.... "	9.40 A.
8.30 A.	....Stockton via Livermore................................	5.40 P.
* 9.30 A.	.... " via Martinez..............................	* 7.40 P.
* 3.30 P.	.... " via Martinez..............................	*10.40 A.
* 9.30 A.	....Tulare and Fresno.....................................	* 7.40 P.

From SAN FRANCISCO Daily.

To East Oakland— *6.00 *6.30 7.00 7.30 8.00 8.30 9 00 9.30 10.00 10.30 11.00
11.30 12.00 12.30 1.00 1.30 2.00 2.30 3.00 3.30 4.00 4.30 5.00 5.30 6 00
6.30 7.00 8.00 9.00 10.00 11.00 *12.00
To Fruit Vale— *6.00 *6.30 *7.00 *7.30 *8.00 *8.30 *3.30 *4.00 *4.30 *5.00 *5.30
*6.00 *6.30 9.00
To Fruit Vale—(via ALAMEDA) *9.30 6.30 ‡11.00 *12.00
To Alameda—*6.00 *6.30 7.00 *7.30 8.00 *8.30 9.00 9.30 10 00 ‡10.30 11.00 ‡11.30
12.00 ‡12.30 1.00 ‡1.30 2.00 3.00 3.30 4.00 4.30 5.00 5.30 6.00 6.30 7.00
8.00 9.00 10.00 11.00 *12.00
To Berkeley—*6.00 *6.30 7.00 *7.30 8.00 *8.30 9.00 ‡9.30 10.00 ‡10.30 11.00 ‡11.30
12.00 1.00 2.00 3.00 4.00 4.30 5.00 5.30 6.00 6.30 7.00 8.00 9.00 10.00
11.00 *12.00
To West Berkeley— *6.00 *6.30 7.00 *7.30 ‡3.00 *8.30 9.00 10.00 11 00 ‡1.00 2.00
3.00 4.00 *4.30 5.00 *5.30 6.00 *6.30 7.00

To SAN FRANCISCO Daily.

From Fruit Vale— *6.23 *6.53 *7.23 *7.53 *8.23 *8.53 *9.23 *10.21 *4.23 *4.53 *5.23
*5.53 *6.23 *6.53 7.25 9.50
From Fruit Vale—(via ALAMEDA)— *5.15 *5.45 ‡6.45 ‡9.15 *3.15
From East Oakland — *5.30 *6.00 6.30 7.00 7.30 8.00 8.30 9.00 9.30 10.00
10.30 11.00 11.30 12.00 12.30 1.00 1.30 2.00 2.30 3.00 3.30 4.00 4.30 5.00
5 30 6.00 6.30 7.00 7.57 8.57 9.57 10.57
From Broadway, Oakland— 7 minutes later than from East Oakland.
From Alameda — *5.22 *5.52 *6.22 6.52 *7.22 7.52 *8.22 8.52 9.22 9.52 ‡10.22
10.52 ‡11.22 11.52 ‡12.22 12.52 ‡1.22 1.52 2.52 3.22 3.52 4.22 4.52 5.22 5.52
6.22 6.52 7.52 8.52 9.52 10.52
From Berkeley — *5.15 *5.45 *6.15 6.45 *7.15 7.45 *8.15 8.45 ‡9.15 9.45 ‡10.15
10 45 ‡11.15 11.45 12.45 1.45 2.45 3.45 4.15 4.45 5.15 5.45 6.15 6.45 7.45
8.45 9.45 10.45
From West Berkeley — *5.45 *6.15 6.45 *7.15 7.45 8 45 ‡9.15 9.45 10.45 ‡12.45
1.45 2.45 3.45 4.45 *5.15 5.45 *6.15 6.45 *7.15

A for Morning.   P for Afternoon.   * Sundays excepted.   ‡ Sundays only.

MONITOR POST, No 112.

WILLOWS, CAL.

OFFICERS, 1886.

E. M. TYLER...Commander
ISAIAH HURLBURT..Senior Vice-Commander
THOMAS KILLEBREW....................................Junior Vice-Commander
W. E. CARMAN...Adjutant
J. E. PUTMAN...Quartermaster
——— ———...Surgeon
O. M. GREELEY...Chaplain
WM. F. MASON..Officer of the Day
IBZAN TODD..Officer of the Guard
F. W. STONE ....Sergeant Major
JOHN E. WILLING..Quartermaster Sergeant

Meeting, First and Third Saturday.

NAME.	CO.	SERVICE.	ADDRESS.
Baird O. A.........		Mich...............................	Willows
Carman W. E........	H	10th Kansas Inf..................	"
Greeley O. M.......	I	31st Maine Inf....................	"
Hurlburt Isaiah.....	F	6th Cal. Inf......................	"
Jenks I. S..........	H	100th Ill. Inf....................	"
Killebrew Thos.....	B	3d Mo. Cav........................	"
Malouey M..........	G	26th Mo. Inf.....................	"
Mason Wm. F.......	A	6th Mo. Cav.......................	Norman
Newsome Thos. F...	A	12th Ind. Inf.....................	Willows
Putnam J. E.......	I	42d Mo. Inf.......................	"
Sell Wm. N.....	I	1st U. S. Cav.....................	"
Stone Fred W........	C	10th Maine Inf....................	"
Todd Ibzan.........	D	5th Mo. Inf.......................	"
Tyler E. M..........	B	20th Ill. Inf.....................	"
Van De Bogart Henry	F	2d Mich. Inf......................	
Wiley Morris B	E	7th Ill. Cav......................	Norman
Willing John E.....	C	10th Ill. Inf.....................	Willows

175

JOHN W. GEARY POST, No. 113.

DIXON, CAL.

OFFICERS. 1886.

E. J. McBRIDE..Commander
CHAS. NEWMAN..Senior Vice-Commander
THEODORE EIMERS..Junior Vice-Commander
F. A. TYLER..Adjutant
J. H. WORTH...Quartermaster
CHAS. E. PLUMMER...Surgeon
S. F. SHAW..Chaplain
WM. H. AMOS...Officer of the Day
CHAS. N. BOCKSTANZ...Officer of the Guard
MYRON ROCKWELL...Sergeant Major
S. T. MOWDER..Quartermaster Sergeant
DENNIS DOWNING...Inside Sentinel

Meeting, Sundays.

NAME.	CO.	SERVICE.	ADDRESS.
Amos William H....	D	36th Iowa Inf......................	Dixon, Cal.
Barber H. D.........	M	2d Mass. Heavy Art.............	"
Bockstanz Charles N.	K	14th Ohio Inf. and K 7th Mich. Inf.	"
Downing Dennis....		U. S. S. Virginia..................	"
Dunning E. C.......	B	1st Nevada Cav...................	"
Duprey A. F.........	D	6th Mo. Inf......................	"
Eimers Theodore....	G	111th Penn. Inf..................	"
Hammond John T...	B	45th Mass. Inf...................	Vacaville, Cal.
Howard W. A........	B	17th Kansas Inf.................	Dixon, Cal
McBride E. J........	I	74th Ind. Inf....................	"
McMaster C. H......	D	2d Maine Inf....................	"
Mowder S. T........	D	14th Ill. Inf....................	"
Newman Charles....		Gunboat Dictator................	
Parker G. L.........	C	28th Ohio Inf...................	Vacaville, Cal.
Plummer Charles E.	G	6th Mich. Inf...................	Binghamton, Cal.
Rockwell Myron	E	32d Iowa Inf....................	Dixon, Cal.
Shaw S. F...........	H	104th Ohio Inf..................	"
Smith David........	D	145th Ill. Inf..................	Batavia, Cal.
Thompson J. A. C...	C	44th Mo. Militia.	Dixon, Cal.
Tyler Frank A.......	A	5th Cal. Inf....................	"
West Thomas	E	7th Ill. Cav....................	"
Worth John H......	H	7th Cal. Inf. and A 11th Maine Inf.	Fairfield

CALIFORNIA

Furniture Manufacturing Co

Successors to N. P. COLE & CO.

FURNITURE,◉

◉ BEDDING,◉

◉UPHOLSTERY

220 to 226 Bush St., San Francisco, Ca

Geo. H Thomas Post, No. 2,
Veteran Guard.

Dr. L. E. Goe,

Dentist,

25½ Post St., San Francisco

San Francisco and North Pacific

~~~ RAILROAD ~~~

The Donahue Broad-Gauge Route.

The Only Direct, and the Shortest, Quickest and Best Equipped Broad-Gauge Road to the Immense

REDWOOD FORESTS OF SONOMA COUNTY,

And the BEAUTIFUL SCENERY of the

—— | RUSSIAN RIVER | ——

The Grandeur and Variety of the Views ou the Line of this Road are unsur-passed, and every facility will be offered to the

Invalid, Tourist, Merchant and Sportsman

IN SEARCH OF HEALTH, PLEASURE OR GAME.

CAMPING PARTIES will find it to their advantage to select their ground on the line of this road; and for **PICNIC PARTIES**

☞ The Accommodations it offers cannot be surpassed. 🖐

STAGE CONNECTIONS.

This is the Only Direct Line to UKIAH and SKAGGS' SPRINGS.
This is the New Line to EUREKA, Humboldt Bay.
This is the Shortest Line to MENDOCINO CITY.
This is the Best Equipped and Most Comfortable Line to LAKEPORT,
BARTLETT SPRINGS, HIGHLAND SPRINGS and SODA BAY.
This is the Most Picturesque Line to the WONDERFUL GEYSERS.
Round-trip Tickets, which are issued via Cloverdale and Calistoga, are under the careful management of world reuowned drivers.

SUNDAY EXCURSIONS.

For a pleasant day and a good time in the Woods, the fields or on the mountains, Go by this Route.

COL. A. W. PRESTON POST, No. 114.

WINTERS, CAL.

OFFICERS, 1886.

JAMES P. TRUMBULL..Commander
P. J. AIKEN ....Senior Vice-Commander
T. E. BOYD.............. ....Junior Vice-Commander
A. N. BABCOCK...Adjutant
D. H. FEATHERS...Quartermaster
———— ....Surgeon
W. H. FREEMAN..Chaplain
JOSEPH CONNOR................... ....Officer of the Day
J. W. BALL..Officer of the Guard
B. R. REINHOLD...Sergeant Major
JOSHUA STEWARD..Quartermaster Sergeant

Meeting, Second and Fourth Saturday.

NAME.	CO.	SERVICE.	ADDRESS.
Aiken P. J., M. D....	D	15th Penn. Cav. and U.S.Sig'l Corps	Winters
Babcock A. N........	B	4th Mich. Cav......................	"
Baldwin A. K........	F	9th Mo. Cav........................	"
Ball J. W............	F	148th Ohio Inf........	"
Boyd T. E............	M	2d Mo. Cav	"
Collins John		U. S. S. Fort Jackson..............	"
Connor Joseph......	D	4th Cal. Inf.......................	"
Feathers D. H.......	E	31st Wis. Inf......................	"
Fisher George W....	H	2d Cal. Inf........................	"
Freeman W. H	E	16th Mo. Cav......................	"
Reinhold B. R.......	E	17th Penn. Cav....................	"
Steward Joshua.....	B	9th Iowa Inf......................	"
Tallman W. M..	K	2d Mo. Cav........................	"
Trumbull James R..	O	20th Conn.Inf.&159th Vet.Res.Cor's	"
Wilson James.......	I	186th Ohio Inf....................	"

CHATTANOOGA POST, No. 115.

NEVADA CITY, CAL.

OFFICERS, 1886.

J. M. WALLING...Commander
J. S. McBRIDE...Senior Vice-Commander
J. G. HARTWELL..Junior Vice-Commander
J. D. CHANNELL...Adjutant
JOHN EVANS...Quartermaster
A. R. PENNINGTON...Surgeon
B. F. THOMAS...Chaplain
L. B. LITTLE...Officer of the Day
OLIVER RAGON...Officer of the Guard
R. LOCKLIN...Sergeant Major
HENRY HURST...Quartermaster Sergeant

Meeting, Second and Fourth Saturday.

NAME.	CO.	SERVICE.	ADDRESS.
Adolph Charles......	A	17th N. Y. Inf........	Nevada City
Ashman William D ..	I	7th Cal. Inf.....................	''
Casey Patrick........	G	2d Maine Inf....****.............	Grass Valley
Channell John D....	E	12th Ohio Inf. and E 23d Ohio Inf..	Nevada City
Charles E. W.......	A	49th Ill. Inf. and 36th Ill. Inf....	''
Crocker J. R........	K	2d Nevada Cav. and K 8th Cal. Inf.	Grass Valley
Evans John	H	62d P. nn. Inf....................	Nevada City
Hallett Albert H....	A	15th Maine Inf...................	''
Hartwell James G...	E	7th N. Y. Cav. and L 5th N. Y. Art.	''
Hogan Michael......	I	2d Maine Inf....................	North San Juan
Hurst Henry........	I	7th Cal. Inf....................	Nevada City
Kempt A. N........	A	18th Ind. Inf....................	''
Little L. B..........	B	9th N. H. Inf....................	''
Locklin Ralph.......	H	1st Vt. Cav.....................	''
Lord James H.......	A	19th Mass. Inf..................	Grass Valley
McBride John S.....	D	79th Penn. Inf..................	North San Juan
Morris F. N...	F	2d Maine Inf....................	''
Pennington A. R....	F	60th Ohio Inf.& 24th Ohio Ind't Ba'y	Nevada City
Pierce Warren H....	E	21st Maine Inf. and O 2d Maine Cav.	You Bet Station
Ragon Oliver........	B	49th Ohio Inf...................	Nevada City
Thomas Benj. F.....	E	8th Penn. Cav..................	''
True George.........	B	4th Iowa Cav...................	''
Walling Julius M. ..	A	8th Iowa Inf.& K 61st U. S. Col'd Inf	''
White Henry........	F	6th Vt. Inf......	''

WILLIAMSBURG POST, No. 116.

WILLIAMS, CAL.

OFFICERS, 1886.

H. C. CROWDER...Commander
H. ARMSTRONG..Senior Vice-Commander
R. E. WOOD...Junior Vice-Commander
B. R. KIRKBRIDE...Adjutant
C. B. CLARK..Quartermaster
B. F. SCOTT..Surgeon
H. H. DYKE...Chaplain
A. MARR..Officer of the Day
LEWIS ELKINS..Officer of the Guard
—— ——...Sergeant Major
—— ——...Quartermaster Sergeant

Meeting, First and Third Saturday.

NAME.	CO.	SERVICE.	ADDRESS.
Armstrong H........	F	7th and F 22d Mich. Inf..........	Williams
Banning Granville W		1st Independent Col. Art..........	"
Clark C. B..........	F	46th Wis. Inf	"
Crowder H. H.......	G	10th Ill. Cav.....................	"
Dyke Hugh D........	C	9th Tenn. Cav....................	"
Elkins Lewis.......	C D	82d Penn. Inf..............	"
Kirkbride B. R......	K	7th Iowa Inf....................	"
Magee James........	C	5th Cal. Inf....................	"
Marr A.............	G	7th Mo. Cav.....................	"
Scott B. F..........	A	44th Mo. Inf....................	"
Wood Reuben E.....	M	4th Penn. Cav....................	"

179

SOUTH MOUNTAIN POST, No. 117.

LOYALTON, CAL.

OFFICERS, 1886.

EDWARD J. WOOD..Commander
JARED BATES...Senior Vice-Commander
ROSCOE G. HAMLIN......................................Junior Vice-Commander
FRANCIS H. CAMPBELL..Adjutant
SHELDEN T. BURTON...Quartermaster
THOS. F. WEST...Surgeon
LEWIS CLYMER... ....Chaplain
H. P. ROBBINS..Officer of the Day
FRANK HAAG...Officer of the Guard
ALBERT HUBBARD...Sergeant Major
———— ———.....................................Quartermaster Sergeant

---

Meeting, last Saturday.

NAME.	CO.	SERVICE.	ADDRESS.
Bates Jared.........		4th Maine Art.....................	Loyalton
Burton Shelden T...	I	8th Cal. Inf............	Sierra Valley, Cal.
Campbell Francis H.	K	7th Cal. Inf........................	Beckwith, Cal.
Clymer Lewis.......	K	7th Cal. Inf........................	Loyalton
Haag Frank.........	K	Minn. Inf. Rangers & 2d Minn.Cav.	"
Hamlin Roscoe G....	D	2d U. S. Sharpshooters...........	"
Houghton James....		28th Maine Inf....................	"
Hubbard Albert.....	I	2d Cal. Cav.......................	Sierraville
Laughton Lee N....	E	5th Maine Inf.....................	Beckwith
Palmer Martin V....	I	8th Kansas Inf....................	Loyalton
Robbins H. P........	D	21st Maine Inf....................	"
West Thomas F.....		....	"
Wood Edward J.....	K	7th Cal. Cav....	Beckwith

RIVERSIDE POST, No. 118.

RIVERSIDE, CAL.

OFFICERS, 1886.

C. J. GILL	Commander
M. M. DAVIS	Senior Vice-Commander
J. H. ROE	Junior Vice-Commander
C. C. MILLER	Adjutant
C. T. RICE	Quartermaster
H. W. ROBINSON	Surgeon
REV. CHAS. BUTTON	Chaplain
E. W. HOLMES	Officer of the Day
V. S. RUNNELS	Officer of the Guard
FRANK COOLIDGE	Sergeant Major
J. P. MITCHELL	Quartermaster Sergeant

Meeting, every Saturday.

NAME.	CO.	SERVICE.	ADDRESS.
Aberdeen John	C	42d Ill. Inf	Riverside
Alkire A. L.	K	18th Ind. Inf	"
Brant D. S	I	11th Ill. Cav.	"
Button Charles, Rev.		20th Ill. Inf.	"
Cady Charles L.	D	1st Bat. Cal. Mountaineers	"
Carr William	B	34th Mass. Inf	"
Coolidge Frank	H	13th Mass. Inf.	"
Cottrell J. O		3d Ind. Battery	"
Cutter John E.	E	23d Maine Inf	"
Davis M. M	H	5th Mass. Inf	"
Dyer Otis T.	B	33d Ill. Inf. and A 137th Ill. Inf.	"
Edmiston Joseph	E	Burgess Sharpshooters	"
Frost David	C	31st Wis. Inf.	"
Gill C. J.	B	33d Ill. Inf.	"
Grico L	E	1st Neb. Inf.	"
Hart Edwin	I	6th Iowa Inf.	"
Hinckley S. B.	D	3d Mass. Inf.	"
Holmes E W	C	35th Mass. Inf.	"
Johnson Robert		Ill. Chicago Board of Trade Battery	"
Kingsley N. H.	A	27th Mass. Inf.	"
Miller C. C.	I	49th Wis. Inf.	"
Mitchell J P	E	29th Ill. Inf.	"
Moore Homer P.	A	7th Minn. Inf.	"
Patchner Frank		1st Col. Inf.	"
Rice C. T.	A	16th Maine Inf.	"
Robinson H W	H	4th U. S. Veterans	"
Roe J. H.	G	134th Ill. Inf.	"
Runnels V. S.	D	136th Ohio Inf.	"
Rustin Nelson	A	42d Ill. Inf.	"
Skinner G. M.	F	58th Mass. Inf.	"
Smith Henry M.	C	3d Wis. Inf.	"
Sprague A. H.	D	4th Mass. Inf.	"
Twogood A. J.	I	6th Iowa Cav.	"
Van Fleet M. B.	F	100th Ohio Inf.	"
Wall W. S.	F	7th Mo. Inf.	"
Wilson W. S.	G	26th Mich. Inf.	"
Woodard J. H.	E	10th N. H. Inf.	"

KEARSARGE POST, No. 119.

UKIAH, CAL.

OFFICERS, 1886.

HENRY L. NORTON..Commander
E. B. HAGANS...Senior Vice Commander
SAMUEL L. RYAN......................................, Junior Vice Commander
E. W. WELLS... ....Adjutant
C. E. NUTTER............................... ....Quartermaster
G. W. GRANT..Surgeon
A. S, BAILEY................... ....Chaplain
JOHN MEWHENEY................ ....Officer of tho Day
E. J. YOUNG ....Officer of the Guard
J. D. CURTIS.....\............ ....Sergeant Major
A. D. DEAN.............. ....Quartermaster Sergeant

---

Meeting, Second and Fourth Saturday.

NAME.	CO.	SERVICE.	ADDRESS.
Bailey A. S..........	B	15th Ohio Inf.& C Bat'y W.Va.Lt.Art	Ukiah
Crain S..............	I	111th Ill. Inf....................	"
Curtis J. D..........	C	20th Ind. Inf. & A 53d Ind. Inf.....	"
Dean A. D..........	A	160th Ohio Inf. & G 198th Ohio Inf.	"
Hagans E. B.........	C	4th U. S. Inf. & C 1st Nev. Cav.....	"
Grant G. W.........	I	14th Iowa Inf....................	Hopland
Mewheney John.....	D	2d Cal. Cav.......................	Potter Valley
Norton Henry L.....	G	2d Mich. Inf.....................	Willits
Nutter C. E.........	E	14th N H. Inf....................	Ukiah
Paxton S. D.........	A	30th Ill. Inf....................	"
Ryan Samuel L......	A	2d Ill. Light Art.................	"
Spubold T		U. S. S. St. Mary and Farralloues..	Potter Valley
Stayner C. R........	A	9th U. S. Inf.....................	Ukiah
Welden Dayton E..	K	8th Ill Cav.....................	Potter Valloy
Wells E. W.........	F	33d Ill. Inf.....................	Ukiah
Young E. J..........	H	4th Maine Inf.......	"

PIONEER
PURE OLD TENNESSEE WHITE RYE WHISKY!

—AN ELEGANT TONIC.—

—GIVE IT A TRIAL.—

A. FENKHAUSEN & CO.
414 Front Street,   San Francisco, Cal.
SAMPLE BOTTLES FREE!

FAIR OAKS POST, No. 120.

SACRAMENTO, CAL.

OFFICERS, 1886.

J. N. LARKIN..Commander
GEO. W. FICKS...Senior Vice-Commander
H. P. WINCHELL...Junior Vice-Commander
E. B. OSLER..Adjutant
J. J. TRARBACH...Quartermaster
C. E. PINKHAM...Surgeon
E. C. JORDAN..Chaplain
J. B. PIERREPONT..Officer of the Day
J S. T. MORRIS...Officer of the Guard
—— ——...Sergeant Major
—— ——,..Quartermaster Sergeant

Meeting, First and Third Thursday.

NAME.	CO.	SERVICE.	ADDRESS.
Ficks George W....	K	50th Penn. Inf......................	Sacramento
Jordan Elmer C.....	E	7th Conn. Inf......................	"
Larkin J. N..... ...	D	13th N. Y. Inf......................	"
Morris J. S. T........	M	2d Penn. Art......................	"
Osler E. B.		Independent Penn. Cav..........	"
Pierrepont J. B	K	10th Conn. Inf....................	"
Pinkham Charles E..	H	1st Maine Cav....................	"
Richards W. H......	H	80th Ohio Inf....................	"
Tebow James O.....	A	35th Iowa Inf....................	"
Thorne W. S.........		U. S. Gunboat No. 1........	"
Trarbach J. J........	F	9th Ohio Inf....................	"
Vogelgesang George.	E	12th Iowa Inf............	"
Walker George A....	G	10th U. S. Inf....................	"
Winchell H. P.......	F	141st Ill. Inf....................	"

J. A. ADDISON POST, No. 121.

SAN JACINTO, CAL.

OFFICERS, 1886.

MILTON MITCHELL...Commander
DAVID HERROD...Senior Vice-Commander
JOHN T. KERR...Junior Vice-Commander
JOEL SPOHN..Adjutant
P. FREY..Quartermaster
JOHN BRYAN..Surgeon
——— ———...Chaplain
L. DURETT...Officer of the Day
JOHN ROBINETT..Officer of the Guard
R. C. DYER...Sergeant Major
——— ———...Quartermaster Sergeant

Meeting, Every Wednesday.

NAME.	CO.	SERVICE.	ADDRESS.
Durett Lewis.......	F	27th Mich. Inf.....................	San Jacinto
Dyer R. E...........	K	5th Cal. Inf.....................	"
Frey P..............	I	33d Ind. Inf.....................	"
Gaston John........	I	17th Ill. Inf.& D 125th U.S.Col'd Inf	"
Haileck H. T........	B	21st Iowa Inf.....................	"
Herrod David.......	E	26th Ohio Inf.....................	"
Kerr J. T...........	A	4th Mo. Cav.....................	"
Lee C. H...........	H	11th Mich. Inf.....................	"
Mitchell Milton.....	E	29th Ind. Inf.....................	"
Morgan Thomas.....	I	28th Iowa Inf.....................	"
Robinett John......	B	8th Ill. Inf.....................	"
Ryan John..........	A	55th Ohio Inf.....................	"
Spohn Joel..........	E	25th Ohio Inf.....................	"

REN DIXON POST, No. 122.

QUINCY, CAL.

OFFICERS, 1886.

JAMES H. WHITLOCK ....Commander
H. S. PORTER..Senior Vice-Commander
B. R. FOSS..Junior Vice-Commander
WM. H. GREVES..Adjutant
M. S. LIGHT..Quartermaster
WILLARD W. SAVERCOOL..Surgeon
A. W. DREW..Chaplain
W. H. WADE..Officer of the Day
ROBERT GAMBLE..Officer of the Guard
CHARLES RUPPERT ....Sergeant Major
J. JACQUEL..Quartermaster Sergeant

Meeting, Fourth Saturday.

NAME.	CO.	SERVICE.	ADDRESS.
Cameron Alex.......		33d Wis. Inf....................	Quincy
Drew Aaron W......	I	10th Iowa Inf....................	"
Foss B. R......	B	7th Cal. Inf............	"
Gamble Robert.....	K	9th Kansas Cav.................. .	"
Greves William H...	K	40th Ohio Inf...	"
Jacquel Julien......	A	2d Cal. Cav.....................	"
Light M. S..........		103d Penn. Inf....	"
Porter H. S..........	G	157th Ohio Inf..................	"
Ruppert Chas.......	F	1st Cal. Inf...............	"
Savercool W.W.,M D.	M	3d Wis. Cav···	"
Wade W. H..........	I	98th Ill. Inf....................	"
Whitlock James H...	F	5th Cal. Inf....................	"

KENESAW POST, No. 123.

ORLAND, CAL.

OFFICERS, 1886.

MICHAEL O'HAIR...Commander
ABBOTT MERRILL..Senior Vice-Commander
MOSES M. BOON. ....Junior Vice-Commander
T. B. BIRCH... ....Adjutant
ISAAC NEIDEFFER .... Quartermaster
ALBERT PAPST... ....Surgeon
THOMAS E. BROWN... .....Chaplain
JOHN H. HICKS ....Officer of the Day
J. GRIFFITH ....Officer of the Guard
T. M. THOMPSON..Sergeant Major
F. WINNE......... ....Quartermaster Sergeant

Meeting, Wednesday.

NAME.	CO.	SERVICE.	ADDRESS.
Birch Theo B........	F	2d Cal. Cav......................	Orland
Boon Moses M......	D	54th Ill. Inf.....................	"
Brown Thomas E...	F	2d Neb. Cav...........	"
Green John V	C	111th Ill. Inf...................	"
Griffith Jonathan...	B	1st U. S. Cav.....................	"
Hicks John H.......	F	1st Mich. Light Art..............	"
Merrill Abbott......	F	13th Ill. Inf....	"
Neideffer Isaac......	A	66th Ind. Inf.........	"
O'Hair John,........	K	7th Iowa Cav....................	"
O'Hair Michael.....	K	7th Iowa Cav....................	"
Papst Albert	E	10th Mich. Inf..................	"
Smith John A.......	A	66th Ind. Inf	"
Thompson T. M.....	C	15th Ohio Inf.......	"
Winne F............	G	33d Wis. Inf....................	"

ONTARIO POST, No. 124.

OFFICERS, 1886.

L. D. GRAVES...Commander
B. S. DENISON...Senior Vice-Commander
M. L. HOMER...Junior Vice-Commander
R. B. MORTON..Adjutant
S. WEAVER..Quartermaster
C. D. WATSON ....Surgeon
W. F. WHEELER...Chaplain
R. R. STAPLES...Officer of the Day
JAMES KING...Officer of the Guard
I. W. WHITTAKER ....Sergeant Major
W. J. BODENHAMER.............................Quartermaster Sergeant

---

Meeting, Saturday.

NAME.	CO.	SERVICE.	ADDRESS.
Applegate James....	K	1st Oregon Inf....	Ontario
Bodenhamer W. J...	E	8th Mo. Cav.......................	"
Denison B. S........		....	"
Graves L. D.........	A	47th Ohio Inf.......................	"
Holdrige A..........	A	6th Ohio Inf....	"
Homer M. L.........	A	19th Ohio Inf....	"
King James.........	B	2d Kansas Inf. & G 11th Kansas Inf	"
Morton R. B....	A	9th Ohio Inf....	"
Staples R. R........	I	7th Cal. Inf.....	"
Watson Chas.D.,M.D.		N. Y. Independent Light Art......	"
Watson William T...	E	51st Mass. Inf.....................	"
Weaver S. P.........	A	33d Ill. Inf.......................	"
Whittaker Isaac W..	G	24th Maine Inf.....................	"

GAYLORD POST, No. 125.

UPPER LAKE, CAL.

———

OFFICERS, 1886.

GODWIN SCUDAMORE..Commander
EMERY BURK...Senior Vice-Commander
WILEY M. SHIMER............................. ....Junior Vice-Commander
ROBERT G. REYNOLDS...Adjutant
WILLIAM WOODARD..Quartermaster
WILLIAM TRAVIS......... ....Surgeon
PETER R. YATES.......................... ....Chaplain
WILLIAM CHRISTIE. ....Officer of the Day
CALEB ANDERSON.. ....Officer of the Guard
JOHN W. CARSON..Sergeant Major
——— ———...Quartermaster Sergeant

———

Meeting, Tuesday on or before Full Moon.

NAME.	CO.	SERVICE.	ADDRESS.
Anderson Caleb.....	E	14th Kansas Cav...................	Upper Lake
Burk Emery.........	G	10th Kansas Inf...................	"
Carson John W.....		2d Kansas Battery................	"
Christie William....		U. S. S. Vermont and Wabash.....	"
Reynolds Robert G..	A	108th Penn. Inf	"
Scudamore Godwin..	A	80th Ill. Inf.....................	Lakeport
Shimer Wiley........	E	8th Ohio Cav.....................	Upper Lake
Travis Wm..........	B	2d Cal. Cav......................	"
Woodard Wm........	C	8th Ohio Cav.....................	Batchelor
Yates Peter R........	E	3d Ind. Cav	Upper Lake

188

ANDERSON POST, No. 21.

FERNDALE, CAL.

OFFICERS, 1886.

O. M. SMITH..Commander
D. F. WILSON..Senior Vice-Commander
J. B. DAVIS...Junior Vice-Commander
W. H. MOORE...Adjutant
E. C. DAMON...Quartermaster
H. B. CHASE..Surgeon
O. B HART..Chaplain
J. N. ADAMS...Officer of the Day
J. W. BLAKEMORE...Officer of the Guard
P. F. HART...Sergeant Major
H. H. NIEBUR..Quartermaster Sergeant

Meeting, Second Tuesday.

NAME.	CO.	SERVICE.	ADDRESS.
Adams J. M..........	H	60th Mass. Inf.....................	Ferndale
Benedict G. L.......	F	27th N. Y Inf. & F Vet.Res.Cor.Bat	"
Blakemore J. W.....	O	4th Iowa Inf. & C 26th Iowa Inf....	"
Bryant D. M.........	K	5th U. S. Inf & C 5th U. S. Cav....	"
Chase H. B..........	E	40th Iowa Inf.........	"
Damon E. C..........	H	3d Kans. Inf. & D 10th Kans. Inf..	"
Davis J. B	C	3d Wis. Inf......................	"
Fike J. A............	F	9th Ill. Inf.......................	"
Hall H. F............	E	16th Vt Inf......................	"
Hart C. B......... ..	G	5th N. H. Inf. & A 24th Vet.Res.Cor	"
Hart P. F............		6th Mich. Cav.....................	"
Moore W. H.	H	6th Iowa Inf.....................	"
Niebur H. H.........	D	2d Cal. Inf. & E 1st Oregon Inf....	"
Nickilson W. G......	G	7th Ill. Inf. & C 64th Ill. Inf......	"
Smith C. M.	K	6th Mich. Heav. Art..............	"
Stevens R. W........	I	26th Ohio Inf....................	Capetown
Stewart Z. P.........	K	1st Mo. Engineers.................	Ferndale
Van Dyke H. E......	B	2d Minn. Inf......................	Eureka
Wilson D. F.........	K	18th R. I. Inf. & K 3d N. H. Inf....	Ferndale

APPENDIX.

NAME.	CO.	SERVICE.	ADDRESS.	POST.
Ahlers Wm......		U. S. S. San Jacinto ..	514 Sixth.........	Lincoln, No. 1, San Francisco.
Lemont Geo. W..	B	1st Maine Inf..........	15 Albion ave....	"
Mooney Geo. W..	E	3d Penn. Inf...........	765½ Howard.....	"
Chesley W. E....		1stR.I.Art.& 5 Mass.Inf	Oakland..........	Geo. H. Thomas, No. 2 San Francisco.
Geran Anthony...	E	4th Cal. Inf.............	35 Natoma........	"
Gilmore C. C.....	H	1st N. Art,..........	823 Valencia.....	"
Jackson J. Ross..	B	37th N. J. Inf...... ...	Alta Office.......	"
Martin Leonard P	H	2 1Me.Inf.&1 16 Me.Inf	148 Ninth	"
Newton E. C....		7th Ohio Inf..........	Lower Lake......	"
Phillips Isidore H	F	165th N. Y. Inf........	1617 13th av.,Ok'd	"
Rush John.......	C	2dN.J.Cav.,K153Pa.Inf	1009 Leavenworth	"
Stoddard Truman	A	27th Iowa Inf..........	Lodi.............	"
Alberger Wm. C .		49th N. Y. Inf,........	1427 Franklin	Lyon, No. 8, Oakland.
Billington Isaac F	I	98th N. Y. Inf.........	618 Eighth........	"
Brown James....	A	3d N, Y. Inf..........	East Oakland	"
Havens Truman..	C	4th & 25th Mich Inf....	1416 San Pablo av	"
HempsteadW.C F	I	104th Ill. Inf...........	729 Tenth........	"
HendersonDan.D	G	187th N. Y. Inf........	320 East Eighth..	"
Laughlin S. B....		19th Ind Battery.......	2020 Union......	"
Little James. .	B	5th Penn Reserves.....	401 Franklin.....	"
Littlefield C. A.,.	K	26th Mass. Inf.........	577 Sycamore....	"
McKay Wm. T..	I	17th Conn. Inf........	2223 Post, S. F...	"
Randall Sam'l L..	E	1st Nev. Cav..........	911 Fifth........	"
Reader Philip...		U. S. S. Juliet........	6th-st.Eng'e Ho'se	"
Todd H. J.... ...		1st W. Va. Art........	1300 Webster.....	"
Wood Walter....	A	10th Wis. Inf..........	Sycamore & Grove	"
Gale C. H........	A	36th Ill. Inf.........	Stockton..........	Rawlins, No. 23, Stockton.
Hurlburt Geo. M.	G	24th Ohio Inf.........	"	"
Strong Nathan...	C	18th Mich. Inf.........	"	"
Wetsell Geo. W..		U. S. Marine Corps....	"	
Goodman John...	A	22d Ind. Inf............	Reese River......	Lander, No. 27, Austin, Nev.
Paull John B....	K	142d Ind. Inf..........	Battle Mountain..	"
Carr Edward S...	M	2d Penn. Cav.........	Santa Cruz.......	Capt. W.H.L. Wallace, No. 32. Santa Cruz.
Copp John.......	C	7th N. H. Inf.........	"	"
Harrington Geo..		16th Mass. Battery.....	"	"
Newcomb Sam'l L	F	6th Maine Inf..........	"	"
Staples S. S......	B	2d U. S. Art..........	"	"
Alexander W. F..	E	1st Mo. Cav.........	San Diego........	Heintzelman, No. 33, San Diego.
Coleman Patrick.	F	2d Wis. Inf........	"	"
Dickson J. T.....	K	2d Cal. Inf............	"	"
Dyo B. U......	E	1st Mich. Eng.........	"	"
Ellsworth C. W..	E	1st Iowa Cav.........	"	"
Eubanks J. J....	C	124th Ill. Inf.........	"	"
Glidden A. P.....	O	1st N. H. Cav........	"	"
Hoefflo J.........		2d U. S. Art.........	"	"
Kroff S. W.......	C	12th Ohio Inf.........	"	"
Large Tompkins..	D	36th Wis. Inf.........	"	"
Long Porter,.....	A	8th Ill. Cav...........	"	"
McIntosh F. J....	B	10th N. Y. Art........	"	"
Moore P. H......	E	15th Mass. Inf........	"	"
Pratt C. W.......	O	2d Mass. Cav.........	"	"

190

NAME.	CO.	SERVICE.	ADDRESS.	POST.
Puterbaugh Geo.,	E	47th Ill. Inf............	San Diego........	Heintzelman, No. 33, San Diego.
Seebold H........	C	14th Md. Inf...........	"	"
Spence S. R......		2d U. S. Vet. Vols....	"	"
Spencer J. R......	E	44th Mo. Inf, ...	"	"
Stone A. B.......	E	41st Penn. Inf.........	"	"
Torris Geo. O.....	E	71st Ohio Inf..........	"	"
Warren D........	G	2d Mo. Cav...........	"	"
Weegar E. H.....	C	1st Cal. Inf..........	"	"
Allen Franklin F.	B	2d & F 33d Wis. Inf....	10 Polk lane......	J. A. Garfield, No. 34 San Francisco.
Burke Peter......		U. S. S. Neptune......	707 Clay.........	"
Cain Thomas.....		U. S. S. Virginia......	207 Linden ave...	"
Carroll Patrick...	E	1st N. J Art,......	112 Hayes.......	"
Frankel Moses...	A	72d N. Y. Inf.........	225 Dupont,......	"
Greenway Thos..		13th Penn Inf........	528 Folsom......	"
Hanson H. J.....		U. S. Navy...........	417 Minna.......	"
Hessler Charles..	I	2d Cal. Cav..........	1 Chatham place.	"
Hohn John M....	K	1st Cal. Inf.........	821 Vallejo......	"
Hughes Wm......	D	1st Bat. Cal. Mt'neers..	10 Sumner.......	"
Hymo Thos,Oscar		U. S. S. Potomac......	Oriental Wareh'se	"
Jessup Henry C..	D	145th Penn. Inf........	1102 Eddy......	"
Kasche Wm......	G	22d Conn. Inf........	506 Montgomery..	"
Lagerman Henry.		U. S. S. Nild, ...	9 6 Howard......	"
Lederer Eman'l M	G	39th N. Y. Inf.......	302 Stockton.....	"
Lentz Henry.....	H	2d Col. Cav..........	925 Market.......	"
Merriam A. B....	E	2d Cal. Cav..........	Industrial School.	"
Reinhold Frey....	A	25th Mo. Inf........	216 Harrison.....	"
Rooney Charles L	F	2d Cal. Cav..........	703 Market.......	"
Stewart William.	G	1st Conn. Inf........	410 Pacific.......	"
Sullivan James ..	A	164th N. Y. Inf.......	522 Folsom......	"
Thompson Rich'd	H	146th N. Y. Inf.......	San Bruno road..	"
Tierney E.P.,M.D		U. S. A...........	703 Montgomery..	"
Walsh Dennis....		U. S. S. Potomac & Tallapoosa	414 Beale........	"
Bolan Peter J....	I	134th Ill. Inf..........	Solomonville,A.T	Negley, No. 35, Tucson, A. T.
Gibson P. M......	B	5th Cal. Inf..........	Tucson.......	"
Hale Heil........	K	1st Ia & D 12th Ia. Inf.	"	"
Kautz John D....	D	1st Ky. Inf...........		
Seward F. B......	D	117th U. S. Col. Inf....	Ventura.........	Cushing, No. 44, San Fancisco.
Heaney John H..	F	69th N. Y. Inf.........		Gen. G. G. Meade, No. 48, San Francisco.
Gardner Jacob W	C	11th Maine Inf........	Eureka..........	Col. Whipple, 49, Eureka.
Mackenzie Alex.R	A	29th Wis. Inf..........	Arcata..........	"
Quinn Thomas...	B	17th Penn. Inf........	Capetown.......	"
Varnum Jefferson	E	7th Cal. Inf.........	Hydesville... ...	"
Cotton L. F......	C	19th O. Inf.& 7 Kan.Cav	714 Castro........	Appomattox, No. 50, Oakland.
Fawcett H. E....	F	4th Ohio Cav..........	700 Sycamore ...	"
Frost W. E......	A	47th & D 62d Mass. Inf.	....	"
Hamm N........	D	3N.J.Mil.& F11N.J.Inf	Alta House.......	"
Murphy Wm.....		U. S. S. Vanderbilt....	1717 Taylor......	"
Owens Wm.....	E	10th N. Y. Art.......	251 Eighth.......	"
Read Geo.R.,Rev.		47th Mo. V. M........	219 Tenth.......	"
Smith H. S.	E	3d Mass. Heavy Art....	....	"
Winsor Serril	I	11th R. I. Inf........	615 Fifteenth.....	"
Gleeson John....	K	10th Minn Inf........	Westport........	Tom Dollard, No. 53, Mendocino City,
Howe Newton B.	B	13th Ill. Inf..........	Potter Valley	"
Snow W. J........	C	43d Ind. Inf..........	Caspar..........	"

NAME.	CO.	SERVICE.	ADDRESS.	POST.
Bedell Edmund..	A	4th Iowa Inf..........	Sacramento......	Warren, No. 54, Sacramento.
Bishop William..	A	1st Ohio Heavy Art....	"	"
Bryan Robert....		....	"	"
Lyons Harvey....	A	1st U. S. Inf...........	"	"
Sefton A. W.....	G	8th Ill. Inf............	"	"
Thompson W.H H	H	15th Ill. Cav.........	"	"
Clayton F. M.....	H	39th Ill. Inf...........	Rocklin..........	Col. E. D, Baker, No. 71, Newcastle.
Corry T. B.......	H	1st N. Y. Arr.........	"	"
Leo John A......	B	30th Ind. Inf.........	"	"
Martin A. L. S...	F	47th Ill. Inf...........	Ophir	"
Symes A..........	I	1st N. Y. Inf.........	"	"
Jewel James.....	C	47th Ill. Inf............	Pescadero........	Gen. Geo. S. Evans. No. 72, Redwood City
Carter J. C.......	I	116th Ill. Inf..........	Napa City........	Kit Carson, No. 74, Napa.
Cook W. T.......		2d Wis. Cav...........	"	"
Deakin W. W....	F	14th Iowa Inf.........	"	"
Dwyer Thomas...	C	2d N. J. Inf...........	Monticello.......	"
Goodenough W.H	K	1st Vt. Cav...........	Napa City........	"
Kennedy W. W..	B	35th Mo. Inf..........	"	"
Neil Henry C.....	G	16th Penn. Cav.......	Monticello.......	"
Nelson D. W.....	F	1st Cal. Cav	Napa City.......	"
Sweetland Seth..	E	3d Maine Inf.........	"	"
Boyle Thomas....		3d Wis. Lt. Art........	Phœnix, A. T....	J. W. Owens, No. 83, Phœnix, A. T.
Breckinridge W.M	B	3d Colorado Cav......	"	"
Drynan Robert...	D	7th Cal. Inf...........	"	"
Baisley George H.	K	75th Ill. Inf...........	East Los Angeles	Gelcich, No. 106, East Los Angeles.
Carlisle E. S......	F	186th N. Y. Inf.......	"	"
Day Isaac........	C	69th Iowa Inf.........	"	"
Duhem Constant.	G	5th Cal. Inf..........	"	"
Gurnea Geo. H..	D	91st Ill. Inf..........	"	"
Tibbitt James M.	K	25th Iowa Inf.........	"	"
Vandusen H. V..	A	11th U. S. Inf.........	"	"

INDEX BY STATES AND ORGANIZATIONS.

CALIFORNIA.

CALIFORNIA.

202 INDEX BY STATES AND ORGANIZATIONS.

ILLINOIS.

		Post
Inf. 35	Miles J. F	33
	Pate W. S	71
36	Bradshaw R. R	47
	Charles E. W	115
	Gale C. H	23
	Jenks Albert	2
	Miles H. C	6
37	Kent J. D	3
	Reed J. W	55
	Roper Spencer	42
39	Dows John	110
	Harty Alfred	54
	Ogle D. W	101
	Patterson W. A	17
	Russell J. H	42
40	Casebolt J. B	1
	Patterson J. L	35
41	Archibald J	42
	Jones J. T	3
	Kelly Thomas	42
	Sandy Wm	79
42	Aberdeen John	118
	Malone Robert P	71
	Petty John	6
	Rustin Nelson	118
	Wilson Chas. S	9
43	Buetel H	73
	Carmichael M. A	73
	Kopmann Frank	56
	Schroeder Chas. F	49
	Woerner B	3
44	Ketchum Myron	35
	Loring Abraham	75
	Parker James	8
45	Beaumont H. E	23
	Boyce H. H	55
	Comstock John	33
	Hamlin Orin C	11
	Scott Robert	27
46	Boyer George	86
	Butz M. Chris	111
	Currey S. T	2
	Inman Henry	7
	Lindsey W. E	69
	Plants W. A	71
	Runyon B. W	69
	Thomas W. H	55
47	Avas John	17
	Bunn Andrew	23
	Foster John C	1
	Hart D. F	67
	Robinson Chas. H	109
	Van Slyke D	55
	Wilson A. J	73
48	Wellman A. F	104
49	Charles E. W	115
50	Davis Bradley S	23
	Decker Chas. F	**75**

ILLINOIS.

		Post
Inf. 50	Jeffrey A. R	69
	Johnson David M	72
	Reese John W	55
	Remley Wm	19
51	Arnold Isaac	101
	Boomer Herman K	80
	Harrison W. H	106
	Magee T. L	33
	McDermott W. J	42
	Rudo Jules	76
52	Laws E. R	1
	Thompson T. H	50
	Tyler F. W	106
53	Archibald J	42
	Condell B. M	23
	Cunningham L	9
	Simmons L. W	64
	Sommers W. H	53
	Tambling V. A	1
54	Boon Moses M	123
55	Cools Wm. E	20
	Dixon Wm. H	118
	Fryer D. F	95
	Taylor R. W	1
56	Dennis John	92
	Garner W. B	57
57	Bloomer R. C	61
	Cole Jesse	6
	Friend W. P	51
	Hayman Al	52
	Mahoney Michael	92
	Wallace Edward L	1
	Wilson J. A	64
	Youngberg John E	2
58	Aiken John J	3
	Brigaerts Joseph	1
	Farhner J. G	79
	Harrison Jay	9
	Van Arnam H. M	8
	Willard J. W	63
59	Anthony Albert	2
	Percival Nicholas	42
	Rea Francis	86
	Shaw Oliver	3
60	Phillips R. O	9
	Senterfey F. M	52
61	Atkins E. S	101
	Corder L. T	61
	Loos Thomas F	111
62	Lambert John C	8
	Mills W. F	32
	Morgan J. D	44
63	Falconer C. D	48
	Glines W. J	75
	Merrifield Wm	95
	Spencer Theodore	42
64	Hardy I. B	52
	Kenney Cyrus	**68**

212 INDEX BY STATES AND ORGANIZATIONS.

MAINE.

216 INDEX BY STATES AND ORGANIZATIONS.

NEW YORK.

		Post
Inf. 80	Wallis Geo. H. W	2
81	Bennett A. G	42
82	Doyle Thos	96
	Smith G. J	2
83	Black Wm	1
	McDermott T	1
84	Smith W. E	45
85	Smith E. B	61
86	Green Miles J	93
88	Dowdall R. E	46
	Mitchell James	4
	Roach Michael	20
89	Lindrob John	1
90	Hickox Gaylord	23
	Pickney Robert S	23
	Ward A. H	11
91	Daly John F	45
	Keefe Walter	36
	McGovern Robert	34
92	Clark W. H	66
	Hall Thomas S	6
	Henagin John	65
93	Lawson James E	38
	Peer Abram	8
	Wallace C. W	54
94	Thomas H. E	2
95	Isaacs Alfred S	34
96	Babbitt John H	34
97	Nichols M. S	66
	Nichols U. S	32
	Robb Charles	106
	Smith J. H	33
	Tuttle John	2
98	Deno William	82
	Manning Sidney	2
	Owen J. A	2
	Slatterly Patrick	80
	Wakeley A	93
99	Clarke F. L	45
	Eustice John H	34
	Farrell Domnick	90
	Morris John	1
	Ryan William	1
	Stanbridge A. H	2
100	Flick Carl	1
	Martin H. N	104
	Wilkins W. P	1
102	Cusack Thomas	1
	Howe Thomas H	2
103	Berkenmeyer Alois	80
	Mayer John	97
104	Chapin John A	7
	Kenny C. A	2
105	Babcock G	1
	Smith David C	2
106	Bitterly Oscar A	49
	Brimson T. W	7
	Henagin David	65

NEW YORK.

		Post
Inf 106	McQuaig John	94
107	Dunn Israel	99
	Dunn Israel	61
	Hopkins T. B	80
108	Craig Hugh	4
	Rockefeller G. W	57
	Ross W. W	2
110	Talcott H. D	2
	Weller H. I	41
111	Gardner I. G	2
	Van Inwagen Leonard	2
112	Ludwick E. A	2
114	Zabriskie J. H	1
115	Gregory Thomas	36
	Staples J. P	78
116	Hutchins C. B	2
	Neff A. D	59
	Stengle J	6
117	Downer E	2
	Wilmarth P. B	42
118	Morse D. A	8
121	Bixby H. H	55
	Hawver H. W	6
	Van Horne J	6
	Yager Myron	75
122	Barnett Geo. A	2
	Farrell James	2
	Myer John	11
123	Martin H. P	3
	Parks Daniel	62
	Shevlin James	34
	Wallis Geo. H. W	2
124	Bateman Emanuel	23
	Monroe Wm	3
125	Hyde Joseph	23
	Hyde W. C	23
	Redfield A. N	92
126	Davis John	6
	Scott Winfield	2
127	Shear Abram	84
128	Card W. D	65
	Ensign Chas. H	8
129	Behan Chas. T	2
	Brown Geo. H	1
131	Anthony A	1
	Banks Chas. W	2
	Wheaton Geo. H	2
	Worrall Joseph A	2
132	Summers J. B	57
133	Jenne Jacob	1
	Seibe Ludwig	50
136	German J. A	32
137	Eggleston A. T	2
138	Royce Frank L	8
140	Fordham M. C	55
	Rutherford Daniel	94
142	Hogan H. H	69
	Sheldon M. M	61

UNITED STATES NAVY.

	Post
Blackburn J. O.	104
Blackmore N. L.	16
Blaisdell I. L.	93
Borton W. F.	42
Boyd John E.	88
Bragdon C. A.	1
Braids John	9
Branch C. H	58
Brittain William	1
Brock Edward M.	1
Bromwell L. L.	2
Brooks Samuel A.	1
Brown Geo. R.	6
Bruce Henry	4
Brundage J. H.	8
Buchanan J	4
Bulfinch Thos. J	44
Burk Edward.	48
Burke Peter.	34
Burke W. L.	3
Burns John	1
Burns Michael	59
Byrnes W. A.	2
Cain Thos.	34
Campbell A. C.	85
Campbell Thos.	45
Carrahan Patrick.	48
Carstens Henry.	1
Cawley John.	2
Chandler L. M.	2
Chapin R. P.	92
Christian Antone.	59
Christie Wm.	64
Christie William	125
Clapp Geo. P.	8
Clark Thomas.	1
Claudianus C. M.	1
Cline Thos.	48
Clough J. F.	1
Cobb W. B.	2
Coghlan J. B.	2
Coleman Michael.	48
Colford John.	80
Collins John	114
Comfort Jos.	65
Commins Job.	75
Conn J. D.	45
Conner Cornelius.	34
Connolly John.	2
Cook C. C.	8
Cooley E. K.	2
Costello M	7
Craig Robert.	4
Crall Geo. A.	34
Crichton R. B.	42
Croft Thomas F.	93
Cruden Albert.	2
Dalton M.	1

UNITED STATES NAVY.

	Post
De Sanno W.	1
Deacon Wm.	2
Dee W.	2
Devine Patrick.	1
Dickinson Albion.	64
Dill A. F.	34
Dodd Jas.	3
Donnelly A. B.	1
Donnelly George A.	4
Donnelly T. S.	10
Donohue Michael.	2
Douglas John.	54
Douty F. S.	2
Downing Dennis.	113
Doyle Philip A.	5
Dunn J. C.	60
Dyer J. D.	36
Eagan L. M.	1
Eckart W. R.	2
Elston George.	48
Enos Joseph.	50
Erickson Conrad.	2
Farciot Chas. C.	1
Fay M. C.	2
Fisher D. F.	48
Foley Michael.	48
Ford Fred W.	1
Fortier S. M.	2
Freeman C. H.	83
Freese Chas. J.	35
French Chas. A.	82
Gardiner F. I.	1
Gee Myron.	57
Gibson John.	8
Gilabert Joseph.	23
Gilmore A. N.	2
Givens W. J.	9
Glass John.	32
Gleason John.	1
Gobertz Martin	1
Golding Thomas.	2
Grant G. W.	33
Graves S. F.	63
Green L. K.	32
Grow A. L	36
Haas Jerome.	23
Hagman Charles G.	48
Hallett Joseph H	72
Hamlin C. L.	98
Hanly Wm.	4
Hanson Geo. W.	7
Hanson H. J.	34
Harding W. T.	48
Harris George L	2
Harrison Joseph.	8
Hart John.	11
Harvey A. W.	7
Haverty John.	42

UNITED STATES NAVY.

	Post
Hawes W. H	2
Hazard A. R	1
Healey Wm	46
Heffernan John	34
Hill John B	93
Hegerup Anthony	83
Henery Samuel	23
Hoeffer E	23
Holst D	34
Hosley Geo. A	2
Howard C. S	1
Howard H. Z	2
Hunt J. H	1
Hyde Marcus D	8
Hyme Thos. Oscar	34
Jagoe R. H	46
Johnson Geo. A	50
Johnson W. H	43
Jones J. P	33
Jordan Franklin	55
Jordan William	48
Josephs William	4
Kano J. H	44
Kelley E	46
Kelley Joseph	67
Kenna James	8
Kenniff J	1
Kidder G. E	2
King David J	1
Kittle William	48
Kraut Charles	1
Laago W. J. F	50
Lagerman Henry	34
Lame R. W	45
Landson Louis	34
Lane Michael	45
Lane W. W	48
Laughton James	34
Laycock T. F	69
Le Chevallier Francis	1
Leachey Thomas	1
Leeds B. F	50
Lewis Nelson	48
Littlefield G. B	93
Lorden W. H	93
Lovejoy Joseph F	45
Lutz W. E	2
Lynch William	1
Macomber David W	108
Mager Henry	1
Malone L. J	48
Mannsell G. M	66
Marsilliot M. G	2
Martin John	34
Martin Michael	50
Mass Peter H	1
Masteller T. C	1
Mathews J. H	2

UNITED STATES NAVY.

	Post
Mathisen O. T	20
Mayer Harry	1
McCarthy Michael	34
McCool D. M	4
McCumisky James	20
McDonald T. H	50
McGinley Daniel	7
McGrath M	46
McKean W. D	4
McKelvey C. W	6
McMahon J. S	11
McMahon Peter	34
McNutt W. F	2
McPeak John	34
McPherson B. R	2
Mellus N. S	54
Melrose K	2
Metzler Theodore C	2
Meyer Adolph	1
Miller Geo. A	1
Miller Henry	4
Monahan D	48
Montagne J. P	50
Montell F. W	48
Morey F. C	6
Morse Obadiah	7
Mullen John	1
Murphy Daniel	34
Murray M	1
Neal Charles S	2
Newman Charles	113
Newman Peter A	1
Nicolaysen J	1
Nicoll Frederic E	2
O'Brien Wm	50
O'Donnell James	8
O'Neil Lawrence	48
Odell Isaac	34
Osborn A. A	2
Owens J. C	1
Pascoe W. H	72
Paulsen Chas. A	1
Paulson Henry	34
Pease G. M	2
Penfield W. H	2
Pennell R. J	2
Perry Fred M	80
Perry Thomas	66
Pittman H. C	1
Place Wm. H	45
Poat J. J	20
Powers Thomas	1
Pracht Max	2
Price C. M	1
Provost Nelson	1
Quinlan D	1
Quinn Edward	34
Quinn Edward, Jr	34

ALPHABETICAL INDEX.

COMRADES, ATTENTION!

Every Comrade visiting the Pacific Coast, should send home a small quantity of

PURE CALIFORNIA WINES.

The Edge Hill Vineyard Co. is located near St. Helena, Napa Valley, and has one of the oldest Vineyards in the State. No Wines are offered by this Company under from three to five years old. They are absolutely pure and possess a bouquet rarely acquired.

Our lowest trade prices will be given all Comrades purchasing from us.

JOHN T. CUTTING & CO.,
SOLE AGENTS,
Nos. 23 & 25 California Street,
San Francisco, Cal.

JOHN T. CUTTING, P. D. I. Dep't Cal.

Geo. H. Thomas Post, No. 2.

PRIVATE: { Taylor's Chicago Battery, and
          { Chicago Mercantile Battery.

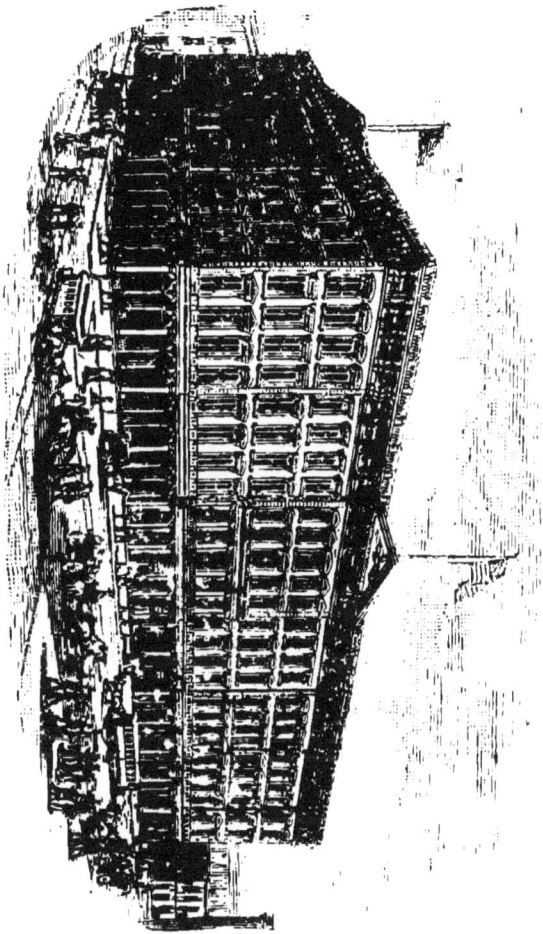

www.ingramcontent.com/pod-product-compliance
Lightning Source LLC
Chambersburg PA
CBHW021112270326
41929CB00009B/846